# HISTORY AND ITS LIMITS

# HISTORY AND ITS LIMITS

## HUMAN, ANIMAL, VIOLENCE

DOMINICK LACAPRA

CORNELL UNIVERSITY PRESS
*Ithaca and London*

First published 2009 by Cornell University Press
First printing, Cornell Paperbacks, 2009

*Library of Congress Cataloging-in-Publication Data*

LaCapra, Dominick, 1939–
History and its limits : human, animal, violence / Dominick LaCapra.
p. cm.
Includes bibliographical references and index.
ISBN 978-0-8014-4786-0 (cloth)—
ISBN 978-0-8014-7515-3 (pbk.)
1. Historiography. 2. Intellectual life—History. 3. Human beings—Animal nature. 4. Animals (Philosophy) 5. Violence—Philosophy. I. Title.

D13.L27 2009
907.2—dc22 2008044158

Cornell University Press strives to use environmentally responsible suppliers and materials to the fullest extent possible in the publishing of its books. Such materials include vegetable-based, low-VOC inks and acid-free papers that are recycled, totally chlorine-free, or partly composed of nonwood fibers. For further information, visit our website at www.cornellpress.cornell.edu.

Cloth printing 10 9 8 7 6 5 4 3 2 1

Paperback printing 10 9 8 7 6 5 4 3 2 1

*For Lotte, Caleb, and Indigo*

# Contents

# Acknowledgments

I would like to thank, for their comments, criticisms, and suggestions, Jane Pedersen and Ethan Kleinberg as well as an anonymous reader for Cornell University Press. I thank Katy Meigs for her editorial assistance and Emma Kuby for her help in preparing the index. I am also grateful to John Ackerman of Cornell University Press and to all of those with whom I have discussed ideas presented in this book, many of whom are mentioned in the text or in footnotes. Chapter 7 of this book is based on an article, "Tropisms of Intellectual History," which appeared in *Rethinking History* 8, no. 4 (2004). I appreciate their allowing me to use it.

# Introduction

For Freud, beyond the explanatory limits of the pleasure principle lay the repetition compulsion, the death drive, and trauma with its symptomatic aftermath—what Lacan addressed in terms of the "real" as a disorienting excess that may be the source not of pleasure but of ecstatic, perhaps sadomasochistic, *jouissance.* How can a critical historiography recognize and give a responsive account of compulsive, typically violent, destructive and at best extremely ambivalent forces that have played such a notable role in so-called limit events and experiences in history? Does the attempt to do so necessarily make the inquirer unguardedly complicit with objects of study by fixating on violence, confusing compassion with identification, even transferentially enacting compulsive repetition?[1] Need one's approach to problems perform or validate some variant of excess (unmitigated negativity,

1. I should note at the outset that the sense of "transference" I employ is revisionary with respect to Freud, does not oppose transference and countertransference, sees Oedipal displacement as only one significant form of broader transferential processes, and stresses the role of repetition as the latter's crux. More specifically, I primarily use transference in the sense of a tendency to repeat, in one's account or critique, the forces active in or projected onto an object of study, including an object of criticism. This sense of transference is not narrowly biographical but related to an understanding of psychoanalysis as critical theory and applies to the analysis of signifying practices in texts as well as in social life. The problem is how to work through inevitable transferential relations and not simply act them out in a compulsive manner.

idealized melancholy, an unqualified aesthetic of the sublime, apocalyptic apprehension if not desire, the affirmation of creation ex nihilo, or blank utopian hope)? How does one understand recent, at times uncanny, invocations of the "postsecular" and the human-animal relation?[2] What, in general, is called for in an attempt to "think" history with respect to the complex problem of limits?

A crucial aspect of any acceptable articulation of history and critical theory is the attempt to address such questions, which requires the elaboration of a cogent yet self-questioning relation between intellectual history, critical theory, and various forms of cultural studies, especially with respect to limit or extreme events and the limit-breaking, radically transgressive, allure of excess. My focus in this book is on the interaction between intellectual history and critical theory, in which critical theory is understood primarily in terms of inquiry into, and interrogation of, basic assumptions in practices and forms of thought. Assumptions set limits to inquiry that may remain unexamined, especially when they are embedded in a habitus or what goes without saying. Critical theory interrogates habitus in order to make it explicit and open it to questioning in ways that may both validate components of it and ready others for change.

There is an important sense in which intellectual history that is correlated with critical theory involves a qualified movement beyond the pleasure principle. It does not offer the reader a captivating narrative with pronounced entertainment value. In fact it often does not tell stories, although it may well recognize their significance and study their procedures.[3] Its principal

2. The turn to the postsecular or to the human-animal relation may be uncanny insofar as it is at times strangely disconcerting or unexpected, possibly transgresses boundaries, and even approximates a returning repressed (the postsecular with respect to religion and theology and the human-animal relation with respect to the quest for a decisive, differential criterion that has had a crucial, albeit at times seemingly marginal, place not only in theology and philosophy but also in everyday life). In chapter 7, I touch on somewhat uncanny dimensions of this turn in my own work.

3. I would in no sense downplay the importance of storytelling. In fact I would especially emphasize the value, on multiple levels, of certain "carnivalized" novels, such as William Gaddis's *The Recognitions* (New York: Harcourt, Brace and World, 1952), and the work of novelists and storytellers, such as Leslie Marmon Silko, who relate to traditions where the story itself both explores at times excruciating problems and may offer ways of engaging them and at least partially working them through. On Gaddis, see my *History, Politics, and the Novel* (Ithaca: Cornell University Press, 1987), chap. 8, and also my discussion of Bakhtin in *Rethinking Intellectual History: Texts, Contexts, Language* (Ithaca: Cornell University Press, 1983), chap. 9. See also Silko's *Ceremony*, intro. Larry McMurtry and new preface Silko (1977; New York: Penguin Classics, 2006). As Silko writes: "You don't have anything / if you don't have the stories. / Their evil is mighty / but it can't stand up to our stories... / And in the belly of this story / the rituals and the ceremony / are still growing. / *What She Said:* / The only

objective is not the discovery of gripping facts or enticing scenarios from the archives and their translation into thick descriptions or richly contextualized renditions of intriguing experiences. Thus one may infrequently, if ever, get a well-rounded allotment of preprocessed information, the "what a wonderful (or horrible) story" feeling, or the conclusive QED effect. While at times calling for work in the archives or a (necessarily reductive) narrative of ideas, if understood in a certain way, intellectual history has, as its primary form of research, extensive critical analysis, involving the reading of difficult texts and artifacts, and its focus is on modes of conceptualization and argument—the way material is or is not thought out, "emplotted," worked over, and set forth.

At the very least, there is a tension between conventional narrative and intellectual history when the intellectual historian does not rely only on summary paraphrase and synoptic content analysis, which may analogize "ideas" to datable events, but instead pauses to offer a pointed reading of a complex text, an analysis of an intricate concept, or an argument about a mode or current of thought. Any closure, terminal date, or periodization is placed in question when one addresses the mutual implication of past, present, and future or the insistence of repetitive temporalities that may come with unsettling disorientation as well as with questions posed to the questioner. In this "essayistic" approach, one at best points things out, makes arguments, and develops lines of thought that one strives to make cogent and convincing but nonetheless recognizes as subject to dispute. Indeed, a recurrent issue is how one is questioned by what one questions, for the mainstay of a critical-theoretical orientation is a constellation formed by questioning, self-questioning, problematization, judgment in selecting issues, at times strenuous argument, and the challenge of responsive understanding. Conceived in this manner, intellectual history often moves on the "meta" level by inquiring into its objects of study, along with the ways they have been studied, through interrogating and at times contesting their assumptions or sense of what is or is not worthwhile and valid. Thought here takes an insistently dialogic form in interrogating the work of others and in opening

cure / I know / is a good ceremony, / that's what she said" (2–3: these lines constitute a kind of paratext, unpaginated in the text). One problem in a critical intellectual history is how to offer commentary on various kinds of stories and their implications for understanding and practice. In this respect, see my discussion in chapter 5 of the story Heidegger tells in "The Origin of the Work of Art" as well as of Borges's "Pierre Menard, Author of the Quixote" in chapter 7. See also my *Preface to Sartre* (Ithaca: Cornell University Press, 1978), esp. chap. 3 (on *Nausea*); *Madame Bovary on Trial* (Ithaca: Cornell University Press, 1982); and *History, Politics, and the Novel* (Ithaca: Cornell University Press, 1987).

itself to interrogation in the interest of both disclosing questionable assumptions or arguments and enabling intellectual movement toward more desirable alternatives. If there is pleasure in this kind of activity or critical and self-critical practice, it is an acquired taste and must be earned. But dismissively to see such an activity as itself elitist is to disparage the competence of a readership (or a student body), to confuse mediation with media effects, and to sell democracy short.

One important implication of my argument is that work within a discipline, such as history or historiography, should, through immanent critique, test boundary limits and raise the problems of interdisciplinarity and cross-disciplinarity, including both the justification or transformation of established practices and the possibility that certain activities might be better housed or institutionalized in different disciplinary and departmental configurations. Intellectual history has been a primary conduit of various forms of critical theory in the historical profession, and it has an uneasy relation to other approaches, such as social, political, economic, and even cultural history, insofar as the latter are limited to practice or methodology and resist theoretical questioning of assumptions. Intellectual history, closely tied to critical theory, might be seen as both a deflationary probe and an enlivening gadfly in the field of historiography, which, without it, might not meet the demands of certain forms of questioning and conceptualization. For the temptation we face when resisting critical-theoretical self-questioning is attempting a premature, unqualified turn to the pleasure principle that confines history to ingratiating narrative and entertaining anecdote, with a reassuring assemblage of "hard" facts and an array of porous formulations, "soft" analogies, or "imaginative" interpolations to fill in the gaps in documentary sources.

Put somewhat differently, intellectual history, closely allied with critical theory, not only investigates problems in the history of thought or representation by narrating sequences of pertinent facts or past formulations and putting forward hypotheses or theses about them (for example: How has trauma been understood over time and associated with violence? What kind of experience has it been taken to be, and when was it identified as a psychic or psychological problem and named? And how do the various understandings relate to one another?).[4] Intellectual history, with a critical-theoretical inflection, also raises questions about the very way problems are articulated. (From

4. See, for example, Ruth Leys, *Trauma: A Genealogy* (Chicago: University of Chicago Press, 2000). See also my discussion of this book in *History in Transit: Experience, Identity, Critical Theory* (Ithaca: Cornell University Press, 2004), 83–93.

what subject position[s] does one put forth a narrative or hypothesis about trauma? How adequate are the basic concepts one is employing? Can trauma be encompassed by the boundaries or established protocols of any given discipline? What are one's own intellectual, cultural, and professional assumptions about understanding and explanation? Can one fully "objectify" trauma and detach oneself from the transferential problems it raises?) It inquires into the implication or mutual involvement of the observer and the observed: Is one's own discourse somehow beyond, or in control of, trauma and its effects by objectifying it as a research problem? And it may even question the questions put to the past: Why the widespread concern with trauma with its links to real or fantasized violence—as well as the sometimes pronounced resistance to an interest in it? Is it specious to talk of "trauma [or compassion, or even radical evil] fatigue"? Can there ever be a "been there done that" response to problems such as violence and trauma? What is assumed about their importance in history and their very definition? What ideological modifications or often sublimating transfigurations do they undergo, perhaps in one's own discourse? Is conventional narrative a suitable "form" with which to try to understand them or to render their often uncannily repetitive, at times distorted, syncopated temporality?[5] Such questions are posed in the interest of generating a more responsive and self-critical interchange between past and present with implications for shaping the future. A key problem in such an interchange is how to come to terms—intellectually, psychically, and sociopolitically—with transferential implication in the problems one studies through various combinations of compulsively repeating them, more or less (in)coherently rendering them, working them over, and trying to work them through. Indeed, what are the "symptomatic" demands and the "redemptive" or transformative limits of replicating or enacting a fragmented, inconsolably melancholic (or impossibly mournful), aporia-ridden, "posttraumatic," and

5. As others have pointed to a "compassion fatigue" as well as a sense of being tired of discussions of trauma, Tony Judt warns, in similar terms, of a kind of "radical evil" fatigue in which the latter is itself banalized: "There is another kind of banality: the banality of overuse—the flattening, desensitizing effect of seeing or saying or thinking the same thing too many times until we have numbed our audience and rendered them immune to the evil we are describing. And that is the banality—or 'banalization'—that we face today." In "The 'Problem of Evil' in Postwar Europe," *New York Review of Books* 55 (February 14, 2008): 35. Judt, who believes with Hannah Arendt that "the problem of evil *remains* the fundamental question of intellectual life, and not just in Europe," apparently has not undergone this "numbing" process himself and even risks writing an article that may contribute to the effect he deplores—a perhaps necessary rhetorical dilemma or performative contradiction in the analysis of various "fatigues." For a discussion of the "fatigue" topos, see Carolyn J. Dean, *The Fragility of Empathy after the Holocaust* (Ithaca: Cornell University Press, 2004).

at times captivating response that may both bear witness to trauma (or the Lacanian "real") and aspire to a certain negative sublimity?[6]

Intellectual history has traditionally emphasized the reading and analysis of difficult texts and artifacts—notably the so-called great texts—but this emphasis is justified only to the extent such texts and artifacts themselves provide exemplars of critical inquiry into assumptions and help to prompt an analysis of ways in which texts may also symptomatically reinforce prejudicial assumptions or become invidious markers of sociocultural superiority and professional elitism. Far from making a fetish of "great" texts, intellectual history is better seen as oriented toward a mutually challenging interaction

6. Prevalent in recent literary criticism and theory are responses that emphasize inconsolable loss, inevitable ruin, transhistorical trauma, idealized melancholia (or endless mourning) detached from severe depression, nonsensically "comic" or bizarre peculiarities, chance "miracles," and epiphanous "events" of sublimity, grace, or asymmetrically excessive generosity. Some of them will be referred to in later chapters. Such seemingly compelling responses tend to resist working-through, see it as naive, or construe it in stereotypical terms of dialectical transcendence or closure. In some measure they account for the almost instant appeal of the hybridized texts of the justifiably celebrated W. G. Sebald. They may also help in understanding the fascination with the virtuoso twists and turns in the important work of Slavoj Žižek. For some impressive works invoking one or more of these responses, see Ulrich Baer's *Remnants of Song: Trauma and the Experience of Modernity in Charles Baudelaire and Paul Celan* (Stanford: Stanford University Press, 2000), and *Spectral Evidence: The Photography of Trauma* (Cambridge: MIT Press, 2002); Sam Durrant, *Postcolonial Narrative and the Work of Mourning: J. M. Coetzee, Wilson Harris, and Toni Morrison* (Albany: State University of New York Press, 2004); David L. Eng and David Kazanjian, eds., *Loss,* afterword Judith Butler (Berkeley: University of California Press, 2003); Ranjana Khanna, *Dark Continents: Psychoanalysis and Colonialism* (Durham, N.C.: Duke University Press, 2003); Slavoj Žižek, Eric L. Santner, and Kenneth Reinhard, *The Neighbor: Three Inquiries in Political Theology* (Chicago: University of Chicago Press, 2005); Eric L. Santner, *On Creaturely Life: Rilke, Benjamin, Sebald* (Chicago: University of Chicago Press, 2006); and Paul Eisenstein, *Traumatic Encounters: Holocaust Representation and the Hegelian Subject* (Albany: State University of New York Press, 2003). Perhaps the paradigm-setting work for the prevalent de Manian deconstructive form of trauma theory is Shoshana Felman and Dori Laub, *Testimony: Crises of Witnessing in Literature, Psychoanalysis, and History* (New York: Routledge, 1992). For views of melancholy over the ages in the West, especially in terms of its relations with acedia, madness, and genius as well as its role in iconography, see *Mélancholie: Folie et génie en Occident,* sous la direction de Jean Clair (Paris: Gallimard, 2005). See also the classical text to which *Mélancholie* is explicitly indebted, Raymond Klibansky, Erwin Panofsky, and Fritz Saxl, *Saturn and Melancholy: Studies in the History of Natural Philosophy, Religion, and Art* (London: Nelson, 1964). My own discussions of melancholy in this book are, by and large, addressed to its recent invocations, especially in certain approaches to psychoanalysis and trauma theory, which are at times rather restricted. As *Mélancholie* and *Saturn and Melancholy* suffice to indicate, any larger inquiry would involve an extensive treatment of melancholy's complex role in areas such as theology, philosophy, literature, and art, along with its medicalization and its ambivalence, notably including its "diabolical" dimensions, its linkage with typically male genius, its affinity with madness, its potential for creativity, its possible alleviation through (other-than-hysterical) laughter and varieties of social activity (including manual labor), and its gendering, particularly with respect to female mourning.

between its own and other historical approaches (including cultural and social history), thus broaching the question of how it relates to, and may even be articulated with, critical-theoretical orientations that are often pronounced in other disciplines and departments, such as literature departments, that are open to the challenges of Continental philosophy.[7]

A leitmotif of this book (and of much of my work) is how—and how not—to think about limits, both limits that bind or impose constraints, prominently including normative constraints that indicate when one is going too far, and the limit in the sense of the extreme or excessive event or experience that transgresses normative limits or suspends constraints and boundaries. In the latter sense, one confronts the crucial problem of how historiography is taken to its limit in attempting to account for extremes. The paradigm case of limit event here is violence related to traumatization. And a key concern is the fascination that violence and traumatization, as in some sense the most excessive forms of excess, have exercised in modern Western thought and practice. This concern becomes acute when violence is not only seen (however contestably) as useful or necessary to achieve certain results (a basic reform, a transformed polity, a hoped-for experimentally discovered cure for a human disease even if it means doing violence to other animals) but is also transfigured in sacred, sublime, redemptive, or foundational terms. There is something both question-worthy and questionable in the prevalent fascination with excess, even violent excess, and the almost compulsive turn to it—a kind of blinding "traumatropism" or "beyond-beyond" syndrome—often at the expense of paying sustained attention to the crucial problem of the actual and desirable interaction between limits and what challenges or exceeds them.[8]

7. For a recent collection of essays, many of which address, in different ways, the question of the relation between history and critical theory, see Keith Jenkins, Sue Morgan, and Alun Munslow, eds., *Manifestos for History* (London: Routledge, 2007). My own contribution to this work, which supplements the arguments in the present book, is entitled "Resisting Apocalypse and Rethinking History," 160–78.

8. One aspect of this phenomenon is the preoccupation with serial killing in both fact and fiction, notably in films. See, for example, the discussion in Mark Seltzer's *Serial Killers: Death and Life in America's Wound Culture* (New York: Routledge, 1998), and *True Crime: Observations on Violence and Modernity* (New York: Routledge, 2007). I would also mention the often uninformed fascination with fascism and especially Nazism, certain Holocaust-related aspects of which I shall touch on at various points in this book. On this problem, see also Saul Friedlander, *Reflections of Nazism: An Essay on Kitsch and Death,* trans. Thomas Weyr (1982; Bloomington: Indiana University Press, 1993). At times associated with "fascinating fascism" is the absorbing interest in what might be termed the grid of victimization, including inter alia the roles of perpetrator and victim, with the inclination to identify with—and to speak for—the abject

At the limit there is a necessary speculative element in historical understanding. But it should be checked and to some extent regulated by empirical research that may never prove or fully substantiate certain contentions but can lend them greater credibility. Empirical inquiry, while never a self-sufficient or free-standing activity, is particularly pointed and fruitful when it is combined with critical questioning and invoked as a "reality check" that may facilitate specificity and interrupt free-flowing, at times self-involved, theoretical speculation. Like the comic and the carnivalesque, an appeal to facts can contest abstract pretensions, bring claims down to earth, and provide critical perspective on certain formulations. Nonetheless, without a speculative dimension, history veers in the direction of restricted social science methods that do not have the thought-provoking relation to theoretical issues, cross-disciplinary initiatives, or problems that agitate the "public sphere," a relation that has been an aspiration of certain approaches to intellectual history.

The chapters of this book form a constellation of interlocking essays. They do not provide a continuous narrative or aim to prove a delimited thesis. But they do enter into sustained dialogic exchange with one another and with the thought of others addressing pertinent issues. They exemplify efforts to recursively think and rethink a set of insistent and often perplexing problems in the attempt to further understanding. By and large the essays are metacritical, interrogating assumptions and indicating directions for basic forms of conceptualization and related research procedures. They also invite, perhaps provoke, questioning and argument directed at the essays themselves and their own assumptions, limits, and limitations. At best they will stimulate others to inquire into the questions I raise or the arguments I explore. They are, of course, related to my earlier work, but they also attempt to engage newer tendencies or prominent figures in the academy and extend inquiry in directions that I think are particularly pressing at present, for example, in reflecting (however tentatively) on the complex question of the human and the animal—not to mention the problems of violence, sacrifice, and the sacred, which are often closely entangled in the relation between the human and the animal. I also touch on the issue of the postsecular. The questions I am interested in are situated both at the heights of "elite" culture, where one finds inter alia the demanding texts of major figures such as Mikhail Bakhtin, Sigmund Freud, Martin Heidegger, and Jacques Derrida, and at the level of

victim, even to transfigure the experience of victimization into the occasion for a sublime act of bearing witness, a problem I explore in chapter 3.

practice or life where the relations among humans, between the human and the animal, or between the secular and the religious are everyday concerns.[9]

One implication is that thought—even what has been seen as thought on its highest, best, or most demanding and provocative level—should not be dissociated from practices and from relational networks that imbricate the human and the animal both within the "human animal" and between humans, other species, and nature more generally. Conversely, practices—at least from a critical-theoretical perspective—should not be dissociated from thought and autonomized in a separate sphere as habitus. Practices, prominently including those resting on unexamined or partially obscure assumptions, are crucial in social life and even in what appear to be lucid forms of thought. But even when practices are quarantined in routines, becoming more or less open secrets or unexamined disciplinary protocols, they still pose problems for thought, for example, with respect to issues related to scapegoating and projection such as marginalization, avoidance, suppression, repression, and disavowal. Those engaged or even immersed in certain practices, especially when they prove unable to furnish sufficiently self-justifying or image-protecting ideological glosses, confront the problem of how to avoid thinking about what they do, how even to maintain a false front in the face of what

9. In what might arguably be read as his own turn to the issue of the postsecular, Derrida makes this arresting comment: "Why then privilege the example of Heidegger? Because of its extreme character and of what it tells us, in these times, about a certain 'extremity'" (59). In "Faith and Knowledge: The Two Sources of 'Religion' at the Limits of Reason Alone," in *Religion*, ed. Jacques Derrida and Gianni Vattimo (1996; Stanford: Stanford University Press, 1998). Note that, as might be expected in a text that problematizes the meaning of religion and even the very possibility of knowing what religion (hence also the secular) is, the very title of Derrida's essay raises issues of translation. *Foi et savoir: Les deux sources de la "religion" aux limites de la simple raison* (Paris: Editions du Seuil, 1996) employs "*aux limites*," which itself connotes a certain extremity if not extremism. It is appropriately translated as "at the limits" rather than "within the limits," indicating the gesture of being or pushing at, even transgressing, the limits (perhaps being at one's wit's end), not simply respecting or remaining within the limits. And the translation of "*simple*" is not that simple. "Alone" is a contestable choice, and why Derrida chooses "*simple*" instead of some other term (say, "*seule*") is an open question. I would merely mention that "*savoir*" is a notoriously difficult term, especially with respect to its complex (at times idiomatic) relations with "*connaissance*," and has as one possible translation "know-how," as in "*savoir faire*." One might suggest that it has a more performative force than "*connaissance*." Derrida himself plays on the meanings of "*foi*." Further complications arise with respect to the titles of the two texts to which Derrida alludes: Kant's *Religion innerhalb der Grenzen der blossen Vernunft* (1793) and Bergson's *Deux sources de la morale et de la religion* (1932). A minimal observation is that "*innerhalb*" would seem to require "*dans*" ("within"), "*blossen*" could be "*nue*" or "*dénudée*" ("naked" or "bare"), and the reference to "*la morale*" is dropped in Derrida's title. Especially in light of the latter consideration, one might speculate that in the move from "*dans*" to "*aux*" there is a shift or at least an inflection from an aesthetic of the beautiful to that of the sublime.

really may not go without saying. The fruitful critique or deconstruction of binary oppositions or total dichotomies, which undercuts the working of a scapegoat mechanism, should have as a key object the frequently unreflective or insufficiently questioned human-animal relation, which has been so important in sacrificial practices and in violent thought and action more generally. Hence, chapter 6, "Reopening the Question of the Human and the Animal," which might superficially seem to be an outlier if not an outcast in this book, cuts very close to the quick of its concerns. The vexed issue of the postsecular, which has recently arisen in a pronounced manner, also raises questions for the binary opposition between the secular and the religious (or the sacred, including the sacrificial), and it exerts pressure on conceptions of secularization even when they do not rely on simplistic developmental models but take the self-questioning form of inquiry into displacements of the religious in the secular and vice versa. Surprisingly, the postsecular may serve, however dubiously, to reassert a radical divide or boundary between the human and the animal, for approaches to the postsecular, along with the posthuman, may remain unquestioningly anthropocentric. They may even appeal to such notions as monstrous excess, "creaturely life," inner psychic split (*Spaltung*), cringing abjection, "signifying stress," and—perhaps most essentially—foundational, originary, transhistorical trauma (paradigmatically including the Fall and original sin along with redemptive hope) in order to differentiate sharply, if at times paradoxically, between the human and the animal, including the animal within, indeed the animal in closest proximity to the human. My discussion of the human-animal problem and my references to the postsecular point to the horizon of this book, which is how to work and play out a self-questioning relational network in understanding and "practicing" interactions both among humans and between the human, the animal, and nature in general.

Taken to the limit of critical theory, history starts interacting with other disciplines in unpredictable and at times strangely disconcerting ways—ways that threaten to escape the habitual confines of a history department and the protocols or criteria of evaluation of established disciplines. This movement to the limit, which may even problematize the dividing line between the human and the animal, raises in pointed form the question of how to define disciplines and justify practices current in them related to hiring and tenuring faculty or evaluating and judging the quality of manuscripts. It certainly raises the question of where certain cross-disciplinary problems (such as trauma, violence, the human-animal relation, the postsecular, the "work of art," even jokes and laughter) fit, including the question of journals or other outlets for publication of work on them. It may also touch on assumptions, emotions, or sensitivities that are so embedded that they evoke positive, negative, or ambivalent responses that result more in rationalizations than in cogent reasoning. Intellectual history has been open to such questions or problems and has served as an avenue for varieties of critical theory in departments of history and, to some extent, in the academy in general.

Intellectual historians continually face the problem of where they "fit" and whether they should "go native" by taking critical theories (including psychoanalysis understood as a critical theory) seriously enough to move beyond objectifying contextualization and conventional narrative in order to engage in some form of critical-theoretical discourse or argumentation. Indeed, where intellectual history belongs in the academy is subject to controversy. So-called slots, along with tenure-track hires, in intellectual history are usually located in history departments, even if other areas—such as departments of comparative literature, German studies, Romance studies, or the occasional humanities center—may include the subfield as an interest or concentration. But, especially when it engages with forms of critical theory, moves across boundary lines, and inquires into cross-disciplinary problems, intellectual history and its practitioners occupy a problematic and often marginal or suspect position in history departments. A history department may decide to do without intellectual historians. Or it may choose one or two whose work resembles closely, or is readily coordinated with, other historical approaches, for example, a type of theory-averse (or at best theory-light) sociocultural history, often stressing, in restricted terms, reception or the larger context that encompasses and sometimes absorbs an area of thought or intellectual/artistic practice. Still, the indispensable concept of "context" (or "field" in Bourdieu's sense), which is often simply taken as a framework of analysis (if not a habitus of sorts), can be productively rethought in a manner that inquires into its construction and the varying, complex ways it interacts with significant texts or artifacts that may "symptomatically" instantiate, critically interrogate, and render contexts ready for transformation. My hope is that the essays in this book contribute to enlarging the possibilities of thought-provoking, critically oriented interaction, both within and without the discipline of history, indeed in the academy in general, while interrogating the limits of disciplines.

My final chapter serves as a conclusion and is somewhat different from the others. The journal *Rethinking History* has an ongoing series in which historians are asked to reflect on their work and their intellectual orientation. Different contributors take different tacks, from the autobiographical to the more restrictedly professional and academic. My own contribution fell somewhere in between these boundary markers and attempted to relate my activity over the years to broader tendencies in the discipline and the academy more generally.[10] A version of my contribution, in concluding this book, provides it with a different discursive context and makes the necessarily tension-laden attempt to provide reflections that situate the earlier chapters, relate more fully to my ongoing concerns, and combine a retrospect with indications of future orientations I expect my work will take (for example, with respect to the key issue of the human-animal relation).

10. See "Tropisms of Intellectual History," in *Rethinking History* 8, no. 4 (2004): 499–529, intro. David Harlan (493–96) and commentaries or contributions Michael S. Roth (531–35), Carolyn J. Dean 537–47), Allan Megill (549–57), and Ernst van Alphen (559–66). The latter are well worth reading in their own right and not simply in relation to my work.

## CHAPTER 1

# Articulating Intellectual History, Cultural History, and Critical Theory

> Articulating. 1. The action of jointing or joining together. 2. Distinct sounding or utterance. 3. The making of stipulations; stipulating. *Obs.*
>
> —*Oxford English Dictionary*

Intellectual history, cultural history, and critical theory (or varieties of critical theory) are undertakings whose mutual articulation is both desirable and problematic. One issue in any proposed articulation is the role of a so-called canon, which has been a concern in intellectual history as in other areas (such as literary criticism, philosophy, or art history). Intellectual history has confronted an anticanonical animus to which it is particularly vulnerable in view of its constitution, notably its focus on "great" texts. But this animus is misplaced if it is directed at an essentialized or fixated concept of the canon itself.

The basic object of critique might well be canonization as a function of the reception and use of artifacts, notably for purposes of ideological legitimation, for example, of the nation-state, a social hierarchy, an imperial hegemony, or even an overly restricted disciplinary matrix, curriculum, or research agenda. But such a critique should not become a pretext to stigmatize certain texts or artifacts. Only a misdirected populism could lead one to dismiss the study of Plato or Freud or to believe that the sole valid approach to religion is to focus on popular practice and to omit theology. Rather, critique should be aimed at an exclusive valorization of "elite" or "high" culture as a label to categorize or corral certain artifacts, separate them from other dimensions of culture, and understand them in an invidious manner. It should also be aimed at the disavowal of the thought-provoking, critical, and possibly disconcerting potential of certain texts or artifacts because of the way they are read or deployed, for example, as school ties or rituals of initiation that assure mutual recognition and admiration in an exclusive elite or clique.

It would seem obvious that the critique of canonization should accompany the qualified valorization of texts that have a thought-provoking potential, including the way they may continue to address readers over time and be internally dialogized such that they help to provide the wherewithal to place in question their own symptomatic and ideologically dubious sides, such as racism, colonial domination, class privilege, or other forms of oppression and victimization. (Hence, for example, the phenomenon of Freud-on-Freud readings whereby Freud's texts are drawn on in a critique of certain tendencies in them such as misogyny.) Self-deconstructive tendencies are empowering to the extent that their critically inflected repetitions and variations supplement or reinforce the type of internal dialogization and self-questioning that serves as ideology critique and wards off dogmatism or self-certainty. This may happen through valuable insistence on the role of anxiety-producing, often victimized or scapegoated, remainders and residues (prominently including the animal in the human and the way the diverse multiplicity of animals cannot be reduced to "animal" as the homogeneous binary opposite of "man" or the human).[1] Texts that are self-critical in this sense are not

1. On this issue, see, for example, Jacques Derrida, *L'animal que donc je suis* (Paris: Galilée, 2006); *The Animal That Therefore I Am*, trans. David Wills, ed. Marie-Louise Mallet (New York: Fordham University Press, 2008). Here the deconstructive insistence on the role of "differences within," along with irreducible supplements, remainders, and residues, converges with the Lacanian notion of the "not-all"—the way any attempted totalization will always leave out something excessive that may act as a point of self-division, contestation, or disorientation, although in Žižek and others the "not-all" attests both to an ineradicable "hole" or void in the symbolic and the necessity of an impossible and itself excessive quest for totalization. For sometimes technical elaborations of the "not-all," exegetically invoked in at times contestable ways, see Slavoj Žižek, Eric L. Santner, and Kenneth Reinhard, *The Neighbor: Three Inquiries in Political Theology* (Chicago: University of Chicago Press, 2005). For example, instead of elaborating a limited, internally self-questioning, never fully "sutured" or stabilized notion of identity, opening to the other and undoing scapegoating (including the scapegoating of exceptions), which might have some political purchase, Santner provides this seemingly apocalyptic exegesis of Giorgio Agamben's understanding of the "not-all" remainder, thereby confining options to the extremes of closed totalities (allowing only for the abject or sovereign "exception") and a bewilderingly enigmatic alterity: "It [the remainder] represents, instead, a cut into the bipolar partition between Jews and non-Jews that allows for the passage to an entirely new sort of logic of being-with, one that no longer operates on the basis of membership in bounded sets or totalities set off against exceptions. For Agamben, the figure that holds the place of this logic (of the noncoincidence of every identity with itself) is that of the 'non non-Jew,' the figure who is *not not-in-the-law*" (129).

restricted either to written artifacts or to what is termed a canon but may well include texts or artifacts that have undergone processes of canonization, often at the expense of a critical potential that a noncanonical reading may reactivate. A subject of debate that cuts across intellectual and cultural history is to what extent and in what ways texts or dimensions of texts are indeed self-critical in this sense and both inquire critically into assumptions and contest more symptomatic or even ideologically saturated tendencies (for example, those prominent in a dogmatic tract or racist editorial). To put the point another way, all texts or artifacts have their blindnesses and are symptomatic of ideological and more generally contextual forces in society and culture—but not in the same way or with the same effects, whether actual or possible. Certain texts or artifacts open the possibility of transformation or what might be termed situational transcendence in the manner in which they come to terms with problems and perform critical work or aesthetic play on contexts of production or reception.[2] In this sense they are significant events in the history of language or signification that both have a complex history and can make a difference in history, including differences that come about through the way in which they may engage other events or processes.

These assertions have a number of consequences. First, there should be an important role for noncanonical and noncanonizing readings of canonical texts in intellectual and cultural history. Noncanonical readings are sensitive to processes whereby texts question themselves, as well as overly restrictive interpretations of them, and are not reducible to their symptomatic, ideologically reinforcing tendencies, however important these may be (for example, in terms of reconstructing collective *mentalités*). Such readings may provide a basis for the critical (not simply empirical) analysis of the way texts are received and deployed in society and politics. They are also attentive to rhetorical, poetic, and performative aspects of texts that do not deny but complicate constative or documentary functions that provide at least rear windows on past empirical reality. Hence they bring out the intricacy of texts and disclose the limits of synoptic readings that are typically adjusted to a restricted contextual understanding that, at the limit, both oversimplifies the problem of contextualization and tries to interpret or explain all texts only as documents that are seen predominantly as objectified symptoms or direct expressions of

2. Situational transcendence points not toward the totally other, or the other-worldly, but toward different possibilities and transformed and possibly more desirable situations in sociopolitical and cultural life.

contexts.[3] For the narrowly historicizing contextualist, contextualization is unproblematically identified with historical understanding in a manner that marginalizes or obviates the ways texts interact with contexts and require responsive understanding, including forms of affective involvement on the part of the inquirer with respect to the "object" of inquiry. Context can even at times become the analog for the tunnel-visioned historicist of the realtor's familiar and familiarizing slogan: "Location, location, location!"

Second, these theoretical assertions create a space for a practice of intellectual history that allows for close reading of texts, especially texts that have a thought-provoking potential for rethinking problems that, however differently, preoccupy readers over time. Closely and critically reading such texts is part of an education that is not restricted to information processing or objectification of the other. Still, it is dubious to find in close reading per se an "ethic," and it is tempting to see close reading, when it achieves quasi-transcendental status, as a form of barely displaced sectarian piety. But this implication is in no sense a necessary feature of close reading, which should be alert to its own limitations, especially when it is fixated on a delimited canon. Indeed, close reading should open onto the problem of how to include and address artifacts and sociocultural processes appearing in non-Western traditions.[4] Such an opening implies an awareness of one's limitations, may

3. Despite its altogether crucial indication of the prevalent complicity of European thought and academic writing in the colonial enterprise, reductively synoptic reading may be seen as one limitation of Edward Said's nonetheless groundbreaking *Orientalism* (New York: Pantheon, 1978), in which all texts are read (without sufficient framing and delimitation of Said's own project) as symptoms of dominant historical forces, similar to the manner in which Foucault reads Descartes as symptomatic of the "great confinement" in one section of *Folie et déraison: Histoire de la folie à l'âge classique* (Paris: Plon, 1961). On its own level, my observation reinforces Robert J. C. Young's argument that "what Said's analysis neglects . . . is the extent to which Orientalism did not just misrepresent the Orient but also articulated [often acting out or at best enacting] an internal dislocation within Western culture"—an unacknowledged ambivalence or "difference within" Western culture (or cultures) that prompted a projective representation of the other. See Young's *White Mythologies: Writing History and the West* (1990; London: Routledge, 2004), 180. On Foucault, see my *History and Reading: Tocqueville, Foucault, French Studies* (Toronto: University of Toronto Press, 2000), esp. 133–41. See also Said's new preface to *Orientalism* in the 2003 Vintage Books edition. What might perhaps be termed Occidentalism simply reverses a stereotypical Orientalism in construing the "West" as a monolithic, essentialized unity whose internal differences and dissensions are ignored even when certain of them might lend support to the valorized practices ascribed to the "West's" others. However problematically, one may attempt to provide a defense of such an "Occidentalist" view of the West as a form of "strategic" essentialism, which turns back on the West certain of its own invidious self-understandings and is undertaken to make a political point.

4. The insistence on such a widening or even shift of focus is now prevalent and requires transnational education in which there is a sustained mutual interrogation of traditions. See,

indicate a need for reeducation, and heightens both the importance and the difficulty of raising pointed questions, especially questions addressing the unexamined assumptions of an approach, profession, or process. Practice in reading texts that are critical and self-critical is crucial to education that is supposed to be critical or, in one possibly "recuperable" sense of the term, "liberal." Intellectual history (and it is not alone here) may offer the possibility of seeking out these texts or artifacts and reading them together, without preestablished national, generic, or disciplinary constraints and in ways that may raise questions about certain boundaries, notably when boundaries become overly rigid. It may also explore the often subtle and overlooked interaction between critical, symptomatic, and less classifiable, perhaps undecidable and uncanny—or at times grotesque and humorous—dimensions of texts and of cultural processes more generally. It may even intimate more desirable institutional configurations, including the organization of departments or programs.[5]

The orientation I am proposing would point toward a discipline or subdiscipline that is flexible in its approach to problems and addresses the question of reading together texts from different genres or areas of culture as well as different cultures in ways that may help to elaborate a critical frame of reference. It would expand the range (but not the proprietary claims) of intellectual history and even interrogate its boundaries with respect to cultural history and critical theory as well as other humanistic disciplines, prominently including those concerned with aesthetic and philosophical issues. I hope it would help to create an intellectual orientation, *forma mentis,* or *mentalité* that is able to address complex issues with an awareness of the interaction between past and present and the way it can be directed toward an openness to possible futures. Such an orientation attests to the value of forms of questioning and exploratory thought that counteract hardening of the conceptual categories and further self-critical understanding but that may not result in the kind of circumscribed theses, clear-cut answers, delimited results, or Q.E.D. experiences often sought by historians and social scientists. (As a former colleague of mine asserted in an interesting metaphor, historians want to pin things

---

for example, the probing argument in Gayatri Chakravorty Spivak, *A Critique of Postcolonial Reason: Toward a History of the Vanishing Present* (Cambridge: Harvard University Press, 1999). See also the approach in Gregory Cajete, *Native Science: Natural Laws of Interdependence,* foreword Leroy Little Bear (Santa Fe, N.M.: Clear Light Publishers, 2000).

5. I shall later indicate why an unmediated appeal to the transhistorical or structural (for example, the Lacanian real) is not a viable alternative to reductive or overly restrictive contextualism but its binary opposite or flip side.

down—an approach that is sometimes necessary and sometimes overly confining or even misleading.)

If undertaken in a certain manner and not autonomized, the study of how things are received can at times further the goals of critical historical understanding, especially when it points to aspects of texts, or ways of reading, rereading, and responding to them, that may not be obvious from an initial reading, one's own response, or an exclusive focus on authorial intention.[6] In this sense varieties of reception may be related to an engagement both with the past and with other cultures that may contribute to the attempt to think through important problems such as the varied relations between sacralizing and secularizing processes or between the traumatic and what may possibly counteract it. This engagement may have implications for the present and future by posing questions to, or even placing in question, the reader or inquirer, for example, by situating genealogically what one takes to be radically innovative (say, aspects of trauma studies or the putative "return" of religion, which never seems to have gone away), by bringing out how the seemingly contestatory or uncanny is commonplace in its historical context or has been adapted to dubious uses (for example, antisemitic or scapegoating dimensions of carnival and the carnivalesque), or by signaling unpredictable readings or adaptations of what may have been intended differently at the time of writing (say, Pierre Menard's reading of the *Quixote,* or Jorge Luis Borges's reading of Menard).[7]

A concern with intention as well as context becomes most accentuated when one believes a text has been misread. Heidegger's own 1933–34 Nazi-inflected readings and uses, if not distortions, of Heidegger, notably his *Being and Time* of 1927, are paradigmatic of these problems, for they show how a text that is for many (including myself) one of the basic contributions to modern thought could be adapted to ideological purposes in a manner that may be argued to be, in certain respects, plausible and, in other respects, called into question on the basis of a reading of *Being and Time* itself. For example, one might argue that the desire for a hero and some movement that would utterly transform and redeem Western civilization plays an important role

6. For excellent studies addressing the problems of reading and reception, see Ethan Kleinberg, *Generation Existential: Heidegger's Philosophy in France, 1927–1961* (Ithaca: Cornell University Press, 2005), and Samuel Moyn, *A Holocaust Controversy: The Treblinka Affair in Postwar France* (Waltham, Mass.: Brandeis University Press, 2005). See also Camille Robcis's 2007 Cornell University Ph.D. dissertation, "The Politics of Kinship: Anthropology, Psychoanalysis, and Family Law in Twentieth-Century France."

7. I discuss the latter question in "Tropisms of Intellectual History," *Rethinking History* 8, no. 4 (2004): 503–5, a version of which is included as chapter 7 of this book.

in *Being and Time,* and one might even contend that there is an implicit antisemitic coding in the critique of *Gerede,* or idle chatter, stereotypically associated with Jews as well as other denigrated groups. One might also argue that *Being and Time* is rather unguardedly open to the rhetoric of conservative revolution (including the notion of a turn away from authenticity and even the loss of some golden age) as well as to Christian motifs (such as fallenness, readily coordinated with notions of loss, degeneration, or decline)—rhetoric and motifs that might abet a blanket condemnation of existing civilization and an apocalyptic desire for total change. But *Being and Time* would seem to resist or even repel the simplistic idea of a return to a golden age as well as the idea that Hitler and the Nazis could be seen as the forces furthering desirable transformation, for such ideas fly in the face of an understanding of *Dasein* ("Being there," which includes but also transforms the understanding of human being) as an open, self-questioning being, especially in light of the Nazis' militant intolerance and virulent antisemitism that were manifest in 1933–34 and later became a basis of a genocidal policy and practice.[8] A different way of raising this question, more in a post-*Kehre* vein (or in terms of the later Heidegger, after his putative "turn" from *Dasein* to *Sein* or Being), is to ask whether *Gelassenheit,* or letting Being be by openly attending to its call, can be identified with obeying the commands, or even being attuned to the voice, of the Führer (as Göring seemed to imply when he asserted that Hitler was his conscience).

A source of the appeal of cultural history (as well as of cultural studies in general) is that its texts (in the broad sense) are not limited to any traditional canon and have an obvious relation to larger social and political processes as well as experiential concerns. They include phenomena or artifacts from various levels or dimensions of culture and society that are not texts in a conventional sense but do involve signifying practices. Moreover, cultural history gives prominence to such issues as gender, sexuality, race, class, religion, colonialism, postcolonialism, and, more recently, species and the human-animal relation—issues that connect with sociopolitical concerns and that have sometimes been marginalized in intellectual history. One reason for the importance of the turn to cultural history is that it expands the scope and revises the understanding of signifying practices to be investigated. It raises the question of the relation of canonical texts to larger signifying practices in society and culture—carnival and carnivalization to give one obvious and much discussed

8. On these issues see my *Representing the Holocaust: History, Theory, Trauma* (Ithaca: Cornell University Press, 1994), chap. 4 and, especially on the question of canons, chap. 1.

example but also discourses and practices of exclusionary categorization, victimization, traumatization, racialization, gendering, and stereotyping in general.[9] It may also go in a more psychoanalytic direction and relate texts and signifying practices to collective phantasms, affects, compulsions, and posttraumatic symptoms.[10] Indeed, what has been especially prominent in the recent past is the movement of intellectual history toward cultural history. This shift or turn parallels that in literary and aesthetic studies toward cultural studies, often combined with an interest in history and historicization. The proliferation in the academy of various cultural "studies" has of course been remarkable in the past generation—gender studies, a revitalized American studies, various "ethnic" studies, French studies, German studies, religious studies, visual studies, postcolonial studies, disability studies, queer studies, trauma studies (mea culpa), memory studies (mea culpa), critical animal studies (mea maxima culpa), and so on.

The inclusion of literature in a larger conception of culture breeds opposition on various fronts (both conservative and theoretically "radical" or at times puristic if not dogmatic). Yet it also opens the way to cooperation as well as informed debate between historians and colleagues in other disciplines. And it may suggest a conception of the aesthetic or the literary as a specific dimension of artifacts that is especially pronounced in works of art but whose specificity cannot be conclusively defined, demonstrated, or made into a secure object of knowledge.[11]

Despite what I would see as the generally fruitful effects of the turn of intellectual history toward cultural history or perhaps their vis-à-vis, I would put forward a few caveats. Cultural history, especially under a hermeneutic impetus that has also marked an important segment of intellectual history, often sees itself as a history of meaning (or ideas) in context—an approach that often is more or less domesticating or "territorializing." Keith Michael Baker expressed the view and the assumptions still shared by many colleagues when he wrote in 1982: "The intellectual historian analyzing a text, concept, or movement of ideas, has the same problem as the historian faced

9. A still pertinent work in this regard is Peter Stallybrass and Allon White, *The Politics and Poetics of Transgression* (Ithaca: Cornell University Press, 1986).

10. See, for example, Michel de Certeau, *The Possession at Loudun,* trans. Michael B. Smith, foreword Stephen Greenblatt (1970; Chicago: University of Chicago Press, 2000).

11. Cultural studies may be dismissed by those who see it as merely contextualizing and historicizing or as opposed to authentic or echt theorizing. This dismissal is shortsighted, especially when it conflates theory with an unhistorical, counterhistorical, or transhistorical, if not universalizing, conceptualization that eliminates or reductively subsumes the problem of the interaction between history and theory.

with any other historical phenomenon, namely to reconstitute the context (or, more usually, the plurality of contexts) in which that phenomenon takes on meaning as human action."[12] But why does a plurality of contexts accompany a homogenization of historians and a nonrecognition of a plurality of historical approaches with significantly different inflections, emphases, and pressures on expression or signification, depending in part on the type of problem investigated? Do the invention of the air balloon, the ideological origins of the French Revolution, Heidegger's Nazi turn, and the nature and dynamic of the Holocaust really pose the same problem to be treated in the same contextualizing way by the intellectual historian, the historian of science, the social historian, the economic historian, and so forth? Is it fruitful to conjure up—except perhaps as an explicitly problematic, heuristic, regulative ideal—the vision of a general historian who combines or synthesizes all of these orientations, particularly as a supercontextualizer? Do certain phenomena raise accentuated if not exceptional questions for representation and understanding?[13] Do certain texts pose distinctive challenges to their contexts of production and reception that may even address or unsettle contemporary readers? And is it only a restricted, anthropocentric understanding of intellectual history to construe it as a history of meaning as human action? Does such an approach at best permit only a very narrow perspective on the lives of nonhuman animals and on ecological issues, perhaps even reducing all others to a natural or human resource, raw material, or mere life-form that is endowed with meaning only through human action?

In its nexus with cultural history, intellectual history is, I think, better understood as a history of the possibility and limits of meaning with respect to various signifying practices and challenges to them, a history that relates past and present with implications for the future and is in intimate, sustained negotiation with critical theory.[14] The horizon of intellectual history thus understood is not the delimitation of a sphere of ideas or of thought but

12. "On the Problem of the Ideological Origins of the French Revolution," in *Modern European Intellectual History: Reappraisals and New Perspectives,* ed. Dominick LaCapra and Steven L. Kaplan (Ithaca: Cornell University Press, 1982), 197–98.

13. On this issue, see the contributions to *Probing the Limits of Representation: Nazism and the "Final Solution,"* ed. Saul Friedländer (Cambridge: Harvard University Press, 1992).

14. The recent turn to practice, especially habitus-type practice as "what goes without saying," threatens to marginalize both intellectual history and its relation to critical theory that articulates and opens for critical scrutiny various unexamined assumptions (or what goes without saying, including in the historical profession). See, for example, Spiegel's introduction to Gabrielle Spiegel, ed., *Practicing History: New Directions in Historical Writing after the Linguistic Turn* (New York: Routledge, 2005), and the comparable introduction by Bonnell and Hunt to Victoria E. Bonnell and Lynn Hunt, eds., *Beyond the Cultural Turn: New Directions in the Study*

an interactive relational network that would have a critical potential with respect to processes of one-dimensional definition, objectification, commodification, and sovereign assertion. One challenge in the study of trauma is that it is in a sense an out-of-context or radically decontextualizing (and disempowering) experience that signals the breakdown of meaning and context (as well as of integrated experience or identity) and poses the problem not only of representation but also (albeit differentially for those with different subject positions) of how to work through that breakdown or unsettlement toward possibly different, significantly transformed, and always threatened reconfigurations of meaning and agency. For, once it occurs, trauma, if not engaged by processes that counter its effects, may itself become an all-consuming "context" that obliterates the experiential relevance of other contexts and extinguishes all sense of possibility.

There are many reasons to maintain and rework the relation between cultural and intellectual history, as well as critical theory, rather than to sever it. Intellectual history has been a principal site for validating the idea that reading counts as a form of research (an idea that does not come "naturally" to some historians and social scientists). It has also been the primary channel in historiography for varieties of critical theory, and it may serve to provide an impetus for critical attentiveness in the use of the culture concept, which in certain ways functions as a kind of floating signifier, at times making culture itself seem like the elusive Moby Dick of the historian's quest for recovered meaning. Conversely, cultural history is a basis for a continually renewed critique of the narrowing of intellectual history in the direction of Western high culture and of any pretension it may have to addressing a transcendental, universal, or perennial level of culture. This pretension may be contrasted with an aspect of intellectual history I have already indicated, that of exploring the extent to which artifacts are situationally transcendent or even may have a transhistorical possibility in their modes of address, indicating how they may be read differently over time and understood as both challenging or disrupting contexts and intervening inventively in changing contexts—a crucial possibility that undergoes questionable reduction when it is hypostatized by a notion of universality. From the perspectives of both intellectual and cultural history, one may insist on an openness to the unpredictable and uncanny, even argue that there is in every other, as in oneself, an enigmatic or unconscious alterity, but nonetheless question a (sometimes

---

*of Society and Culture* (Berkeley: University of California Press, 1999). I return to this issue in chapter 2.

all-too-predictable) fixation on the aporia, the totally other, the "real," or the unrepresentable, including a centering of history on an abyssal, all-consuming quest for an ecstatic, sublime, or nauseating *Erlebnis*—an unmediated, intuitive experience to be found somewhere at the end of the line. Such options become especially attractive when one is moving away from or even fleeing an opposing extreme perspective, such as formalism, radical constructivism, or systems theory. Especially noteworthy in this respect is Frank Ankersmit's move from radical constructivism to a bold attempt to center history on a seemingly sublime, immediate experience in direct contact with the past.[15] One finds similar initiatives in literary criticism, especially in the attempt to link if not identify trauma with the sublime.[16] In my judgment, the sublime is better approached in a nondismissive but critical and self-critical manner that inquires into its manifold variations, uses, and abuses, including the way it has become prominent as a transfiguration of trauma and may even at times impede historical and critical inquiry, for example, into the violent and traumatic events of the Shoah.[17] For example, Linda Belau, who finds fault even with Claude Lanzmann and Shoshana Felman in this regard, argues that the only truly "ethical" approach to trauma is to affirm its radical incomprehensibilty or unreadability.[18] (Here the "ethical" seems to encrypt an abstractly theoretical or "theoreticist" displacement of the religious and theological, however empty or void.) And, in their provocative study, Michael Bernard-Donals and Richard Glejzer oppose bearing witness, as a sublime moment of blank, ineffable, awe-struck apprehension, to giving testimony, as the fall or descent into discourse.[19]

But genuine alternatives are not provided by an unqualified, "diremptive" or radically disjunctive turn to the traumatic, the incomprehensible, or the sublime, on the one hand, and a conflation of historical understanding with familiarizing contextualization (or "territorialization"), on the other. Important as it is, contextualization (including a concern for both intention and its

15. F. R. Ankersmit, *Sublime Historical Experience* (Stanford: Stanford University Press, 2005).

16. I return to this problem in chapter 3.

17. For a useful study of the sublime over time in Western thought, see Philip Shaw, *The Sublime* (London: Routledge, 2006). Shaw, however, may pay insufficient attention to desires for radical transcendence, or at least its traces, in certain initiatives.

18. Linda Belau, "Trauma and the Material Signifier," *Postmodern Culture* 11 (2001), http://jefferson.village.virginia.edu/pmc/current.issue/11.2belau.html. See also the measured discussion in Stef Craps, *Trauma and Ethics in the Novels of Graham Swift: No Short-Cuts to Salvation* (Brighton: Sussex Academy Press, 2005), 9–13.

19. *Between Witness and Testimony: The Holocaust and the Limits of Representation* (New York: State University Press of New York, 2001). See my discussion in chapter 3.

insertion in a larger social field) is a necessary but not sufficient condition of historical and critical understanding. And adding "plurality" to context does not account for the mutually overdetermined relations of texts and contexts. One might even suggest, as does Michel de Certeau in *The Possession at Loudun* (227–28), that an extreme contextualizing, objectifying history serves a carceral and exorcistic function by eliminating a threatening "other" from our society and confining it to the past, where it is rendered initially opaque but in a canny fashion that simultaneously promises full meaning if the other (the sorcerer or the sacrificer, not to say the cat-killer) is grasped in context. In its more extreme, unself-questioning, presumably explanatory forms, contextualization may also oversimplify the complexity, internal divisions, and uncertainties of a riven past and, through unchecked objectification, function to obscure or deny one's own implication in the problems one studies. The issue is rather how an unfinalized notion of contextualization may help both to avoid misunderstandings and to open readings of cultural artifacts that have a renewed ability to address and question both their contexts and the reader. To work in this way, contextualization is better understood as an active, internally contested process, and at the very least it is conjoined with belated recognitions related to the passage of time. Such recognitions, which take seriously our involvement in temporality, enable us to supplement questions raised in the past with other questions that those in the past were not in a position to raise (including such questions as whether atheism was even thinkable in a given time and place—a question Rabelais, for example, did not explicitly raise for himself).[20]

20. See Lucien Febvre, *The Problem of Unbelief in the Sixteenth Century, the Religion of Rabelais,* trans. Beatrice Gottlieb (1962; Cambridge: Harvard University Press, 1982). Of course belated recognition raises the knotty problems of anachronism and projection, but it cannot be reduced to them. And one need not agree with Febvre's response to the important question he raises about the possibility of "unbelief" in a given context—a response that may be too self-certain. More cautious and qualified but still controversial is Max Weber's approach in *The Protestant Ethic and the Spirit of Capitalism,* trans. Talcott Parsons, foreword R. H. Tawney (1904–5, 1920; New York: Charles Scribner's Sons, 1958). Weber poses questions concerning the relations between a religious orientation in early modern Christianity (epitomized in Protestant sects such as Calvinism and the ambiguously termed Puritanism) and the "qualitative formation and the quantitative expansion" of a capitalistic "spirit over the world" (91) with its broader consequences for "the historical development of modern culture" (92). People during the Reformation period could not possibly have addressed or even raised these questions for themselves. He also finds resistance to (as well as misunderstanding of) his views concerning those complex relations at his own time, as evidenced in his voluminous and sometimes heated footnotes, where at one point he exclaims: "One should really only criticize things which one has read, or the argument of which, if read, one has not already forgotten" (201). In contrast to orthodox marxist theories concerning "a reflection of material conditions in the ideal superstructure," which he here finds to be "patent nonsense" (75), he asserts that Benjamin

Nonteleological recognitions attest to the role of a self-questioning dialogic exchange with the past requiring responsive understanding and interpretation sensitive both to the challenge of alterity and to the limits as well as the possibilities of meaning. Moreover, responsive understanding has an affective dimension involving the problem of empathy or compassion in a sense not equated with identification or tantamount to the foreclosure or evasion of sociopolitical problems but rather requiring the affirmation of the "other" as in significant ways "other," the experience of empathic unsettlement with respect to the traumatic and the disorienting, and the attempt to connect the notion of working through the past to sociopolitical practice. The consequence of these admittedly contestable assertions (which require extensive unpacking) is that a cognitively responsible approach to the past is obligated to frame and justify the selection and validation of what one counts as pertinent contexts, notably in terms of their relative weight, limitations, and relation to other contexts. For example, how does one estimate the relative significance of, or trace the interaction between, Heidegger's sustained engagement with past philosophers or with theological and religious traditions (including mystical tendencies), on the one hand, and his implication in contemporary currents, such as the ideology of conservative revolution or the Nazi movement, on the other—a question that does not arise for those who see Heidegger as a Nazi ideologist or, on the contrary, as a thinker who, after 1934, thought in a manner totally disengaged from anything to do with

---

Franklin—a paradigmatic figure for him—had the time-is-money spirit of capitalism before its prevalence as an economic system. And Franklin's ethic of "money-making as an end in itself to which people were bound, as a calling" (73) would have been "simply unthinkable" (74) to Thomas Aquinas and others in the Middle Ages. Still, the ruptures over time are not total, and the specters of Franklin and the Puritans continue to haunt the world Weber himself inhabits, for "the idea of duty in one's calling prowls about in our lives like the ghost of dead religious beliefs" (182). Aside from the issue of the often-disguised displacement of the religious in the secular (or postsecular), a question Weber's study helps to raise is that of the possible, if unintentional, effects—both for religion (the "death of God") and for the unlimited exploitation of nature and its inhabitants—of a total "investment" of the sacred in the radically transcendent or "totally other." From the Calvinist perspective that stresses "in its extreme inhumanity" (104), the doctrines of predestination and the salvation only of a Hidden God's freely chosen elect, Weber observes that "for the damned to complain of their lot would be much the same as for animals to bemoan the fact they were not born as men. For everything of the flesh is separated from God by an unbridgeable gulf and deserves of Him only eternal death, in so far as He has not decreed otherwise for the glorification of His Majesty" (103). For informative approaches to Weber, see Fritz Ringer, *Max Weber: An Intellectual Biography* (Chicago: University of Chicago Press, 2004), and Hartmut Lehman and Guenther Roth, eds., *Weber's "Protestant Ethic": Origins, Evidence, Contexts* (New York: Cambridge University Press, 1993). See also my comparison of Weber and Emile Durkheim in *Emile Durkheim: Sociologist and Philosopher* (1972; 1985; Aurora, Colo.: Davies Group, 2001), 165–70.

National Socialism? And how does one approach the ways in which the more inventive or uncanny aspects of his thought cannot be reduced to his various contexts but continue to pose a challenge for us and our contexts, at times even tempting the intellectual historian to become an intellectual by engaging actively with the thought processes being studied (an undertaking in which thought becomes a possibly dangerous supplement to research—somewhat as "going native" does for the anthropologist)?

I think such questions are becoming widely acknowledged and investigated with respect to undoubtedly "useful" or even insistently pressing contexts or categories such as gender, race, ethnicity, class, and religion as well as less recognized or developed categories such as displaced religiosity or secular faith and operative ideology, even so-called postsecular thought, notably on the level of basic assumptions and their role in the formation of subjects. I do not think this means engaging in political theology in the manner of Carl Schmitt, but it does imply a critical examination of the relation of one's thinking to theological concepts and their displacements in political thought.[21] Whether there should be a general opening to what is termed postsecular thought, is a provocative question, but how that opening should be made and the critical and self-critical processes it may require are intricate questions.[22] In any event, it has become evident that one needs a more complex concept of ideology that is not situated at the extreme of fully articulated systematic thought functioning in a binary manner opposed to "culture," whose own discursive components are left undeveloped and at times seemingly divorced from practice and a so-called logic of practice.[23]

21. See Schmitt, *Political Theology: Four Chapters on the Concept of Sovereignty,* trans. George Schwab (1922; Cambridge: MIT Press, 1985). With respect to sovereignty and related notions such as decision and the state of exception, Schmitt's oversimplifying, categorical assertion was: "All significant concepts of the modern theory of the state are secularized theological concepts not only because of their historical development—in which they were transferred from theology to the theory of the state, whereby, for example, the omnipotent God became the omnipotent lawgiver—but also because of their systematic structure, the recognition of which is necessary for a sociological consideration of these concepts. The exception in jurisprudence is analogous to the miracle in theology" (36). Of course a key problem in Schmitt is the relation between identity (or homology) and analogy, whereby the latter often seems absorbed by the former.

22. In this book, especially in chapter 2, I indicate my reservations about the ambitious attempt to address the postsecular and political theology in Slavoj Žižek, Eric L. Santner, and Kenneth Reinhard's *The Neighbor: Three Inquiries in Political Theology,* and Eric L. Santner's *On Creaturely Life: Rilke, Benjamin, Sebald* (Chicago: University of Chicago Press, 2006), as well as in Žižek's thought in general. In a somewhat different key, see Jane Bennett, *The Enchantment of Modern Life: Attachments, Crossings, and Ethics* (Princeton: Princeton University Press, 2001).

23. For the notion of a logic of practice, see Roger Chartier, *On the Edge of the Cliff: History, Language, and Practices,* trans. Lydia G. Cochrane (Baltimore: Johns Hopkins University

Ideology should rather be understood in its flexible and multifarious forms that cannot be reduced to the opposition between systematic articulation, on the one hand, and practice that is divorced from discourse, on the other (with a Hegel at one extreme and a militarized automaton, or perhaps an idealized, "pious" participant in a "traditional" religious practice, at the other—beings [to the extent they exist] whose own formation raises the question of possible roles of ideology). Ideology should also be seen in terms of subject formation involving the role of fantasy and (positive or negative) identification. In summarizing one current of recent thought about Nazi ideology and antisemitism, notably in the work of Saul Friedländer, Alon Confino observes in his interestingly entitled "Fantasies about the Jews: Cultural Reflections on the Holocaust" (a title indicative of the concern with fantasy in the study of culture):

> At the center of Nazi anti-Semitism were nonpragmatic, redemptive fantasies aimed at extirpating the Jews from German society. . . . The fantasies of extirpating the Jews were malleable, contingent, and thus a proof of how uncertain the Nazis were in building their racial civilization. They were internalized, but also rejected, opposed, doubted or just ridiculed. There were many ways Nazi society could have developed within the framework of racial ideas. It is a mistake to interpret the Nazis as camouflaging "real" intentions, for their real intentions changed with time. Differently put, thinking with fantasies avoids telling a story of the orderly and continuous progression of a radicalized war context coupled with Nazi ideas reduced to the instrumental rationality of a class of professionals and racial-biological zealots. Instead, it appreciates that the making of the Nazi universe must have been tremendously messy, where irrational, redemptive images came to possess the aura of logical, scientific and proven truths.[24]

I would add that such a perspective (which would require some qualification and reformulation) indicates not the irrelevance but the limitations of a means-ends or narrowly instrumental schema in analyzing the Nazi phenomenon and developments relating to it, including the schema that presents a culture in which means-ends rationality went berserk, with violent means

---

Press, 1997). See also Gabrielle Spiegel's introduction to *Practicing History,* which I discuss in chapter 2.

24. *History & Memory* 17 (2005): 307. See also Enzo Traverso, *Le passé, modes d'emploi: Histoire, mémoire, politique* (Paris: La Fabrique éditions, 2005) and Federico Finchelstein, *Transatlantic Fascism: Ideology, Violence, and the Sacred, 1919–1945* (Durham: Duke University Press, 2009).

exceeding ends or with rationality reaching a mysterious point of dialectical reversal.[25] Moreover, one pertinent context of understanding is always our own, and the problem of self-contextualization has to be on the agenda of a critical use of contextualization, as does the related issue of the subject positions of historians or other scholars in relation to objects of study. In brief, the relation of texts or signifying practices to contexts (as well as the nature of contexts themselves) is complex and divided. This relation is in variable ways informative, symptomatic or ideologically reinforcing, critical, and possibly transformative or situationally transcendent, pointing to the problematizing as well as utopian dimension of texts and to the complex, contingent, and contested dimensions of contexts. Hence, the appeal to context does not simplify the problem of how to read but complicates it in necessary and unavoidable ways.

There have been some recent pressures in the discipline of history that repeat and displace older pressures and reinforce reductive or integral contextualism, at times in the form of a born-again positivism. One prominent pressure is the widespread resistance to theory and especially to forms of critical theory, which may be accompanied by a resistance to intellectual history, particularly in its linkages with critical theory. There are numerous markers of resistance if not reaction in history, for example, such books as *Telling the Truth about History, In Defense of History, Sur la "crise" de l'histoire, Reconstructing History: The Emergence of a New Historical Society,* and *Beyond the Cultural Turn.* At the outer limit, there is the seemingly unsurpassable *The Killing of History: How a Discipline Is Being Murdered by Literary Critics and Social Theorists.*[26] Telling the truth, defending, bemoaning crises, forming new societies, going beyond, fantasizing death threats, and so forth, may well

25. The first view is briefly suggested toward the end of Isabel V. Hull's study of German military culture with respect to the latter's implications for the Nazi regime. See *Absolute Destruction: Military Culture and the Practices of War in Imperial Germany* (Ithaca: Cornell University Press, 2005). (I discuss this book in chapter 4.) The second is that of Max Horkheimer and Theodor Adorno in *Dialectic of Enlightenment,* trans. John Cumming (1944, New York: Seabury Press, 1972). Horkheimer and Adorno's discussion of antisemitism, however, has points of intersection with Confino's comments, for it indicates that scapegoating and sacrificialism are not simply a dialectical reversal of instrumental rationality. See also the thought-provoking discussion in Carolyn J. Dean, "History Writing, Numbness, and the Restoration of Dignity," *History of the Human Sciences* 17 (2004): 58–96, which addresses problems of identification in the writing of history, with probing discussions of the work of Daniel Jonah Goldhagen, Inge Clendinnen, and Omer Bartov.

26. Joyce Appleby, Lynn Hunt, and Margaret Jacob, *Telling the Truth about History* (New York: W. W. Norton, 1994); Richard Evans, *In Defense of History* (New York: W. W. Norton, 1997); Gérard Noiriel, *Sur la "crise" de l'histoire* (Paris: Belin, 1996); Elizabeth Fox-Genovese and Elisabeth Lasch-Quinn, *Reconstructing History: The Emergence of a New Historical Society* (New York:

function as pretexts or screens. Important figures in the discipline have not only reconsidered youthful enthusiasms and put forward measured, possibly salutary critiques but at times have undergone a hardening of conceptual categories in what seems to be an unfortunate spirit of retrenchment.[27] But one should avoid erecting a composite "straw man," for there are important, more measured counterforces at work and at play in the historical discipline, and further analysis would require differentiations among the works I have mentioned. Indeed, developments have been uneven. Recent theoretical initiatives have had some effect in changing the discipline, and they have been taken up in a number of ways, at times in a critically selective manner or an unassuming fashion whereby they are integrated without fanfare into an analysis or a complex and at times self-questioning narrative.[28]

My basic point is that the turn to cultural history (like the earlier turn and the recent return to social history) should not displace or even eliminate intellectual history and should not become a rationale for aligning cultural history either with the most objectifying, contextualizing historiography or with relatively atheoretical or antitheoretical forms of cultural studies or social history. It should be conjoined with intellectual history and critical theory and exist in a fruitful tension with more conventional or standard approaches to historiography. It requires not only research in the conventional sense,

---

Routledge, 1999); Keith Windschuttle, *The Killing of History: How a Discipline Is Being Murdered by Literary Critics and Social Theorists* (Paddington, Australia: Macleay Press, 1996).

27. For a strong, well-argued defense of the role of critical theory in history, along with a pointed critique of tendencies toward retrenchment, see Joan W. Scott, "History-writing as Critique," in *Manifestos for History,* ed. Keith Jenkins, Sue Morgan, and Alun Munslow (London: Routledge, 2007), 19–38.

28. As an effective effort at integrating complex narrative and critical-theoretical awareness, I would recommend, inter alia, Jeremy Varon's *Bringing the War Home: The Weather Underground, the Red Army Faction, and Revolutionary Violence in the Sixties and Seventies* (Berkeley: University of California Press, 2004). This book might be read as a historical counterpart and at times a countervoice to Michael Hardt and Antonio Negri's *Multitude* (New York: Penguin, 2004), which often returns to the orientation and some of the rhetoric of the 1960s without providing a genealogy that would help situate and at times elaborate its various claims. See also the theoretically informed narrative of Tracie Matysik, *Reforming the Moral Subject: Ethics and Sexuality in Central Europe, 1890–1930* (Ithaca: Cornell University Press, 2008). On the level of more overtly experimental overtures, I would mention the journal *Rethinking History* as a site where such ventures are occurring, of course with the necessary unevenness of results from more or less experimental efforts. *History and Theory,* especially with the editorial participation of Ethan Kleinberg; *The Journal of the History of Ideas;* and *Modern Intellectual History* (launched in 2004) are also important reference points. Also notable is Elizabeth A. Clark, *History, Theory, Text: Historians and the Linguistic Turn* (Cambridge: Harvard University Press, 2004). Clark is a historian of early Christianity teaching at Duke, and she attempts to make a case for the applicability of historiographical and critical theory both in general and in relation to the material on which she works (patristic literature).

whose importance should not be underestimated, but reading, reflection, criticism, and self-criticism addressed not only to the methods and results of research but to its assumptions and possible implications.

One may question aspects of "conventional" history but nonetheless attempt to recuperate many of its legitimate concerns in a different framework of research and inquiry. One may also raise doubts about its excesses, exclusions, and limitations. By the same token, one may self-critically question the excesses and limitations of theory that is insufficiently tested and contested by historical resistances. It is obviously necessary to explore the question of the approaches to theory that are most fruitful in an exchange with historiography, an issue of interest not only to professional historians but to others with an interest in history.

Theory need not be identified with theoreticism or thought that operates primarily on a speculative, purely conceptual, often self-referential, level that feeds on itself (at times to the point of tying itself in quasi-transcendental knots) and construes history as a source of illustrations or signs, a repository of incommensurable particularities or singularities, or a transhistorical abstraction (equated with trauma, for example). I think this inadequately qualified conception of theory is prominent in figures such as Agamben and Žižek.[29]

29. For a defense of theoreticism à la Žižek, including impossible totalization via a counterintuitive Žižekian reading of Hegel as theorist of the "not-all" Absolute, see Paul Eisenstein, *Traumatic Encounters: Holocaust Representation and the Hegelian Subject* (Albany: State University Press of New York, 2003). In Eisenstein a structural or transhistorical concept of trauma, in the guise of the Lacanian real, leads to an illustrative and derivative use of history. In a blurb on the back cover of Eisenstein's book, Žižek hails it as "a forceful redemption of the power of theory." Despite the book's brilliance, I would see it as an overextension, or all-or-nothing version, of theory in an abstract theoreticism that obviates an analysis and engagement with historical traumas in their specificity, thereby failing to confront the problem of articulating the relations between theory and history instead of reducing one to the other. It amounts to an inverted mirror image of the reductively contextualizing historicism it rejects (and curiously ascribes to my approach), not a genuine alternative to it. Eisenstein is unable to see how the very problem of the intricate relation (articulation or at times disarticulation) of structural and historical trauma is itself explored in texts to which he refers, such as Thomas Mann's *Doctor Faustus* or David Grossman's *See Under: Love,* where the importance of the specifically historical and, in the latter novel, the intergenerational is insistent, although there are problematic aspects of both novels in these respects (the invocation of the devil in *Doctor Faustus* or Anshel Wasserman's appeal to seemingly transhistorical forces, especially in light of his complicitous relationship as storyteller to Neigel, the concentration camp commandant in Grossman's novel). Eisenstein even sees *Doctor Faustus* as "provid[ing] us with a manifesto or blueprint for how to proceed" in and through the character and approach to music of Adrian Leverkühn. Not the novel as a whole or the intricate relations in it of writer, interposed narrator (Zeitblom), "mad" musical genius (Leverkühn), Germany, and the reader but, rather, Leverkühn's own "diabolical" quest for the aesthetic breakthrough is taken to eventuate in "fundamentally a music of witnessing... to that structural trauma for which [the Nazi] regime promised redress"

Of course one should not reject all theoretical speculation. But the problem for intellectual and cultural history linked to critical theory is to elaborate approaches to theory that are in a mutually provocative, in part unpredictable, relation to history and to historical as well as sociopolitical questions.

It does not suffice, for example, to show how Auschwitz illustrates the Lacanian "real" or Jean-François Lyotard's "differend." Moreover, as I have already intimated, one may insist that a multidimensional understanding of the Nazi genocide cannot be based only on a theoretical conception of *homo sacer* or biopower. Such an interpretation is curiously aligned in a rather unreflective way with an important current in mainstream historiography itself that one-sidedly stresses the machinery of destruction, modernization, bureaucratization, means-ends rationality, and pest control, thereby occulting the role of "nonrational," quasi-sacrificial dimensions of Nazi ideology and practice directed against a perceived source of ritual or phobic pollution and aimed at collective redemption as well as the fulfillment of the sacred orders of the Führer.[30] It is noteworthy that the only historical text in the bibliography of

(120–21). Hence Leverkühn is seen as a Žižekian tragic or posttragic hero who takes problems to an implosive limit and thereby does not give up on his desire, traversing the fantasy into a consuming abyss. Perhaps this understanding might apply to an imagined filmic version of *Doctor Faustus* made by David Lynch. And one might well argue that the parallel between Leverkühn's music and the onset of, or preconditions for, the Nazi regime (not the regime itself) is at best offset and problematic. (For example, three years elapse between Leverkühn's subsidence into a coma, with a return to his mother's womblike protection, and the Nazi seizure of power in 1933.) One might also suggest that Leverkühn in some sense undertakes on the level of personal tragedy and self-sacrifice what the Nazi regime, by scapegoating others and projectively construing them as causes of pollution and dislocation in the phantasmatic *Volksgemeinschaft,* came to enact on the level of collective atrocity and murderous excess. But it is dubious in the extreme to take Leverkühn as the hero of his time and a model for ours. In Mann's novel, Leverkühn is figured as an altogether equivocal being who embodies the best and the most questionable, if not the worst, in Germany, someone whose transgression of limits is bound up with a repetition compulsion and does not lend itself to a heroic, rather one-dimensional, symptomatic reading. For a different approach, see chap. 6, "History and the Devil in Mann's *Doctor Faustus,*" in my *History, Politics, and the Novel* (Ithaca: Cornell University Press, 1987). Eisenstein even argues that the acknowledgment, or indeed what he sees as the reexperience, of transhistorical or structural trauma (the Lacanian real) serves, and apparently suffices, ethically and politically as a counterforce to fascism. Like Žižek, he not only skirts specific historical issues but ignores the possibility that some fascists and Nazis may have been fascinated by, played out, or indulged the structural dimension of trauma related to excess, unheard-of transgression, risk, sublimity, and the so-called death drive. I discuss Žižek's comparable argument in chapter 2 of this book.

30. On these problems, see Saul Friedländer's *Memory, History, and the Extermination of the Jews of Europe* (Bloomington: Indiana University Press, 1993), *Nazi Germany and the Jews, 1933–1939: The Years of Persecution* (New York: HarperCollins, 1997), and *Nazi Germany and the Jews, 1939–1945: The Years of Extermination* (New York: HarperCollins, 2007), as well as my own books: *Representing the Holocaust, History and Memory after Auschwitz* (Ithaca: Cornell

Agamben's *Remnants of Auschwitz* is Raul Hilberg's *Destruction of the European Jews,* the classic exposition of the machinery-of-destruction analysis that stresses the role of bureaucracy.[31] Like many others, Agamben avoids one of the most intricate problems in the understanding of Nazi ideology and practice, to wit, the seemingly paradoxical relation between various, at times very different, registers. For example, how should we view the relation between the reduction of the other to "mere life" or the role of bureaucratically administered pest control (which is indeed important) and the response to a sense of pollution or contamination in the *Volksgemeinschaft* associated with a quasi-sacrificial quest for purification and redemption (with the *Endlösung* as *Auslösung* and *Erlösung,* that is, the "Final Solution" as release or liberation and redemption)? To give another instance, one cannot have an acceptable analysis or rewriting of Heidegger or Georges Bataille that does not include a careful, more than perfunctory, inquiry into the former's affiliation with the Nazis or the latter's fascination with fascism. Theory on a sustained conceptual level is valuable in testing and contesting categories and expanding the range of conceptual and imaginative possibilities. But it also facilitates questionable elisions through a quasi-transcendental self-understanding that does not allow for an explicit, significant, mutually challenging relation to history. Its inverted mirror image, not its alternative, is conventional contextualizing history or objectifying historicism that embeds interpretations in narratives or descriptions without critically examining interpretations as interpretations and lacks a significant relation to critical theory, especially theory that addresses the assumptions of historiography. To put the point metaphorically, conventional contextualizing history tends to fly below, or at times even in, the cloud cover, while overly abstract conceptual theory (or theoreticism) may sometimes move in the stratosphere with an occasional appropriative look at objects far below.

Implicit in what I have been saying is the idea that the defense of a cogent articulation of intellectual history, cultural history, and critical theory opens the problem of the understanding of critical theory to be elaborated and argumentatively defended as pertinent to historical inquiry. At a minimum, this problem challenges the historian to engage critical theories argumentatively in the attempt to work out an approach that addresses both

University Press, 1998), and *Writing History, Writing Trauma* (Baltimore: Johns Hopkins University Press, 2001).

31. On Agamben, see my *History in Transit: Experience, Identity, Critical Theory* (Ithaca: Cornell University Press, 2004), chap. 4. See also chapter 6 of this book.

historiographical assumptions and the manner in which research is conceptualized and conducted.

Allow me to give one brief example of such engagement that has occupied me at various points in my work. There are of course others, notably deconstruction, which I have discussed elsewhere.[32] Here I shall mention only psychoanalysis, which has often been conjoined with deconstruction. I would contend that psychoanalysis should not be understood as individual psychology, as an anodyne hermeneutic, or as an object to be analyzed only in context. Nor should it be seen only or even primarily as objectifying psychohistory that unreflectively applies psychoanalytic concepts (such as the Oedipal complex) to presumably explain the behavior of individuals or groups from the past. At least in its articulation with historiography, psychoanalysis should rather be seen, and in significant measure rethought, as a critical theory with sociocultural dimensions. Its basic concepts are to be construed as undercutting the opposition between individual and society and seen as individuated or collectivized in different contexts or situations. Here there may well be tensions. For example, fabricating a different past as a therapeutic way to make the present more livable or the future more possible *may* be justified clinically in certain extreme individual cases, marked by incapacitating suffering, but I doubt whether it would be justified on a collective level or with respect to sociopolitical analysis and critique. (This consideration is perhaps one reason for different responses to *Life Is Beautiful,* which is a kind of filmic analog of the therapeutic idea of imagining a flower growing on the selection ramp at Auschwitz.)

For the historian a primary concern of psychoanalysis is historiography itself, its assumptions, and its relation to its objects, raising the question of the relation of the historian to the past, including the role of transferential implication in the object of study with the tendency to identify with, repeat, or performatively reenact forces active in it. A key problem is how to engage that often denied or avoided transferential tendency to repeat, in terms of modulations of acting-out, working-over, and working-through. In other words, instead of being taken as a license for putting past individuals or groups on the couch, psychoanalysis may be understood primarily as a self-critical mode of

32. See, for example, my discussion in *A Preface to Sartre* (Ithaca: Cornell University Press, 1978); *Rethinking Intellectual History: Texts, Contexts, Language* (Ithaca: Cornell University Press, 1983); and *Soundings in Critical Theory* (Ithaca: Cornell University Press, 1989), esp. 5–8 and 18–20; and *Representing the Holocaust,* esp. 125–33. On the role of deconstruction in professional historiography, including the prevalent, marked resistances to it, see the excellent article by Ethan Kleinberg, "Haunting History: Deconstruction and the Spirit of Revision," *History and Theory* 46 (2007): 113–43.

inquiry, indicating the way the historian is placed in question by investigation of the object of study and emphasizing the problem of the relation between the present—including professional historians in the present—and the past with possible implications for the future. This larger context would itself serve as the framework for legitimate but limited forms of contextual objectification.[33] (Here one has the problem of how to understand and undertake legitimate and necessary forms of contextualization that do not simply objectify the past or detach and "disimplicate" oneself or the present from an involvement with it and its aftermath. Certain attempts to drive a sharp wedge between history and memory, at the expense of their tangled interactions, are, I think, motivated by a desire for "disimplication" of the historian and the historical profession from a fully objectified past.)[34]

I would immediately add that the very attempt to combine intellectual history, cultural history, and critical theory itself generates tensions or even aporias in that the three cannot be synthesized without leaving remainders or unresolved problems. But these tensions are necessary. How different historians negotiate them will justifiably vary without eliminating the need for debate and mutual criticism. The most convenient and conventional option is to avoid or foreclose the tensions by taking one or another critical theory as at best an object of contextualizing research and not investigating its bearing on one's own research protocols and procedures. Hence one may study psychoanalysis, trauma theory, deconstruction, or Frankfurt school critical theory without asking how their concepts or concerns affect, or exert pressure on, one's own inquiry and its assumptions, typically with the effect of unself-consciously enacting what a critical theory signals as problematic (for example, objectification and seeming closure in Martin Jay's nonetheless impressive, widely read, early book on the Frankfurt school, *The Dialectical Imagination: A History of the Frankfurt School and the Institute of Social Research, 1923–1950*).[35] One should be wary of advocating any specific combination

33. I have already referred to my analysis in *History in Transit* (83–93) of the implications of resistance to self-reflective engagement with critical theory, notably in the form of psychoanalysis, whose concepts are deceptively taken only as objects of study, with respect to Ruth Leys's important work *Trauma: A Genealogy* (Chicago: University of Chicago Press, 2000).

34. See chap. 1, "History and Memory: In the Shadow of the Holocaust," in my *History and Memory after Auschwitz*.

35. Boston: Little, Brown and Company, 1973. Jay's approach to intellectual history has to a significant extent changed over the years and combines the thorough scholarship and erudition that characterized his first book with a more "dialogical" and critical-theoretical orientation to his material. See, for example, his *Fin-de-Siècle Socialism and other Essays* (New York: Routledge, 1988), *Force Fields: Between Intellectual History and Cultural Critique* (New York: Routledge, 1993), and *Songs of Experience: Modern American and European Variations on a*

of intellectual history, cultural history, and critical theory. But one can and, I think, should argue that the attempt be made to articulate their relations and to engage the tensions, both enabling and disabling, that this attempt brings about.

A clear and obvious implication of what I have been saying is that there should not be a single dominant, exclusionary model of acceptable history that establishes the professional identity of the historian and serves as the institutional charter for such crucial practices as vetting graduate students or hiring and tenuring faculty. One may certainly argue for approaches but not impose them or simply assume their dominance in evaluating work, making appointments, or recommending promotions. In fact one may seek out colleagues whose approach both poses a challenge to one's own orientation and provides alternative models for students. A department that studies all

---

*Universal Theme* (Berkeley: University of California Press, 2005). A compelling and in good part defensible recent case of synoptic reading provides an impressive analysis and critique of colonial violence, which is seen in relation to later genocides, including the Holocaust. I am referring to Olivier Le Cour Grandmaison's *Coloniser. Exterminer* (Paris: Fayard, 2005), which, in a manner reminiscent of Georg Lukács's approach, reads Joseph Conrad's 1902 novel *Heart of Darkness* as an instance of critical realism in its analysis and indictment of colonial practices. Unlike more simplistic advocates of contextual reading, Le Cour Grandmaison does not present Conrad himself as an exponent of colonialism and imperialism. Rather, following the lead of Sven Lindqvist (*"Exterminate All the Brutes": One Man's Odyssey into the Heart of Darkness and the Origins of European Genocide* [1992; New York: The New Press, 1996]), he understands *Heart of Darkness* as drawing from documentary sources and Conrad's own experience to render a literary account of colonial activity typical not only of the Congo but of colonialism in Africa more generally. For Le Cour Grandmaison Conrad's novel is in point of fact a more reliable history of these empirical processes than were actual histories of the time and even subsequently, histories that were misleading vehicles of ideologies of progress, imperial glory, and the "civilizing mission." He concludes that "the literature of Conrad, at least that which has held our attention, is a literature of radical and brutal disenchantment. That's why it was rebellious at its time; it remains so today, for it allows one to take the just measure of what was the conquest and colonization of Africa for the populations that were subjected to it" (167; my translation). Despite his trenchant formulations and incisive analyses, Le Cour Grandmaison, while not reducing texts to symptoms of contexts and instead recognizing their critical power of provocation, does not inquire into their internal tensions or self-contestations, for example, that between Tocqueville's violent, at times exterminatory response to North African peoples (or to the working class in France after 1848) and his democratic liberalism, reserved for "civilized" peoples. (On Tocqueville in these respects, see my *History and Reading: Tocqueville, Foucault, French Studies,* chap. 2). In part because of his very limited attention to formal dimensions of analysis, he also does not look into the different if not divergent movements in *Heart of Darkness* itself. In Conrad's text there is both a radical condemnation of, and a fascination with, the violent excesses personified in Kurtz, a fascination that affects the narrator Marlowe and even the implied author and may well be conveyed to the reader as well, who is drawn in by the way a quest narrative almost inevitably endows its object (be it "the heart of darkness") with an at least ambivalent allure, an allure that includes the fascination of violence and its "dark" excesses. I thank Marie Muschalek for bringing Le Cour Grandmaison's text to my attention and return to it in notes in chapters 4 and 6.

regions of the world and contains members of various origins is altogether desirable. But it does not amount to an intellectually diversified department if it is ruled by one norm of professional identity and an unexamined professional identity politics, even an ethos of "fitting in" and conforming to one model of research. Indeed, a criterion of a strong and viable department is the willingness not only to tolerate but actively to seek out colleagues whose perspective is not well represented and may well pose a challenge to prominent if not dominant research orientations. Despite its undoubted value, the recent emphasis on narrative (often understood in other than experimental terms) may have gone astray both by downplaying the role of other historical approaches, including the critical essay, and by underwriting the already privileged status in the historical profession of archival research and the translation of archives into narratives. Contextualization, archival research, and translating archives into narratives are mainstays—indeed the three pillars—of conventional history at the present time. And they are indeed very important dimensions of historiography. But they call for continual rethinking that itself requires an inquiry into assumptions and modes of conceptualization implying a nexus between history, including intellectual and cultural history, and critical theory.

# CHAPTER 2

# Vicissitudes of Practice and Theory

> The repressive intolerance to the thought that is not immediately accompanied by instructions for action is founded on anxiety. Untrammeled thought and the posture that will not let it be bargained away must be feared because of what one deeply knows but cannot openly admit: that the thought is right.
>
> —Theodor W. Adorno, "Resignation"

A crucial question at the intersection of history and critical theory is how to intervene in the historical discipline in informed and cogent but flexible, noncodifiable ways that address its current configuration and try to point it in more desirable directions.[1] Such interventions should be attuned to the dimensions of historiography that are not confined to the present but have a longer history and a possible future in that they continue to pose, in different ways, thought-provoking questions over time. These dimensions of historiography make one mindful of the interaction between the historical and transhistorical forces that affect the historian—forces that may bring into question the possibilities of the historical enterprise and indicate the manner in which the historian, like others, is internally challenged by what has been figured in terms of the "transhistorically" (or structurally) traumatic, the dangerous supplement, the "extimate" other, the disorientingly uncanny, or that which leaves residues and remainders that set

1. Although I here go for the most part in distinctive directions, for lines of argument that supplement or at times parallel formulations in this chapter, see my "Resisting Apocalypse and Rethinking History," in *Manifestos for History*, ed. and intro. Keith Jenkins, Sue Morgan, and Alun Munslow (London: Routledge, 2007), 160–78, as well as my recent books, notably *Writing History, Writing Trauma* (Baltimore: Johns Hopkins University Press, 2001) and *History in Transit: Experience, Identity, Critical Theory* (Ithaca: Cornell University Press, 2004).

limits to a history of meaning in that they cannot be fully mastered or integrated meaningfully into a historicized narrative or interpretive account.[2] A break or event (in Alain Badiou's sense) may in some sense be a creation ex nihilo that is forged on the edge of an indeterminacy or void (a "madness" of sorts), but possibly traumatic indeterminacies or voids are themselves situated historically in changing ways that may be elucidated. A challenge here is to recognize and confront the importance of trauma in history relating to extreme or limit events, while not only questioning an identification of history with trauma but also allowing for, even insisting on, the significance of less dramatic yet debilitating phenomena (such as poverty) and the role of forces in history that may counteract the occurrence and the radically disorienting effects of trauma itself.

The interest in figures such as Giorgio Agamben, Alain Badiou, and Slavoj Žižek came about unpredictably and quite suddenly but can nonetheless be situated and contextualized within limits.[3] All three are in a significant sense

2. Derrida's deconstructive reading of Foucault's history of madness might in certain respects be taken as paradigmatic with reference to these questions. In Foucault himself, despite some inconsistency in usage, unreason (*déraison*) would seem to be the transhistorical force and madness (*folie*) its reduced modern form or figuration. Derrida asks whether the project of writing the history of madness itself—or rather unreason—is mad and whether one can write only a history of one or more of its figures or figurations over time, including madness in a more specifically modern sense. See Derrida's "Cogito and History of Madness," in *Writing and Difference,* trans., intro., and additional notes Alan Bass (1967; Chicago: University of Chicago Press, 1978), chap. 2, as well as my *History and Reading: Tocqueville, Foucault, French Studies* (Toronto: University of Toronto Press, 2000), chap. 3. On the concept of "extimacy" in Lacan, the entry in Dylan Evans's *Introductory Dictionary of Lacanian Psychoanalysis* (London: Routledge, 1996) is helpful: "Extimacy (*extimité*) Lacan coins the term '*extimité*' by applying the prefix 'ex' (from '*extérieur,*' 'exterior') to the French word '*intimité*' ('intimacy'). The resulting neologism, which may be rendered 'extimacy' in English, neatly expresses the way in which psychoanalysis problematises the opposition between inside and outside, between container and contained. . . . For example, the real is just as much inside as outside, and the unconscious is not a purely interior psychic system but an intersubjective structure ('the unconscious is outside'). Again, the Other is 'something strange to me, although it is at the heart of me'. . . . Furthermore, the centre of the subject is outside; the subject is ex-centric" (58–59).

3. One should not simply amalgamate these three thinkers, although there are lines of intersection between them as well as attempts to conjoin them. And one need not disparage the importance of their work in observing that their relatively recent rapid rise to prominence, in spite of the fact that both Agamben and Badiou have been working and publishing for quite some time, is in part related to the disappearance or eclipse of many figures in an earlier generation of high-theory superstars. Moreover, they take theory to its most extreme "theoreticist" limit and foreground tendencies that were at points qualified by earlier figures such as Foucault or Derrida, or even Lacan at times. The empty utopianism and at times the apocalyptic, violent fantasies that accompany theoreticism might be seen as the complement of disempowerment if not despair in the bleak political context of the recent past or even in the aftermath of 1968 with its hopes and disappointments.

unhistorical (or at times counterhistorical) thinkers who at best rely on very sweeping historical categories (such as modernity or "post-Auschwitz"), and they often subordinate history to the transhistorical or even the universal, at most referring or alluding to specific historical phenomena to illustrate transhistorical forces (such as the Lacanian real [in Žižek] or abjection, *homo sacer,* mere life, and the state of exception [in Agamben]). One may also note that history is not one of Badiou's four areas of ontological concern (science, art, politics, and love). For him mathematics seems more important philosophically than does history, and set theory is tantamount to fundamental ontology.[4] Obviated or reductively construed in such approaches is the complex relation between the transhistorical and the historical, along with the challenge of working out a mutually questioning interaction between historiography and theory.[5]

I would open a parenthesis to note that Žižek has objected in the following terms to an earlier version of my contention that he tends to subordinate the historical to, if not collapse it into, the transhistorical:

> This also enables us to answer Dominick la Capra's [*sic*] reproach according to which, the Lacanian notion of lack conflates two levels that have to be kept apart: the purely formal "ontological" lack constitutive of the symbolic order as such, and the particular traumatic experiences (exemplarily: holocaust) which could also NOT have occurred—particular historical catastrophes like the holocaust thus seem to be "legitimized" as directly grounded in the fundamental trauma that pertains to the very human existence.... Against this misunderstanding, one should emphasize that the quasi-transcendental lack and particular traumas are

4. Badiou sees himself as an insistently secular antiphilosopher. But his conception of the secular is problematic, especially when he invokes notions of grace, and his exemplar of the radical militant is Saint Paul. See, for example, his *Saint Paul: The Foundation of Universalism,* trans. Ray Brassier (1997; Stanford: Stanford University Press, 2003) and *Manifesto for Philosophy,* trans., ed., and intro. Norman Madarasz (1989; Albany: State University of New York Press, 1999).

5. The relation between the transhistorical and the universal as well as the (quasi)transcendental is problematic, and I am tempted to moot the question and even to argue that what is asserted to be universal or even (quasi)transcendental (notably some kind of foundational or originary trauma [including the Lacanian real] or, in Judith Butler, the closely related notion of the formation of subjectivity on the basis of a constitutive melancholy) is at best transhistorical and repeated (at times compulsively) in given traditions, such as dimensions of Christianity and Judaism. See Butler, *The Psychic Life of Power: Theories in Subjection* (Stanford: Stanford University Press, 1997), esp. 197–98. See also my more nuanced discussion in *Writing History, Writing Trauma,* 72–74. The approach I am suggesting would resist both "theoreticism," closely allied with universalism or (quasi)transcendentalism, and narrowly historicizing contextualism.

> linked in a negative way: far from being just the last link in the continuous chain of traumatic encounters that reaches back to the "symbolic castration," catastrophes like the holocaust are contingent (and, as such, avoidable) events which occur as the final result of the endeavours to OBFUSCATE the quasi-transcendental constitutive lack.[6]

I agree with Žižek's critique of a one-dimensional, unself-critical historicism and his important supplementary point that a historical trauma should not be seen as the last link in a chain leading back to the transhistorical. But I take issue with the manner in which he formulates the argument I make in "Trauma, Absence, Loss."[7] I distinguish analytically between transhistorical absence (or void) and historical losses or lacks but do not see the transhistorical as purely formal or argue that the two levels have to be kept apart. In fact I argue that in empirical cases, the two will be imbricated but that the analytic distinction is still important in that it resists the collapse of the transhistorical and the historical that subordinates the one to the other and leads either to confusion or to a deceptive explanation of one in terms of the other. (Also deceptive is the opposite of Žižek's tendency: the contextualizing explanation of everything transhistorical, for example, dimensions of anxiety and vulnerability, in terms of particular historical circumstances or situations.) I do not assert that an explanatory venture necessarily has legitimizing functions, although, as Žižek's comment itself indicates, it may always be read or misread in that manner. Still, Žižek's rejoinder, I think, actually supports the view of him as, in significant ways, an unhistorical thinker, or at least a thinker for whom history is in a very subordinate if not derivative position.[8]

6. "Death's Merciless Love," available at http://www.lacan.com/Žižek-love.htm, 19n.

7. A version of this essay is included as chapter 2 of *Writing History, Writing Trauma.*

8. Certain tendencies prominent in the influential work of Agamben, Badiou, and Žižek might be seen as threatening to undermine historical "consciousness" itself, with its relation to critique, that Hayden White did so much to elucidate and defend. Witness White's recent assertion: "Critique means, as Jameson says, 'Always historicize!' but not in the conventional way of the professional historian, that is to say, not as a way of providing an event with a past from which it must have derived, but rather as a way of restoring events to their presents, to their living relations with their conditions of possibility. But more: it means treating the present as well as the past as history, as a condition adequate to its possibility but also as something belonging to history—which is to say, as something worthy of being overcome and escaped from—that links critique to a particular kind of modernism or feeling of modernity characteristic of our time" ("Afterword: Manifesto Time," *Manifestos for History,* 225). I see processes of working through problems as intimately related to the historical attempt to understand and overcome—or situationally (not totally or annihilatingly) "transcend"—aspects of the past. I would further note that figures such as Agamben, Badiou, Santner, and Žižek do not share White's humanism, and White's work is not a reference point for them. But I think

Historical trauma may to some extent be prompted by an avoidance of an encounter or engagement with transhistorical trauma (or the Lacanian real). But such an encounter is never unmediated, and historical traumas have to be understood in nonderivative terms and not construed simply as radical contingencies. Transhistorical trauma is better figured as an absence or void than as a (constitutive) lack, even though confusion or misprision may induce an unsettling if not traumatizing experience (or fantasy) of transhistorical absence (most notably, the absence of absolute foundations or of full community and unity with the other) as a lack—indeed induce the feeling that one has lost or lacks what one could not possibly ever have or have had. (Conversely, not experiencing transhistorical absence as a lack or loss may not eliminate all traumatizing potential but may nonetheless facilitate an experience of that absence or void as an affirmative opening to possible futures, including [as Nietzsche saw] an invitation to improvisation.)[9]

While one may undertake historically traumatizing activities in order to obfuscate or avoid anxiety and vulnerability attendant on transhistorical trauma by projecting the source of anxiety and vulnerability onto scapegoats, the opposite is also possible. In other words, one may traumatize others and risk

---

their seeming posthumanism remains anthropocentric in that their concerns are fixated on the human and its relation to the theological or the "postsecular," and, however paradoxically at times, they assume or insist on the radical difference or divide between the human and the animal. In Santner, the divide is conceived in terms of the role of trauma, signifying stress, and "cringing" abjection in the human—all of which are reminiscent of notions of original (or originary) sin (and fallenness)—also evoked by certain elaborations of the Lacanian real and (in Žižek) of distinctive "inhuman," all-too-human monstrous excess. See *On Creaturely Life: Rilke/Benjamin/Sebald* (Chicago: University of Chicago Press, 2006). See also Slavoj Žižek, Eric L. Santner, and Kenneth Reinhard, *The Neighbor: Three Inquiries in Political Theology* (Chicago: University of Chicago Press, 2005).

9. Santner's notion of "signifying stress" gives a semiotic twist to anxiety. In commenting on Peter Gordon's *Rosenzweig and Heidegger: Between Judaism and German Philosophy* (Berkeley: University of California Press, 2003), Santner objects to Gordon's notion of Rosenzweig's "holism" and its relation to "the context of a historically determined matrix of relations." He opposes to it a notion of social formations "permeated by a lack by which we are, in some peculiar way, addressed, 'ex-cited,' and for which we are in some fashion *responsible.*" He argues that Rosenzweig's "more radical claim pertaining to Judaism is that it opens the possibility of community on the basis of a shared orientation with respect to a nonrelational remainder/excess, to the signifying stress that every 'normal' community attempts to gentrify by way of some sort of simulated 'holism'" (*The Neighbor,* 107). The difficulty here is the unmediated opposition to an understanding of historical context by an appeal to a transhistorical, constitutive lack or trauma (the Lacanian real) that eventuates in a now-familiar yet extreme notion of an impossible community of neighbors as radical others and possible monsters. There is no investigation of a possible "holism" not as a homogeneous or fully unified whole but in terms of a relational network that conjoins community and alterity, does not scapegoat "remainders" or outsiders, and both encounters and counters the temptation or threat of excessively transgressive breaches, including that between the human and the animal.

traumatization oneself in order to enact or act out (rather than work through) transhistorical trauma and the "death drive," compulsively engaging in traumatizing, often violent scenes and even thereby attaining a sublime sense of transcendence. (As Žižek may be read as intimating, working through transhistorical trauma means at the very least learning to live with inevitable anxiety and not projecting it onto scapegoats.) Himmler's fascination and repulsion in the face of gloriously extreme and unheard-of transgression, which surfaces in his oft-quoted Posen speech, could be construed in such terms. One could even, albeit implausibly, see Himmler and other elite Nazi perpetrators as obeying a higher call and undertaking genocide for a pure, honor-bound sense of duty and a refusal to betray Hitler, despite their own personal desire to act otherwise ethically, hence becoming similar, in their own unconditional *actus purus,* to the Princesse de Clèves in Žižek's reading of her "heroic" action. (This conception of the SS and their killing operations is in fact suggested in Jonathan Littell's novel *Les Bienveillantes.*)[10]

Any response other than psychosis may be interpreted as in some way an obfuscation (if not "gentrification") of the putative "transhistorical constitutive lack." The historical as well as ethicopolitical problem is to specify the nature, validity, and implications of the "obfuscation." Construing something as an obfuscation of the transhistorical is not sufficient for an analysis or understanding of the historical in its specificity and singularity. To believe that such a construction is sufficient would make very short shrift of historiography and might well accord with a sweepingly apocalyptic or postapocalyptic politics that takes itself as engaging directly with the traumatic real, perhaps typically through some form of often sacralized or divinized violence.[11] The broader problem is how to articulate the complex, variable relations between the transhistorical and the historical, which is not accomplished by the view that historical catastrophes come about through a diversionary avoidance or obfuscation of the transhistorical—an argument that situates history vis-à-vis the real in a position analogous to that of worldly *divertissement* in Pascal's insistent affirmation of the anxiety-ridden yet authentic relation to the *Deus absconditus,* or Hidden God.

10. Paris: Gallimard, 2006. For a discussion of this novel, see chapter 4 in this book.

11. In the preceding chapter, I discussed in a note the spirited defense of such an antihistoricist (as well as unhistorical), seemingly unmediated, engagement with the "real," as well as of Žižek's thought and his conception of Hegel, in Eisenstein's *Traumatic Encounters.* For an opposed, historicizing approach to Hegel, Hegelianism, and their contexts, see John Toews's, *Hegelianism: The Path toward Dialectical Humanism, 1805–1841* (New York: Cambridge University Press, 1980) and *Becoming Historical: Cultural Reformation and Public Memory in Early Nineteenth-Century Berlin* (New York: Cambridge University Press, 2004).

In Žižek, who shares with Agamben and Badiou a pronounced antinomian strain that stresses grace transcending (but not necessarily transgressing) the "dead letter" of the law, there is also an ascetic insistence on law, voided of an "obscene superego supplement" or bonus of pleasure, as necessary to control monstrous excess. Here a seemingly extreme leftism merges with an extreme conservatism reminiscent of theologians for whom the radical evil or ontologically warped nature of "man" requires strict and even cruel normative strictures. As the old saw has it, "les extrêmes se touchent," and a Bakhtinian notion of the desirability of a viably alternating rhythm of social life (ordinary obedience to the law relieved by periodic legitimated carnivalesque transgression) is firmly rejected in favor of a strict Pauline (or Kantian) insistence on adherence to a decathected law, stripped of its "obscene superego supplement" and sustained by the hope of transcendent acts of grace.[12] Thus Žižek can offer the totally speculative, implausible interpretation of the acts of refuseniks in Israel, who refuse to fight in the occupied territories, not only as a move away from seeing Palestinians as Agamben's *homo sacer* toward a vision of them as Judaeo-Christian neighbors (what happens to Islam here?), but also as designating "the miraculous moment in which eternal justice momentarily appears in the temporal sphere of empirical reality"—in effect as acts of transcendent grace conflated with (or incarnated in) this-worldly miracles.[13]

The initiatives of such influential figures as Agamben, Badiou, Santner, and Žižek pose challenges to historians who are trying to rethink history in ways that make the admittedly tension-laden attempt both to connect with problems deemed significant in professional historiography and insistently to relate historical inquiry to work in other disciplines and to larger social and political issues. One way to define the desirable, historically pertinent intervention is as an essayistic attempt (*essai*) to make available for critical inquiry the often unexamined assumptions informing a practice. The point of such an intervention would not be simply to take one or another critical theory (Foucauldian genealogy, Derridean deconstruction, Frankfurt school *Kritik*, Freudian or Lacanian psychoanalysis) and to "apply" it to historical material that is reprocessed unilaterally in its terms. Indeed, I would stress that,

12. See, for example, *The Puppet and the Dwarf: The Perverse Core of Christianity* (Cambridge: MIT Press, 2003), 113. To use an older terminology (which Žižek would probably reject), one says "yes" with the body but a saving "no" with the spirit in confronting *la condition humaine* that is essentially a Kafkaesque horror film in which relief comes only from radically "other," often violent incursions of grace and "love."

13. *Welcome to the Desert of the Real* (London: Verso, 2002), 116.

in the approach I am proposing, these orientations, including psychoanalysis, are to be conceived as critical theories (not simply, for example, as therapeutic techniques, methodologies convertible into research procedures, forms of experimental writing, or cutting-edge sources of insight). In such an approach, there would be a mutually thought-provoking interaction between historical understanding and critical theory that would sensitize the historian to otherwise avoided or underconceptualized issues and enable him or her to explore questions of cross-disciplinary significance. (Here theory might be contrasted not with practice but with habitus in the sense of critically unself-reflective practices and assumptions.)

No one has been more important than Hayden White in disclosing and criticizing the limitations of unself-reflective practice and of a narrowly conceived, self-sufficient "conventional" research paradigm, which reaches its extreme form in positivism.[14] But he has at times been tempted by its opposing number or even its "flip side": radical constructivism (at times open to a sublime notion of creation ex nihilo that may seem almost miraculous). In the latter perspective, referential statements making truth claims apply at best only to events and are of restricted, perhaps even marginal, significance. By contrast, essential are performative, at times radically creative, figurative, aesthetic, rhetorical, ideological, ethical, and political factors—factors or forces (not involving truth claims) that "construct" structures—stories, plots, arguments, interpretations, explanations—in which referential statements are embedded and take on meaning and significance. Radical constructivism often restricts itself to a strategy of reversal in its critique of positivism—a strategy that is useful in bringing out the limitations of positivism and of a restricted research model of historical understanding in general. In comparison with a documentary or restricted research model, radical constructivism's significant twist (or reversal of the binary relation) is that the dis-implicated subject, in full creative existential freedom, presumably imposes meaning and, on epistemological and even political levels, constructs or fashions the object ex nihilo in a "radical" (violent?) break with the past that brings with it a sublime elevation of the human subject to the quasi-transcendental heights of an "endower" of meaning, with the simultaneous reduction of the object or other

14. How Hayden White, who has a strong but existentially humanist utopian impulse, would respond to the kind of quasi-theological or "postsecular" apocalyptic utopianism in Agamben, Badiou, and Žižek is something one would like to know. He has not, to my knowledge, provided sustained commentary on their thought, despite its significance in the current critical scene.

to raw material, unprocessed record, or mere life. (One obvious problem here is the implication of this perspective for other-than-human animals and the rest of nature.) As White himself at times seems to sense, the limitations of a strategy of reversal indicate the need to articulate problems and relations in a significantly different manner that is encompassed neither by a restricted research model, however refurbished in putatively postlinguistic or postcultural terms, nor by its radical constructivist reversal.[15] A self-sufficient research model and radical constructivism tend to converge in foreclosing the knotty question of the relation between the historical and the transhistorical along with the need for responsive understanding and the attempt to work through one's "transferential" implication in the object of study, with the tendency to repeat, rather than critically rework or respond to forces active in it. Indeed the sublime sense of creation ex nihilo that seems tantamount to the modernist moment is itself something perhaps best glossed not in the quasi-transcendental, humanist, and existential terms of the purely performative, projective "endowment" of others with meaning but simply as the easily misconstrued subjective experience of shock or traumatic break.

I would mention here revisionist initiatives or perhaps gestures of restoration that may in certain cases invite returns to earlier forms of documentary or self-sufficient research models, even though they present themselves as moves beyond radical constructivism, which is construed in the guise of cultural and linguistic turns. Such initiatives are apparent in Gabrielle Spiegel's introduction to the book she edits, *Practicing History: New Directions in Historical Writing after the Linguistic Turn,*[16] which parallels if not echoes much

15. This sense of needing a significantly different articulation of problems is perhaps most acute in White's reflections on the Holocaust and other extreme or limit events. See his "Historical Emplotment and the Problem of Truth," in *Probing the Limits of Representation: Nazism and the Final Solution,* ed. Saul Friedländer (Cambridge: Harvard University Press, 1992), 37–53, reprinted in *Figural Realism: Studies in the Mimesis Effect* (Baltimore: Johns Hopkins University Press, 1999), 27–42.

16. New York: Routledge, 2005. There are only a few references to White in this book, and the one by Spiegel is rather dismissive and overly amalgamating: "How does the historian write up [*sic*] the multi-dimensional, semi-coherent, semi-articulate dynamics of practice in the face of traditionally felt needs to represent the past in some kind of narrative logic and/or form of emplotment, a not insignificant problem when one remembers the origins of linguistic turn historiography in the narrativist schools of White, LaCapra, Kellner, Ankersmit, and the like, who argued that *no* historical account is possible without some form of troping or emplotment?" (23). I would note that at no point in my work have I made the generalized type of tropological or narrativist argument Spiegel seems to ascribe to me in this assertion. In fact I have repeatedly criticized it. For explicit statements about my relation to White's thought, see, for example, chapter 7 of this book and "Resisting Apocalypse and Rethinking History,"

of Lynn Hunt and Victoria E. Bonnell's introduction to *Beyond the Cultural Turn*.[17] In "valorizing once again a fundamentally and deeply ingrained historicist posture" (25), Spiegel adopts from the German sociologist Andreas Reckwitz the oxymoronic term "Practice Theory" as a name for the "new directions" she advocates in the historical discipline. In her conception, what does "Practice Theory" criticize, what does it defend, and what does it play down or omit? The answers to these questions indicate, I think, that Practice Theory is manifestly directed against attempts to rethink history in ways indebted to the work of Hayden White. Yet Practice Theory is itself, perhaps unavoidably, an uneven undertaking that is misleading as a general theory but, disentangled from its more dubious dimensions, may well have application to the important areas it in fact privileges as well as broader implications for rethinking historical studies.

Most evidently, Practice Theory marks a putative move beyond radical constructivism, at least in the guise of the cultural and linguistic turns that Spiegel tends to conflate. (Important cultural turns were not in the direction of language but, for example, of visual studies or artistic forms such as music, notably opera.)[18] Plausibly enough, Practice Theory rejects the idea that all of social life and history are the products of discourse, but it retains a so-called weak or attenuated notion of discourse (25) as playing a role in society and culture. Without sufficiently explicating its conception of discourse, it rejects an identification of discourse with language, particularly in a structural-Saussurian sense, as well as textualism, understood in Geertzian (rather than Derridean) terms, as the idea that all of sociocultural existence and experience may be understood and read as text analogs, especially as narratives.[19] One limitation in the unobjectionable if unsurprising idea that not

---

164–7, as well as *Rethinking Intellectual History: Texts, Contexts, Language* (Ithaca: Cornell University Press, 1983), chap. 2.

17. Berkeley: University of California Press, 1999.

18. See, for example, Michael Steinberg, *Listening to Reason: Culture, Subjectivity, and Nineteenth-Century Music* (Princeton: Princeton University Press, 2004). In a subsequent article, Spiegel queries the conflation of the linguistic and cultural turns. "Comment on [Geoff Eley's] *A Crooked Line*," *American Historical Review* 113 (2008): 409. Her argument still follows closely the outlines of her introduction to *Practicing History*, but she stresses what she sees as the rejection of phenomenology in structuralism and poststructuralism and argues for a return of phenomenology, especially in terms of what Reckwitz calls "social phenomenology," reinstating the intentional subject as social agent. She also calls for a partial return to social history and "for a historiography that acknowledges both the social, contextual determinants of thought and behavior in the past and the mediating role played by language and culture in their functioning," what David Nirenberg refers to as a "unified field theory" (410).

19. In my view, discourse is best seen as language—or more broadly, signifying practice—in historical use and perforce linked in complex ways to other practices. "Text" in the Derridean

all social life may be reduced to discourse or language is that it may obviate sustained inquiry into the role and importance of the complex, nonintuitive workings of language in history, which were of concern to White and those whose association with the linguistic turn was more than a half-hearted pirouette. It may also divert attention from the relations between forms of language and forms of life that were of concern to Wittgenstein. And it does not enable one to broach the question of the role of language in animal societies.

I would note that Spiegel, in her appraisal of current historiography, joins others in the perception of a recent turn, not so much to the history of, say, language or discourse in rhetorical, religious, philosophical, and poetic traditions (much less in animal societies), but from social to cultural history in a broad and somewhat vague sense. And she shares their apprehensions concerning why this putative shift has occurred. For example, Jay Winter writes with an assurance that indicates the extent to which he believes he is simply stating conventional wisdom about recent tendencies in historiography:

> Cultural history is in the ascendancy these days, occupying a position which the sub-discipline of social history enjoyed in the 1960s and '70s. The French and Germans have no trouble eliding the two, and have done so for decades. But in the Anglo-Saxon world, the shift from one to the other has been palpable. The British Social History Society's journal *Social History* was renamed *Cultural and Social History* in 2004. The study of working-class movements and social and demographic structures, so fruitful in an earlier generation, is now out of fashion. Instead of learning about "the making of the working class" in a host of nations and towns, students are more likely to focus on the memory of past events, and especially traumatic ones.

Winter continues:

> Since remembrance varies radically among different groups, the emphasis in such studies is more about multi-vocality and fragmentation than on linear historical narratives such as class formation and class conflict. Why this shift from social to cultural history has occurred is a complex question, touching on the eclipse of the transformational politics of the 1960s, the loss of faith in social scientific models in historical

sense is not identified with a book or a literal text. Rather it indicates a network of instituted traces, a notion that applies to contexts as well as to literal texts and to signifying practices in general (ritual, music, dance, painting, and so forth).

study, the influence of trends in critical theory, and the emergence in the 1970s and after of trans-disciplinary studies of the witness as the essential voice of historical narratives.[20]

As in some sense one of the shape-shifters with an interest in such problems as memory, multivocality, trauma, and witnessing, as in his own way Winter is, I would not press too hard on his formulations. But I would note that the change in title of the journal he mentions would indicate an "Anglo-Saxon" desire to combine cultural and social history, and rather than an eclipse or loss of faith, one might refer to a more critical if not skeptical approach to social-scientific models and a revised conception of the role of culture in political life (affirmed in the 1960s and by Winter himself in his insistence on the importance of political culture). Moreover, the role of critical theory is not simply a question of trendiness, and the witness's voice and the very status of the witness, along with memory and trauma, are hotly contested issues across the disciplines. In any case, Winter's assertions have parallels in Spiegel's introductory essay, and her sense of what is to be done is worth analyzing, for it is not unique to her even if its prevalence cannot simply be assumed.

What then does Practice Theory defend or postulate as a truly historicist alternative to the linguistic and cultural turns? Here one is theoretically on shaky ground, for as Spiegel observes: "'Practice Theory' as such has scarcely attained the status of a viable 'theory' in any real sense of the word." And it hardly seems to point in new directions in that "the accent it places on the

20. "Got the T-Shirt," a review of Donald Sassoon's *The Culture of the Europeans: From 1800 to the Present, Times Literary Supplement,* 5416 (January 19, 2007): 4. Based in part on an autobiographical perspective, Geoff Eley also sees "a huge tectonic shift from social history to cultural history" over the last four decades (xii), and he attributes it in part to the loss of conviction among marxist social historians that "class relations are *the* constitutive element in the history of industrialized capitalist states" (110–11). He points out that he experienced "the so-called linguistic or cultural turn of the 1980s as a vital empowering of possibilities." But, referencing the work of such historians as Carolyn Steedman, Catherine Hall, and Leora Auslander, he nonetheless wants to explore "how and in what forms the earlier moment of social history might be recuperated" (xii). He cogently argues that "we may still want to talk about class, about capitalism, about the structural distribution of inequalities, about the varying political capacities available to different social categories of people depending on their access to resources, and so on" (199)—inquiries that depend on a viable form of social history that accounts for the achievements of other approaches, including those related to the so-called cultural and linguistic turns. Eley's distinctive approach may be compared with Spiegel's. See *A Crooked Line: From Cultural History to the History of Society* (Ann Arbor: University of Michigan Press, 2005). See also William H. Sewell's attempt to relate history and the social sciences, notably by way of the concepts of temporality, event, and structure, in *Logics of History: Social Theory and Social Transformation* (Chicago: University of Chicago Press, 2005).

historically generated and always contingent nature of structures of culture returns historiography to its age-old concern with processes, agents, change, and transformation, while demanding the kind of empirically grounded research into the particularities of social and cultural conditions with which historians are by training and tradition most comfortable." Moreover, "as a form of historical reasoning that focuses on the selective cultural organization of experience 'Practice Theory' seems sufficiently capacious to accommodate a host of revisionist impulses, whose ultimate configuration remains to be realized" (25–26). It nonetheless could be argued that Practice Theory, as envisaged by Spiegel, is very close to the initiative of Hunt and Bonnell in advocating, at least in significant measure, a return to a supposedly reconceptualized social history that emphasizes experience and practice, including routinized bodily techniques that are untheorized and inculcated in disciplinary formations—in general, what Pierre Bourdieu termed habitus (14, 19).[21] It also seems to advocate a restoration of empiricist historicism that, as itself a habitus or craftlike practice stressing "know-how," threatens to emulate (or transferentially replicate) its largely atheoretical objects of study. Its clearest, and perhaps most significant, field of application is in *Alltagsgeschichte* or what Michel de Certeau termed "the practice of everyday life"—a field in which much noteworthy work has indeed been done recently.[22] But its at times bewildering array of ill-assorted, diverse and divergent formulations (presumably including "some of the most powerful insights of poststructuralism," which it simultaneously seems to disavow) may, I think, facilitate a return to conventional practices, including the unargued, ad hoc appropriation of concepts or discursive strategies as fuzzy tools in a heteroclite "tool kit" adapted to established or preset problems and procedures.

More precisely, what does Practice Theory underplay or omit? It pays scant attention to earlier initiatives that were at times misconstrued in terms of restricted linguistic or cultural turns but in reality attempted to rethink culture in terms of signifying practices that raised the problem of the possibilities and limits of meaning and did not unproblematically see culture or society exclusively in terms of codes, narratives, or discursive structures. Here John Toews's influential article on the "linguistic turn," which some

21. Isabel V. Hull's book could be read as instantiating "practice theory," while dismissing, with respect to her object of study, the relevance of ideology (understood in restricted terms as tantamount to systematic "theory" or philosophy). See her *Absolute Destruction: Military Culture and the Practices of War in Imperial Germany* (Ithaca: Cornell University Press, 2005), as well as my discussion in chapter 4.

22. *The Practice of Everyday Life* (1980; Berkeley: University of California Press, 1984).

twenty years after its publication remains a key reference even for those affirming "new directions," had the limitations of its remarkable virtues. For it was perhaps too influential in the masterful way it stylized and prefigured historians' understandings of theoretical initiatives and actually may, however unintentionally, have offered historians a seeming shortcut to understanding complex texts or problems. It may thus have diverted attention from specific articulations that did not fit its own Hegelian-phenomenological insistence on construing developments in terms of a triadic structure involving language, meaning, and experience—with seemingly privileged experience as a largely unexplicated residue or remainder.[23] In any event, Practice Theory, in Spiegel's formulation, does not address the crucial problem of the relation of practices to ideology understood not narrowly as systematic "theory" or rationalistic philosophy but in terms of the problem of subject formation, which involves not only discourse (in some restricted sense) but all that goes into the making of a significant if problematic world—self-presentation, justification, prejudice, fantasy, and affect as well as experience that is not reducible to immaculate perception. In addition, a reductive historicism simply excludes the problem of articulating relations between the historical and the transhistorical. And it does not face up to the intricacies and demands of a critical analysis of artifacts, including uses of language and modes of discourse, which raise complex issues of reading and interpretation

23. John Toews, "Intellectual History after the Linguistic Turn: The Autonomy of Meaning and the Irreducibility of Experience," *The American Historical Review* 92 (1987): 879–907. See my discussion of the essay in *History and Reading: Tocqueville, Foucault, French Studies* (Toronto: University of Toronto Press, 2000), 56–62. Toews provides a generous but reductive reading of my *History & Criticism* (Ithaca: Cornell University Press, 1985) and, especially, *Rethinking Intellectual History: Language, Texts, Contexts.* In both books, my analysis invokes Bakhtin as well as Derrida, is critical of a restricted Saussurian-structural approach, and emphasizes the role of signifying practices, including language in use or "practice" (*langage* in contradistinction to the *langue/parole* binary). I raise the problem of the relation among "levels" or dimensions of culture (elite, popular, and mass) and, especially in *Rethinking Intellectual History,* reiterate the importance of what was indeed important for Hayden White but not prominent in historiography at the time: a close, critical reading, along with the problematic contextualization, of significant texts involving problems of language and rhetoric or, more broadly, signification not reducible to codes, narratives, or structures, although obviously not simply ignoring their role. I do, however, suggest that language understood, not as autonomous or self-referential "discourse," but as an institution and a practice, might, in important ways (for example, the interaction of repetition and variation or difference, including traumatic breaks), be paradigmatic of other institutions and practices. In my later work the scope of concern is broadened, and the question of the relation of texts and contexts, including the limitations of an exclusive focus on canons, is stressed. See, for example, *Representing the Holocaust: History, Theory, Trauma* (Ithaca: Cornell University Press, 1994), chap. 1. For an attempt at a critical analysis of the concept of experience in its multiple dimensions, see my *History in Transit,* chap. 1.

that, while not exhaustive of society and culture, do demand differential theoretically informed attention and cannot simply be reduced to the social contexts that inform or constrain them.

In addition, Practice Theory sidesteps or disavows the issue of the implication of the observer in the observed (or what may be termed the transferential relation) and, with it, the need for a responsive understanding of the object of study that cannot be totally objectified and may even raise problems for one's own prereflective disciplinary habitus or unexamined assumptions. It marginalizes, brackets, or even excludes the type of intellectual history for which the preceding questions have been vital—the type of intellectual history that has itself been a primary site and conduit for the introduction into the historical discipline both of a sustained inquiry into the problem of language as a signifying practice and of critical theories addressed to assumptions and orientations. Practice Theory tends to shift attention from such problems and critical theories to insufficiently rethought social history and social science approaches that emphasize methodology and downplay self-reflective and self-critical theoretical questions. It also tends not to consider psychoanalysis as a crucial form of critical theory that bears on the relation between the observer and the observed and that has been very significant in its mutual articulation with other critical theories, those stemming both from tendencies in and around the Frankfurt school (for example, in the work of Theodor Adorno and Jürgen Habermas) and from poststructuralist, including deconstructive, developments. Thus, particularly in the terms Spiegel offers, Practice Theory may promise much, but it also downplays or misconstrues a great deal. I would note that one could not make this statement about certain figures to whom Practice Theory presumably looks.[24]

Here I would make special mention of Michel de Certeau whose notion of practice challenged overly restricted humanist assumptions and was not presented as an alternative to psychoanalysis, poststructuralism, or intellectual history. De Certeau's work, along with that of others (perhaps Derrida's, most forcefully) would also indicate that any pure binary opposition between theory and habitus is dubious, for theory is never a fully self-reflective, masterful metalanguage, and habitus as a totally prereflective experience or phenomenon

24. In his ambitious *Formations of the Secular: Christianity, Islam, Modernity* (Chicago: University of Chicago Press, 2003), Talal Asad employs a Foucauldian notion of embodied practice that he links to habitus, although the relation of habituslike practice to critical theory is unclear (including the role of critical theories as themselves self-critical practices embodied in traditions and the manner in which such theories need not be totalizing or foundational but instead involve the questioning of assumptions in ways that Asad himself engages).

is itself a reflective myth. The affirmation of habitus either as a disposition or as an object of study typically comes with a resistance to theory or at least certain forms of theory but may itself be "theorized" in very abstract terms, as in Bourdieu. In the volume Spiegel edits, Andreas Reckwitz, in his defense of the study of habituslike practice, makes the questionable assertion that Practice Theory, despite its seeming diffuseness, provides a "basic vocabulary" that "amounts to a novel picture of the social and of human agency" (247). A leitmotif of de Certeau's approach was the effort to undercut a confining conception of the social and of human agency and to explore the notion of practice in a way that might jeopardize the postulation of any criterion that would establish a sharp divide or gap between the human and the animal—at times even the plant. In terms reminiscent of Derrida, de Certeau clearly asserted that "the question at hand [in *The Practice of Everyday Life*] concerns . . . an operational logic whose models may go as far back as the age-old ruses of fishes and insects that disguise or transform themselves in order to survive, and which has in any case been concealed by the form of rationality currently dominant in Western Culture" (xi). He even ventured to say that "many everyday practices (talking, reading, moving about, shopping, cooking, etc.) are tactical in character" and may be related to "the immemorial intelligence displayed in the tricks and imitations of plants and fishes. From the depths of the ocean to the streets of modern megalopolises, there is a continuity and permanence in these tactics" (xix–xx). If taken seriously, such an approach would indeed introduce what might be called "new perspectives" in history and related areas. It might even assist in the elaboration of a nonanthropocentric conception of critical thought as a practice that is distinctive but also related to other practices.

The caveats I have put forward about "Practice Theory," insofar as it marks an unproblematic return to a restricted if not one-dimensional historicism centered on social history and social science, may also indicate that constructivism, even in its radical form, continues to be relevant in the often sharply etched, discomfiting challenges it poses and the way it provokes a process of rethinking and of rearticulating historical inquiry. But, despite its important power of provocation, it also tends to assume or assert an excessively narrow humanism or anthropocentrism in terms of which all meaning and value are derivatives of specifically human endowment, projection, or will. And it becomes misleading when it takes the valid notion that there are structural similarities between historiography and art or literature and exaggerates it, at times to the point of identity, hence downplaying the role (as well as the difficulty) of research and truth claims in historiography. The question of how to relate history and art or literature in a nonreductive manner, neither seeing the work of art merely as a historical document nor, by and large, converting historiography itself into a work of art, is a complex issue that calls for endless inquiry, reflection, and rearticulation. This question also requires attention to attempts to effect a more or less unmediated "postsecular" combination of melancholic immersion in lost, stranded, or ruined objects and chance occurrences, miraculous encounters, epiphanic openings, messianic longings, or events of grace.[25]

Also prevalent in much recent thought is a resistance to the very concept of working-through, which, I think, derives from a limited if not stereotypical understanding of it as a form of closure, therapeutic cure, or even turning the page of the past. It also stems from a related valorization of melancholia, inconsolable attachment to lost (at times transfigured into sublime) objects, and even a belief, as in Žižek, that at the very core of the human is a monstrously inhuman excess or death drive that renders all working-through a deceptive form of obfuscation, evasion, or "gentrification." (One may recall here Žižek's moving self-image in *Žižek!,* the excellent film directed by Astra Taylor, as an energized void resonating with quantum theory.) There may even be a tendency to identify radicalism with extremism or going to an implosive or explosive limit that violently bursts apart all existing formations, both intellectual and practical, and looks toward a blank utopia related to notions of grace, the miraculous, and the transcendent.[26]

One may acknowledge the significance of "inhuman," uncanny excess (or the Lacanian real) as well as of an enigmatic dimension (or unconscious) in humans without dismissing or undervaluing the role of processes that counter the unlimited play of excess and are related to intimately interacting thought and practice, including the crucial role of institutional transformation. One need not become fixated on particular concepts such as working-through, and it is of course possible to appeal to other conceptualizations in making comparable arguments. But the concept of working-through has had a very restricted role in academic appeals to psychoanalysis, and it stands in need of the type of elaboration that only dialogue and debate can give it. Such elaboration may offer a more critical approach to the postsecular (for example, in terms of inquiry into the possible role of rituals and ceremonies, including

25. In *On Creaturely Life,* Santner develops and valorizes this view of the work of W. G. Sebald, which he relates to that of others, including Kafka and Anselm Kiefer. See also "Miracles Happen: Benjamin, Rosenzweig, Freud, and the Matter of the Neighbor," in *The Neighbor,* 76–133.

26. See, for example, Žižek's contribution to *The Neighbor,* "Neighbors and Other Monsters: A Plea for Ethical Violence," 134–90.

carnivalesque ones) and indicate alternatives to a seemingly compulsive return to aporia and paradox that has carried over from certain forms of deconstruction into trauma theory. The point here is not to deny the role of aporia or paradox but to seek ways of negotiating double binds without simply postulating and endlessly reiterating their terminal or interminable nature and perhaps turning to "violent" ways of decisively cutting through the Gordian knots or impasses they present. Working-through is a form of negotiating problems that is not tantamount to repression, denial, or obfuscation. And it may occur in many processes and practices, including narrative, but also in other genres (the essay, the poem, ritual, dance, music, and so forth). It is in general an articulatory practice with political dimensions: to the extent one works through trauma and its symptoms on both personal and sociocultural levels, one is able to distinguish between past and present and to recall in memory that something happened to one (or one's people) back then while realizing that one is living here and now with openings to the future.[27]

An attempt to work over and through problems may also enable a differential approach to the aesthetic of the sublime (and its possibly displaced relations with the sacred) that neither dismisses it nor remains uncritically within its frame of reference. Such an attempt does not signal total critical distance, full emancipation, or complete mastery of problems, including one's sometimes haunting implication in, if not possession by, the past. Nor does it imply that there is a pure opposition between past and present or that acting-out—whether for the traumatized or for those empathetically relating to them—can be fully transcended toward a state of closure or full ego identity (as a professional historian or in terms of any other delimited identity). And it should not induce the conflation of subject positions (for example, with everyone becoming a victim and survivor). But it does mean that processes of articulation crucial to working-through may counteract both unchecked identifications and the symptomatic force of acting-out or the repetition compulsion, whereby the past not only haunts but intrusively erupts in the present and is compulsively relived or reenacted, however inappropriate, or

27. An interesting question is the way music may be understood in terms of a problematic process of working through the past, for example, how jazz, the blues, and sorrow songs have differential relations to one another and to African-American experience as well as that of other oppressed groups. For a discussion of the articulatory practice, including a critique of the way "liberal" philosophies may obscure the role of conflict and antagonism only to allow them to run rampant in unacknowledged, undemocratic ways, see Ernesto Laclau and Chantal Mouffe, *Hegemony and Socialist Strategy: Towards a Radical Democratic Politics* (London: Verso, 1985). Despite its own "theoreticist" tendencies, this important text remains a pertinent reference point.

politically disastrous, its scenarios may be in current conditions and however much it may be conducive to endless cycles of violence. (Bizarrely, acting out a repetition compulsion approximates abstractly routine behavior and might even be seen as an extreme form of "pure" practice or habitus.) Processes of working-through may also enable victims not to be overwhelmed or even crushed by a single identity that preempts all others and blocks access to possible futures.

Such processes, including mourning and modes of critical thought and practice, involve the possibility of making—not dichotomous binary oppositions (say, between the human and the animal or even between acting-out and working-through along with melancholia and mourning) but—variable, complex distinctions or specific articulations that are recognized as problematic but still function as limits, necessary bases of judgment, and possibly desirable resistances to confusion and the obliteration or blurring of all distinctions. (The latter states may indeed occur in trauma or in compulsively acting out posttraumatic conditions.) In general, perhaps the best way to understand the complex, never finalized process of working-through is as the attempt to work and play out counterforces to acting-out, the repetition compulsion, and denial—an attempt that, to be in any measure effective, must combine psychic "work" on the self with larger sociopolitical and cultural processes. Hence, for example, mourning should not be reduced to individual grieving but seen as a social practice, indeed in some sense a critically tested ritual process, which has political dimensions, for one may undertake the difficult effort to divest psychically and politically from an abusive authority figure who merits not mourning but sustained critique. Mourning and critique in general also may involve laughter and jokingly carnivalesque forms (prominent in the wake) as significant ways of negotiating aporias and engaging perhaps intractable problems.

There is a crucial sense in which one begins investigation already inserted in an ongoing historical process, a positioning toward which one may attempt to acquire some transformative perspective or critical purchase. A critical aspect of this positioning is the problem of the implication of the observer in the observed, what in psychoanalytic terms is treated as transference. Transference indicates that one begins inquiry in medias res (or what Hayden White might term a "middle-voiced" position), which one engages in various ways.[28] As I have indicated, a basic sense of transference is the tendency to

28. I have noted elsewhere that in the academy there are transferential relations between inquirers (especially pronounced in the relations between professor and graduate student and at

repeat or reenact performatively, in one's own discourse or relations, processes active in, or projected into, the object of study or critique. Transference in this sense occurs whether one recognizes it or not, and the problem is how one comes to terms with it in ways involving various combinations, more or less subtle variations, and hybridized forms of acting-out, working-over, and working-through. Indeed, to the extent one does not explicitly engage transferential implication and the problem of repetition, one tends blindly to act them out, often living a habitus run amok, engaging in destructive, even violent, behavior, or at the very least becoming involved in performative contradictions.[29] Working-through offers the possibility of enacting variations in repetition that may be significant (at times decisive) enough to bring about effective change, including transformations analogous to conversion experiences that, within the context of working-through, are not simply bolts from the blue or radically transcendent, aleatory acts of grace.

Can historiography participate, at least in limited ways, in the complex, self-questioning process of working through the past? This may be possible, especially on collective levels, notably in the effort to critically examine and monitor memory, counteract compulsive repetition, elaborate viable if contestable distinctions, disclose unrealized possibilities in the past, problematize by historicizing the present, and open possible—and possibly more desirable—futures.[30] Simultaneously, however, it may lessen one's enjoyment

---

times between the scholar and his or her critics) and between inquirers and the past, its figures, and processes. See also my cautionary discussion of the notion of a middle voice in *Writing History, Writing Trauma,* 19–42. I am here attempting to indicate certain possibly fruitful aspects of the concept.

29. Among innumerable instances of performative contradiction due to unreflected repetition or acting out of problems one studies, I would refer to the criticisms put forward in the controversial case of David Abraham, which were instrumental in forcing his departure from the historical profession. See my discussion in "Resisting Apocalypse and Rethinking History," in *Manifestos for History,* 172, where I note: "A typical charge against Abraham was his use of structural explanation or interpretation that went beyond any possible empirical substantiation. Yet those leveling the charge (such as Gerald Feldman and Ulrich Nocken) at times accused Abraham of conscious fabrication or lying, a charge that itself went beyond available evidence and could not be substantiated."

30. For extensive discussions of acting-out and working-through as they apply to historiography, see especially my *Representing the Holocaust; History and Memory after Auschwitz; Writing History, Writing Trauma;* and *History in Transit.* See also the convergent argument in Françoise Davoine and Jean-Max Gaudillière, *History beyond Trauma: Whereof One Cannot Speak, Thereof One Cannot Stay Silent,* trans. Susan Fairfield (New York: Other Press, 2004). Still relevant is Theodor W. Adorno's 1959 essay "What Does Coming to Terms with the Past Mean?" in *Bitburg in Moral and Political Perspective,* ed. and intro. Geoffrey Hartman, trans. Timothy Bahti and Geoffrey Hartman (Bloomington: Indiana University Press, 1986), 115–29 (also translated as "The Meaning of Working Through the Past," in *Critical Models: Interventions and Catchwords,* trans. and preface Henry W. Pickford (New York: Columbia University Press, 1998), 89–103.

of symptoms and apocalyptic or postapocalyptic hope in miracles, messianic acts of grace, or blank utopias, not to mention vague, insufficiently qualified appeals to violence. The view I am proposing does not imply a simplistic "Enlightenment" faith or an equally simplistic understanding of secularization as the opposite of the religious or as the culmination of a linear teleological process of "modernization." Instead, it leads to the question of intricate nonlinear displacements, repetitions, and variations in the complex interaction of the secular and the "religious." It also induces a critical inquiry into the notion of the "postsecular," which may be deceptive in that it, like the seemingly endless host of "post" terms, implies a linear temporality that it simultaneously denies. (An inconsistently linear temporality also characterizes the notion of *posthistoire* with which the universalizing, dehistoricized, at times radically transcendent impetus of certain prevalent uses of the "postsecular" seem implicitly bound up.) But the notion of the postsecular has a possibly fruitful role as an invitation to scrutinize critically certain assumptions, especially those wherein working-through itself is (mis)conceived as the secure attainment of secular maturity (Kant's *Mündigkeit*), which is complacently assumed to resolve or even transcend problems related to religion, the sacred, sacrifice, transcendence, and so forth.

Like working-through itself, any process of achieving secular "maturity" must be repeatedly undertaken or worked (and jokingly played) out in a self-questioning manner. It should also raise the critical question of the limitations of anthropocentric humanism (and certain anthropocentric posthumanisms) as well as the possible dimensions of religion that have complex displacements in secularity (including notions of human creation [and endowment of the world or the past with meaning] and of the "real" as comparable to a willfully arbitrary, demonic *Deus absconditus*). But one may also raise the question of possible aspects of "religion," in all its complexity and multidimensionality, that may be rearticulated in a critical framework.[31] Here

---

As becomes quite clear by its end, the essay criticizes a facile attempt to turn the page of history (to clear or "blow" off the past) but is in fact a strong defense of working through the past in both psychoanalytic and sociopolitical terms close to the ones I have been employing. The term in the title of Adorno's essay is *Aufarbeitung,* whereas the term Freud used for "working-through" was *Durcharbeitung.* See also Michael S. Roth's, *Psycho-Analysis as History: Negation and Freedom in Freud* (Ithaca: Cornell University Press, 1987) and *The Ironist's Cage: Memory, Trauma, and the Construction of History* (New York: Columbia University Press, 1995), as well as Ernst van Alphen, *Caught by History: Holocaust Effects in Contemporary Art, Literature, and History* (Stanford: Stanford University Press, 1997).

31. For an intricate if problematic inquiry into how little we know about the very concept of religion, as well as for a discussion of the various senses in which it may be taken, see Jacques Derrida, "Faith and Knowledge: The Two Sources of 'Religion' at the Limits of Reason Alone,"

I would not look to political theology, however seemingly deconstructed, or to a “psychotheology of everyday life”—tendencies that retain doctrinaire dimensions (for example, the postulation of Lacan or Žižek as the basically unquestioned authority or even the “subject-supposed-to-know”) as well as the rather uncritical treatment of objects of inquiry as sacred texts whose typically ahistorical, decontextualized exegesis will yield insight if not truth.[32] In however tentative and self-questioning a manner, I would rather point in the direction of both fallible notions of belief and commitment, involving trust and possible forms of critical thought and practice, crucially including carnivalized ones, that resist victimization (prominent in sacrificialism) and instead help generate articulations for crucial transitional points in life (for example, with respect to mourning as a critically informed process of working through losses of legitimately valorized [not all] others).

The broadest question here is the insertion of the human, as well as any form of the postsecular or posthuman, in a nonanthropocentric relational network that includes other animals and the rest of nature—a relational network that would itself indicate the need for historically and situationally overcoming certain existing institutionalized forms (prominently including runaway capitalism that excessively depletes, constrains, and impoverishes many to allow for multiple excesses in some). Such a network would also limit human (and posthuman), often excessive assertiveness that is typically legitimized by a decisive criterion or gap separating the human from the animal along with nature in general (reducing the latter to a bizarre combination of raw material or mere life and quasi-sacrificial victim—or even to a split-off, opaque, enigmatic “other”). This relational network, obviously requiring ecologically informed elaboration, would give a different valence to the notion of a middle voice, here genuinely situated in medias res, and indicate the need both for a more expansive, nonanthropocentric (as well as other than theological) frame of reference and for a revised, insistently critical-theoretical understanding of psychoanalytic concepts (such as trauma, transference, repetition, the unconscious, acting-out, working-over, and working-through).

---

in *Religion,* ed. Jacques Derrida and Gianni Vattimo (1996; Stanford: Stanford University Press, 1998), 1–78.

32. For a contrasting approach, see Eric L. Santner, *On the Psychotheology of Everyday Life: Reflections on Freud and Rosenzweig* (Chicago: The University of Chicago Press, 2001).

# Chapter 3

# "Traumatropisms"

## *From Trauma via Witnessing to the Sublime?*

> Traumatropism. A peculiar growth or curvature of an organism (esp. a plant) resulting from a wound.
>
> —*Oxford English Dictionary*

> The sublime can be described thus: it is an object (of nature) *the presentation of which determines the mind to think of nature's inability to attain to an exhibition of ideas*. . . . The imagination thereby acquires an expansion and a might that surpasses the one it sacrifices; but the basis of this might is concealed from it; instead the imagination *feels* the sacrifice or deprivation and at the same time the cause to which it is being subjugated. Thus any spectator who beholds massive mountains climbing skyward, deep gorges with raging streams in them, wastelands lying in deep shadow and inviting melancholy meditation, and so on is indeed seized by *amazement* bordering on terror, by horror and a sacred thrill; but, since he knows he is safe, this is not actual fear; it is merely our attempt to incur it with our imagination, in order that we may feel that very power's might and connect the mental agitation this arouses with the mind's state of rest. In this way we [feel] our superiority to nature within ourselves, and hence also to nature outside us insofar as it can influence our feeling of well-being.
>
> —Immanuel Kant, *Critique of Judgment*

> The communication of Christianity must ultimately end in "bearing witness," the maieutic form can never be final. . . . In the end the maieuticer will not be able to bear the responsibility because the indirect method is ultimately rooted in human intelligence, however much it may be sanctified and consecrated by fear and trembling. God becomes too powerful for the maieuticer and so he is the witness, though different from the direct witness in that he has been through the process of becoming one.
>
> —Søren Kierkegaard, *Journals* (1848)

Trauma studies has arisen as one of the most significant and at times controversial areas in psychoanalytic thought with significant implications for history and critical theory. And it has played a key part in the analysis of testimonies of survivors, notably Holocaust survivors but also victims of other genocides and extreme events such as rape and assault as well as longer-term processes such as domestic violence. The noted French historian Annette Wieviorka has referred to the present as the "era of the witness."[1] Other important scholars, such as Geoffrey Hartman and Aleida Assmann, have presented testimony as a new genre-in-the-making that characterizes this era.[2] Of course testimonies and witnesses have existed in other times and places. But the extent and intensity of traumatic events and experiences, notably including genocides and other forms of violence, abuse, and victimization (as well as "natural" disasters), seem to mark our time in a distinctive manner and to lend credibility to its prevalent figuration as the era or age of the witness who gives testimony.[3]

1. Wieviorka, *The Era of the Witness,* trans. Jared Stark (1998; Ithaca: Cornell University Press, 2006). I would observe that Kant asserts a few pages after the quote serving as one of my epigraphs: "Perhaps the most sublime passage in the Jewish Law is the commandment: Thou shalt not make unto thee any graven image, or any likeness of any thing that is in heaven or on earth, or under the earth, etc." *Critique of Judgment,* trans. and intro. Werner S. Pluhar, foreword Mary J. Gregor (1790; Indianapolis: Hackett, 1987), part 1, section 274, p. 135. This prohibition on images and likenesses of what is often termed creation would, one would infer, include any "idolatrous" attempt (however impossible) to represent the radically transcendent Hidden God—the "totally other" and arguably the most sublime of sublimities. With respect to my epigraph from Kierkegaard, the *Oxford English Dictionary* defines *maieutics* as "pertaining to (intellectual) midwifery, i.e., to the Socratic process of assisting a person to bring out into clear consciousness conceptions previously latent in the mind." This definition relies on the latent/manifest opposition that was also important for Freud. But, as in Freud, one may argue that for Kierkegaard maieutics is a more problematic and indirect process, not reducible to binary oppositions, which involves irony and the uncanny as the return of the repressed or disavowed. In the quotation from Kierkegaard one may also detect a duality (not a dualism) concerning the human being who is not immediately the direct witness but who also is not able to lead an entire life of irony or, more generally, of indirection. The latter is reserved for Christ as the God-man who always spoke to the people in parables, that is, indirectly in what Paul de Man might term a "permanent parabasis," which for Kierkegaard is not the prerogative of humans.

2. See the special issue of *Poetics Today* 27, no. 2 (2006) entitled *The Humanities of Testimony,* ed. Geoffrey Hartman, including essays by Geoffrey Hartman, Aleida Assmann, and Annette Wierviorka.

3. Such was the self-understanding of Albert Camus, for example, as well as that of many others, including, in certain ways, W. G. Sebald and the more obvious but significantly different cases of Jean Améry, Charlotte Delbo, Victor Klemperer, Ruth Klüger, Primo Levi, and Elie Wiesel. It is noteworthy that in Michael Donovan's 2007 film *Shake Hands with the Devil* the Canadian general Roméo Dallaire is represented as falling victim to extreme melancholia and depression after the failure or subversion of the peace-keeping mission he headed in Rwanda. He averts breakdown and suicide by finding what I think could be termed his calling as a

The complex issue of witnessing and testimony seems to call for an initial distinction. The problematic distinction, which should not be taken to binary or dichotomous extremes, is between bearing witness, giving testimony, and offering commentary of one sort or another.[4] Bearing witness in this usage refers to the act of someone having the experience of an event, and it can take various forms that are nonverbal, including posttraumatic symptoms.[5] Traumatic experience itself has attracted special attention and poses distinctive problems, notably in terms of its aftermath and bearing on the problem of giving testimony. Trauma is a shattering experience that distorts memory in the "ordinary" sense and may render it particularly vulnerable and fallible in reporting events. What has been called traumatic memory refers to symptoms of the traumatic experience such as nightmares, flashbacks, startle reactions, and compulsive behavior. Giving testimony involves the attempt to address or give an account of the experience one has had oneself and through which one has lived. In a sense, one might understand giving testimony as the fallible attempt to verbalize or otherwise articulate bearing witness. Testimony is itself both threatened and somehow authenticated or validated insofar as it bears the marks of, while not being utterly consumed and distorted by, the symptomatic effects of trauma. But testimony may

witness. See also Sam Durrant, *Postcolonial Narrative and the Work of Mourning: J. M. Coetzee, Wilson Harris, and Toni Morrison* (Albany: State University of New York Press, 2004). Durrant makes the important attempt to approach postcolonial literature in terms of trauma and bearing witness, although his thought-provoking book does so in terms I question. Durrant's variant of trauma theory collapses the distinction between melancholy and mourning and often relies on a binary, yet at times paradoxically fragile, logic (collapsing melancholy and mourning but placing in stark opposition history and what is beyond or resistant to it). He allows theoretically only for an idealized, totalizing conception of working-through, which he rejects. Yet in practice he invokes a more nuanced understanding of it and of mourning as one of its important modalities that is not simply conflated with melancholy or compulsive repetition. He nonetheless explicitly puts forward an affirmation of an ethic of inconsolable, impossible mourning and quasi-transcendental or meta-metaphysical resistance to history in the postromantic, empty (or fully open) hope for total transformation. Durrant sees this orientation most clearly enacted in the work of Coetzee on the insufficiently differentiated levels of character, text, and author. While this reading is in certain ways contestable, Durrant's approach, as I have indicated, may be experienced as compelling and has considerable currency in recent thought.

4. Of course many more distinctions remain implicit here, some of which emerge in the course of my discussion. One would at least have to distinguish further among experience, event, symptom, bearing witness, memory, and giving testimony. Moreover, commentary covers many different genres and forms that from another perspective would require more detailed and differential treatment.

5. One might suggest that a symptom bears witness but alone does not give testimony. It is made to give testimony though interpretation or some supplementary activity. The question is: To what does it then give testimony? I argue that it gives testimony to experience with a problematic but at times crucial relation to events.

shade into various kinds of commentary on experience and the events it involved.

We, of course, seek knowledge of traumatic events from testimony and even from bearing witness. But, at least within certain contexts, the distinctive interest of both bearing witness and giving testimony is in their relation to experience, especially traumatic experience.[6] And it is well known that testimony and witnessing may be unreliable with respect to an accurate reporting of events, in large part because of the uncontrollable, disorienting effects of trauma itself. A survivor who gives testimony may also produce various kinds of commentary and even have testimony influenced or shaped by commentary and by exposure to the media or signifying practices such as films, novels, or histories, on the levels both of construing events and of templates for narratives or interpretations. Although I do not devote to it the sustained attention it warrants, the interaction between testimony, memory, and the shaping role of media events and templates is very important.

We often use bearing witness and giving testimony (or witnessing) interchangeably, and this practice itself bears witness to the proximity of the terms or processes in common usage. A distinction arises when we restrict bearing witness or witnessing to those having the experience itself or at least something very close to, or in intimate contact with, the experience. This sense of contact is conveyed in the frequently employed expression in testimonies of eyewitnesses who are not simply bystanders but themselves what might be termed "body-witnesses" or even victims of abuse: "I have seen it" or "I have seen it with my own eyes." This expression validates an object of testimony other than in a narrowly empirical or positivistic sense. It also has a performative force with respect to the often devastating experience of being there, for example, seeing and feeling an intimate tortured, killed, or dying in one's arms. It may even mean something like: "My very eyes have been marked or even scorched by what I have seen."

Michael Bernard-Donals and Richard Glejzer, in a provocative and heartfelt book, turn the distinction between bearing witness and giving testimony into a sharp opposition and an aporetic or paradoxical demand, and they do so in a manner that is related to broader tendencies in the approach to trauma and witnessing that I find both questionable and question-worthy (to use a Heideggerian turn of phrase).[7] For them bearing witness is the excessive,

6. See my parsing of the concept of experience in *History in Transit: Experience, Identity, Critical Theory* (Ithaca: Cornell University Press, 2004), chap. 1.

7. Michael Bernard-Donals and Richard Glejzer, *Between Witness and Testimony: The Holocaust and the Limits of Representation* (New York: State University Press of New York, 2001). See

indeed negatively sublime, moment of apprehension—the unmediated vision, the ineffable or unrepresentable experience itself, or something so intimately close to the experience as to be indistinguishable from it. By contrast, giving testimony is tantamount to a pressing, even necessary, descent or fall into inadequate discourse. One might say that bearing witness is a sublime *Erlebnis* (unmediated experience) or intuitive *Augenblick* (moment of apprehension), one having a melancholic aftermath but also a possibly redemptive potential. As such, bearing witness in its immediacy cannot itself be articulated but can only be identified with and relived.

From this point of view, testimony is secondary; commentary is at best derivative; and pedagogy, while requiring commentary and knowledge, seeks to transmit, almost as stigmata, the witnessing and the kind of testimony that conveys the impossible, aporetic attempt to express what exceeds knowledge. The point is apparently to get as close as possible to the experience of bearing witness and to become the kind of secondary witness who somehow relives or is marked by what the trauma victim has lived. It is also to undergo a supplementary, possibly sublime, suffering or anguish in the necessary if impossible attempt to translate witnessing into testimony. For many commentators, the authentic or appropriate affect of testimony, or of any attempt at representation or signification with respect to trauma, is melancholy, indeed inconsolable and interminable, possibly anguished, melancholy, which may even be conflated with (impossible) mourning. Such melancholy is in a sense the affect or "feel" of aporia and absolute paradox. (Its "manic" complement may be a sense of total openness or possibility—a kind of empty, blank utopianism or messianism.) This orientation certainly prevents closure or turning the page of the past. But it may also block any significant counterforce or mode of working through traumatic symptoms, however hesitant, limited, or self-critical. Interminable or perhaps terminal melancholy in the response

---

also Jacques Derrida's *Gift of Death,* trans. David Wills (1992; Chicago: University of Chicago Press, 1995) with respect to the story of Abraham and Isaac, in which Abraham seems to become a traumatic and sublime figure of sacrifice who lives the aporia in fear and trembling. One may raise the question of the relation between the unrepresentable (or unsayable), the traumatic, and the sublime in the work of Maurice Blanchot, especially *The Most High* [*Le Très-Haut*], trans. Allan Stoekl (1948; Lincoln: University of Nebraska Press, 1996) and *The Writing of the Disaster* [*L'écriture du désastre*], trans. Ann Smock (1980; Lincoln: University of Nebraska Press, 1986). (The title of the first book employs a term often used to refer to God, and the title of the second book evokes a writing of the stars.) But Blanchot's sense of paradox and ambiguity is so intense and sustained as to make any definite correlations problematic. See the allusion to this question in my *History in Transit,* 149, as well as the discussion of Blanchot in Ethan Kleinberg, *Generation Existential: Heidegger's Philosophy in France, 1927–1961* (Ithaca: Cornell University Press, 2005), chap. 6.

to trauma seems to transcend history and to keep in touch with (or at least honor) the lost object—both the dead or the victimized and the putative negative sublimity of evanescently bearing witness to them. This response is at least suggested in the approach of such figures as Lawrence Langer and Claude Lanzmann, even at points in W. G. Sebald, among others.[8] In a different register, it may also be evoked in Derrida's "impossible mourning" that succeeds most when it most fails—arguably a sublime mourning that seems to be in imperceptible proximity to inconsolable melancholy that encrypts, without integrating, the "totally other."[9] The approach to testimony and witnessing takes a distinctive inflection in the frequently invoked, occasionally mantra-like, formulation of Shoshana Felman and Dori Laub, whereby the witness to trauma bears witness to the impossibility or breakdown of witnessing.[10] As Bernard-Donals and Glejzer put it:

> We have endeavored, in this book, to reexamine a relation between witness and testimony that can account for what exceeds the limit of knowledge. Witnessing in this sense is founded upon a moment of seeing, of glimpsing what escapes understanding. What we glimpse in such moments is not history but the event [others here might say the "real"] as it precedes our ability to bring it into language at all.... We will argue that the disaster of the Shoah—in which the victim and the survivor find it impossible to know or put words to, the experience in which they find themselves—is located at the junction of the compulsion to speak and failure of speech, where the witness manages to redeem the moment (to finally see what lies beyond or behind what can be told by history), to "fall victim" to it, and leave a trace of it in language. The witness, confronted with the sublime object, is rendered both [*sic*] speechless and is nonetheless compelled to speak.... The sublime moment, presented by means of a failure of representation, has an effect on the secondhand witness, but it is not an effect of knowledge.

8. After the completion of this book, there appeared Thomas Trezise's excellent critical analysis of Dori Laub's identificatory, sublimely overinterpretive, and at times inaccurate rendition of survivor testimony, "Between History and Psychoanalysis: A Case Study in the Reception of Holocaust Survivor Testimony," *History & Memory* 20 (2008): 7–47.

9. See, for example, *The Work of Mourning*, ed. Pascale-Anne Brault and Michael Naas (Chicago: University of Chicago Press, 2001) in which Derrida even questions the role of impossible mourning as itself a betrayal of the uniqueness of a friend. Much in Derrida, however, resists tendencies evident in the orientation of Bernard-Donals and Glejzer, for example, their notion of unmediated vision or glimpsing.

10. Felman and Laub, *Testimony: Crises of Witnessing in Literature, Psychoanalysis, and History* (New York: Routledge, 1992).

> It is, instead, a mark of the traumatic, and whatever knowledge the student tries to produce will likewise be affected by the sublime object [here the sublime object of trauma and aporia].[11]

As I indicated, I find these views to be questionable, but they are significant, for some compelling, and they resonate in different ways with a number of important tendencies. One tendency is the extreme, at times exclusive and intransigent, investment in an aesthetic of the sublime and the melancholic (with the aporia as a sublime textual trauma or *mise en abîme*). What may well accompany it, as a rejected alternative, is a truncated, stereotypical idea of working-through, not as (what I take it to be) a mode of immanent critique related to social and political practice (including carnivalesque contestation as in the wake), but as a facile form of uplift, closure, identity formation, integration of the lost other, taking leave of the past, and denial of loss. (Much depends on what one understands by the contested notion of working-through and what it is one rejects when one rejects it.) Another tendency is the collapse, via the sublime and its excess, of any distinction between event and experience, both of which exceed knowledge and representation to the point of becoming ineffable, yet paradoxically demanding impossible testimony (the double bind). An accompanying phenomenon is the collapse or conflation of subject positions, especially through identification or at least extreme proximity vis-à-vis the victim or witness, along with a labile or insufficiently framed rendering of the victim's perspective or voice in a participatory or free indirect style. This conflation of subject positions may well involve the confusion of empathy or compassion with identification. Unlike empathy or compassion (at least as I use the terms), identification assimilates or appropriates the experience of the other rather than (as in empathy) responding to it affectively while recognizing the difference or alterity of the other and the distinctiveness of his or her experience (which need not be taken to the extreme of total otherness or the *tout autre*). I would argue that there may well, perhaps even should, be a form of empathic unsettlement in the commentator who addresses the traumatic experiences of others, and this unsettlement places a special stress on modes of address, including forms of writing or representation, in ways that cannot be legislated or programmed and may even be understated or subdued (as, for example, in Sebald who at times writes in a style of subdued empathic unsettlement).[12]

11. Bernard-Donals and Glejzer, *Between Witness and Testimony,* ix, xi, and xiii.

12. Without turning to a rhetoric of the sublime or to sacralization of victimhood, Samuel Beckett in *The Unnamable* wrote something relevant to this point in what are now almost

In any case, empathic unsettlement or compassion respectful of the other does not mean identification, denial of important differences, and appropriation or incorporation. Nor does it imply that one is entitled to speak, however paradoxically, for the other, somehow vicariously reexperience, or become melancholically immersed in a putatively sublime object and even be led to deny that victims may indeed work through trauma to become, in significant measure, not only survivors but social and political agents. Of course it is possible that a victim may, at least in crucial ways, live on without surviving and be overwhelmed by a traumatic past—an eventuality regarding which a commentator (such as myself) may not have a viable subject position to enable worthwhile or even relevant commentary. And identification with the victim may take place on an unconscious level such that one may be haunted or even possessed by another in whose halting or broken voice one may find oneself speaking. This possibility may be especially likely in the case of intimates of victims and survivors. Such a state of affairs, which would be misconstrued if seen as merely pathological or as a simple choice, is, however, not the same as that of a commentator who rhetorically validates or advocates vicarious identification and takes up the gap-ridden voice of the victim or survivor, attempting to speak for and in that voice rather than with respect to, and respect for, it. (The latter undertaking is, at the very least, problematic and would minimally require careful framing in which, say, an attempt at reenactment of the voices of victims is not tantamount to appropriation or vicarious identification.)[13] Insofar as there is a form of secondary witnessing, it comes about not through identification, reexperiencing what is taken as sublime, affirming the authenticity of endless melancholy, and speaking or writing for the other. Rather, secondary witnessing, to the extent this locution makes any sense, proceeds by way of a very problematic process whereby one offers commentary that is not narrowly factual but motivated by a respectful compassion or empathic unsettlement that need

---

classical terms, which are echoed in certain formulations of Bernard-Donals and Glejzer: "You must go on, I can't go on, you must go on, I'll go on, you must say words, as long as there are any, until they find me, until they say me, strange pain, strange sin, you must go on, perhaps it's done already, perhaps they have said me already, perhaps they have carried me to the threshold of my story, before the door that opens on my story, that would surprise me, if it opens, it will be I, it will be the silence, where I am, I don't know, I'll never know. In the silence you don't know, you must go on, I can't go on, I'll go on." *Three Novels by Samuel Beckett: "Molloy," "Malone Dies," "The Unnamable,"* trans. Patrick Bowles in collaboration with the author (New York: Grove Press, 1955), 414.

13. Henry Greenspan's performances are attempts at explicit reenactment of voices of victims, which can be disconcerting, but one may question whether they are reducible to vicarious identification.

not be narcissistic or ecstatically self-immolating but in the best of cases is coordinated with sociopolitical analysis and practice. (Here political criticism and empathy [or ethics] are not necessarily alternatives.)[14] And, while one may not legislate an appropriate or "authentic" form of response, including a form of commentary, or deny the compelling role of identification (which does occur, at times unconsciously, even in Sebald), one may certainly argue about the suitability or appropriateness of various forms of response in the critical and self-critical attempt to work out a viable ethic of response. Such an ethic would be mindful of, but not fixated on, the paradoxes and aporias of representation as well as the differences in subject position and context of those to whom one is responding.

I have intimated that a further questionable tendency that the formulation of Bernard-Donals and Glejzer helps one to identify is an insufficiently differentiated, at times uncritical, relation to an aesthetic of the sublime, including a rendering sublime or even sacralization of traumatic experience. The tendency to transfigure trauma (including at times violence) into the sacred or the sublime is, I think, very prevalent. And it may occur in different ways in perpetrators, victims, and commentators. The idea that trauma is something like a negative sublime is very forceful and appealing. Hence, even Saul Friedlander, with specific reference to the understanding of extremely disconcerting passages of Himmler's 1943 Posen speech, can write: "For further analysis, we would need a new category equivalent to Kant's category of the sublime, but specifically meant to capture inexpressible horror"—in a sense, a decidedly negative sublime.[15] Others, such as Jean-François Lyotard, Hans-Jürgen Syberberg, Slavoj Žižek, and Giorgio Agamben, have turned to a discourse of the sublime at times without the qualifications and discriminations evident in Friedlander's own work, and the sublime exerts a pervasive fascination that is difficult for any commentator to approach critically.

14. Of course empathy itself, when autonomized or made to function as a substitute (rather than a motivation) for social and political action, notably with respect to victims, is highly suspect. Empathy is at best one component of a larger constellation of forces or factors in both historical understanding and sociopolitical action, and it must be approached situationally and in terms of its differential deployment. Nor should empathy or compassion be seen as implying an initial separation between self and other that needs to be bridged by some special mental act—a view beholden to atomistic individualism. While there certainly are differences and even forms of separation between different groups and individuals that may require insistent effort in engaging and understanding others, empathy is best seen as a way of negotiating transferential relations that are related to the manner in which there are always co-implications between individuals and groups.

15. Friedlander, *Memory, History, and the Extermination of the Jews of Europe* (Bloomington: University of Indiana Press, 1993), 115, n. 13.

A variant of this fascination is found even in Hayden White, for example, in the admonition that historians have traditionally avoided the sublime, an admonition that Frank Ankersmit has heeded to the extent of arguing both for a formal analogy between trauma and the sublime and for an unmediated sublime experience as the very goal or point of historiography.[16] Still, Friedlander's hesitancy and accentuation of the negative may indicate a casting about for a general category where none may be available. And the new category that readily suggests itself—the postsublime—is of course not very novel; like other "post" terms, it may attest to a crisis in naming as well as conceptualization and signal the turn to a label in the absence of a concept. But such a term (and others like it) may be necessary, and at least it points to the dubiousness in certain cases of invoking the sublime in one's own voice, even when its negative valence is accentuated.[17]

This dubiousness marks a thought-provoking essay by Liliane Weissberg that, through a montage technique, approaches the problems of the sublime and the sacred.[18] Weissberg addresses the way the Holocaust and art related

16. See Hayden White, "The Politics of Historical Interpretation: Discipline and De-Sublimation," in *The Content of the Form: Narrative Discourse and Historical Representation* (Baltimore: Johns Hopkins University Press, 1987), chap 3, and Frank Ankersmit, "The Sublime Dissociation of the Past: or How to Be(come) What One Is No Longer," *History and Theory* 40 (2001): 295–23, and *Sublime Historical Experience* (Stanford: Stanford University Press, 2005). For an appreciative account of Ankersmit's recent turn to the unmediated experience of the sublime, see Martin Jay, *Songs of Experience: Modern American and European Variations on a Universal Theme* (Berkeley: University of California Press, 2005), 255–60. Jay quotes Ankersmit as asserting (in terms reminiscent of the argument of Bernard-Donals and Glejzer): "Essential to the notion of historical experience is that it provides us with a *direct* and *immediate* contact with the past; a contact that is *not* mediated by historiographical tradition, by language or aspects of language (like tropology), by theory, narrative, ethical or ideological prejudice, etc." (quoted, 256–57). See also the sympathetic yet critical review of Ankersmit's *Sublime Historical Experience* by Michael Roth, *History and Theory* 46 (2007): 66–73. White also has proposed a tortuous combination of extreme realism and extreme formalism in the idea that there are intrinsically "holocaustal," ineffably sublime, uniquely modernist events, of which the Shoah is the epitome, and their seemingly appropriate or authentic representation demands the formal techniques and innovations of modernist literature. See "The Modernist Event," in *Figural Realism: Studies in the Mimesis Effect* (Baltimore: Johns Hopkins University Press, 1999), chap. 4.

17. A notion such as the postsublime may indicate a destabilization and questioning of the sublime, at least as it is invoked in certain situations. At times, however, one may want to contest the invocation of any form of the sublime, including the "postsublime." One may see the sublime (notably in Kant) as involving three aspects: an excess or overwhelming of understanding, a blockage of some sort related to that excess, and a feeling of elevation or exhilaration. I would argue that, with respect to acts of violence and victimization, one should resist or attempt to undercut and deflate the third movement, even if negatively tinged, and, more importantly, seek ways of counteracting and eliminating the sociopolitical sources of victimization and related violence.

18. Weissberg, "In Plain Sight," in *Visual Culture and the Holocaust,* ed. Barbie Zelizer (New Brunswick, N.J.: Rutgers University Press, 2000), 13–27.

to it seem to place in radical jeopardy an aesthetic of beauty (a now familiar theme). Forms of art seem to call for Adorno's notion of an aesthetic of pain that parallels a scream, indeed the anguished absence of even the scream (what might perhaps be seen as an arresting form of posttraumatic art—one thinks of Munch's *The Scream* [1893] in the form of an anguished, petrified open mouth—or, perhaps even better from Adorno's perspective, because more formalized and less manipulative, the open mouth of the corresponding figures, including the horse, in Picasso's *Guernica*). Weissberg goes on to discuss Heidegger's evocation of the pair of shoes, which he attributes to a peasant woman, in *The Origin of the Work of Art* and Meyer Schapiro's opposed reading of these shoes, in van Gogh's famous painting, as van Gogh's own.[19] Weissberg contrasts both readings, which, even in their difference, refer to bearers who may be figured, with the anonymous pile of shoes from Majdanek included as an exhibit in the Holocaust museum in Washington. Then she proposes a sublime conception of the traumatic origin of the work of art that surprisingly if not shockingly aestheticizes the remains of Nazi genocidal crimes:

> Individuality has turned into this faceless mass. The pile of shoes revises van Gogh's painting as an installation that resembles conceptual art. Here, too, may rest the truth of its objects, of the material residue that is "equipment" and has reached the limits of this definition. Thus, the display of objects results in another story of the origin of art. The installation of a mountain of shoes translates the experience of the vastness of a crime; it is a peculiar form of the sublime. (23)

The reference to the sublime almost converts the pile of shoes into a Benjaminian ruin. Yet it comes, after a semicolon, almost as an afterthought, punctuated by a lack or void in transition—a black hole that, I would suggest, marks a kind of transfiguration of wound or trauma into the sublime, however indentured to the melancholic the latter may be. But how does the "translation" of the (traumatic) experience of the vastness of a crime—via the seeming objective correlative of a "faceless" pile of shoes—itself become further translated into a peculiar form of the sublime? Are we getting lost in translation (from genocide to shoes to the sublime)? And is the violence, typically associated with trauma, itself aestheticized and rendered sublime, however unintentionally or unconsciously? The force of these questions is intensified

19. Weissberg does not treat Jacques Derrida's *La vérité en peinture* (Paris: Flammarion, 1978); trans. as *The Truth in Painting* by Geoff Bennington and Ian McLeod (Chicago: University of Chicago Press, 1987), which I discuss in chapter 5.

by Weissberg's earlier discussion of the way Daniel Libeskind writes about the Jewish Museum in Berlin in terms of an absent or voided sacred that also seems to be "a peculiar form of the sublime." (Here we are, I think, swimming in the most troubled and troubling waters of the "postsecular.")

> Libeskind's deconstructionist [*sic*] building... offers a challenge for exhibitors. In Libeskind's writings, it is interesting to note how the notion of the void and the invisible shifts from the impossibility of the depiction of the Holocaust to the invisibility of a higher power in which faith may rest: "[It is a] conception, rather, which reintegrates Jewish/Berlin history through the unhealable wound of faith, which, in the words of Thomas Aquinas, is the 'substance of things hoped for; proof of things invisible.'" Lessing's imagination [in his 1766 essay on the *Laocoon*] that tries to complete the sculpture's narrative is here replaced by the unhealable wound of faith and the paradoxical projection of hope. (21)

An extensive discussion of this passage would take us into the recent constellation that brings together the traumatic, the sublime, the sacred (including sacrifice), the postsecular, political theology, and the apocalyptic or postapocalyptic—a constellation that has had the Shoah as a special point of reference. (In it St. Paul is a more frequent, if still disconcerting, source of citations than Thomas Aquinas.)[20]

I have intimated that the sacralization of trauma and the traumatic experience may be interwoven with its figuration as sublime, since in both cases trauma becomes unrepresentable, awesome, beyond the ordinary, and somehow elevating—even redemptive—in its very excess. Trauma itself can be presented as accompanied by a sublime or ecstatic elation or exhilaration, however ambivalent or even decidedly negative, only if it is affectively transfigured as an experience through some supplementary effect or perhaps ideological refashioning, which may misunderstand itself in terms of immediacy. One might also observe that elation may come not from what Kant saw as a self-preservative step back to safety but from the onrush of negative and destructive affect itself, indeed the thrill of violence and unheard-of transgression, that Freud related to the death drive and Lacan to

20. See Eric L. Santner, *On Creaturely Life: Rilke, Benjamin, Sebald* (Chicago: University of Chicago Press, 2006) and his contribution "Miracles Happen: Benjamin, Rosenzweig, Freud, and the Matter of the Neighbor," in Slavoj Žižek, Eric L. Santner, and Kenneth Reinhard, *The Neighbor: Three Inquiries in Political Theology* (Chicago: University of Chicago Press, 2005), 76–133. Santner indicates the crucial importance of Paul for Agamben, Badiou, and Žižek.

the "real." The so-called real—what one might see with Žižek as the extremely traumatic—is itself related to *jouissance,* an orgasmic, limit-shattering experience beyond the pleasure principle and deeply equivocal in nature, that is, combining attraction and repulsion or eroticized desire and obscenely monstrous horror.[21]

But sublimity or sacralization may also be associated with resistance to any form of elevation, *jouissance,* or thrill. It may be experienced or figured as a blow or a void that signals an abyssal descent without ascension or an interminable melancholia without a manic complement. Or its elation may be ecstatic in a more sanctified and perhaps subdued or ascetic key (including the form of asceticism related to a minimalist style). Still, the same phenomenon or figure may be seen as both sublime and sacred, for example, Claude Lanzmann's film *Shoah* or at times even Lanzmann himself as a martyrlike, stigmata-bearing figure who is larger than life. One may even transfer to

21. A critique of a generalized, indiscriminate aesthetic or rhetoric of the sublime (along with an ethos of hyperbole) does not imply a generalized, indiscriminate dismissal or exclusion of hyperbole or the sublime. Rather, it raises the difficult question of how to judge situationally when an openness to the sublime or a turn to hyperbole is indeed warranted. This point seems to escape Sara Guyer, in her at times misplaced deconstructive reading, when she asserts of both Amy Hungerford (in *Holocaust of Texts: Genocide, Literature, and Personification* [Chicago: University of Chicago Press, 2003]) and myself (in *History in Transit*): "Not only do they demonstrate the importance of a vigilant awareness of the violence sustained by tropological substitution, they also dramatize the fallibility of any effort to exclude particular tropes from discourse." "Remembering, Repeating...," *Contemporary Literature* 46 (2005): 736–45 at 744. The very idea of excluding particular tropes from discourse is unacceptable if not absurd. Nor does questioning certain turns to the hyperbolic or sublime imply that one is in total control of one's response, although attentiveness to the problem may conceivably affect response. I quote, with a couple of interpolations, my response to John Zammito's critique of some of my own work as excessively hyperbolic ("Are We Being Theoretical Yet? The New Historicism, the New Philosophy of History, and 'Practicing Historians,'" *Journal of Modern History* 65 (1993): 784–814: "Hyperbole and even opacity (or at least difficulty) may be understood and in a qualified manner defended [as warranted], especially when they are framed in certain ways and are not simply indulged in all contexts. One might provide a limited, contextualized defense of hyperbole as a stylistic indication of one's involvement in the excess of an excessive or extreme (indeed, at times traumatic) context or situation—a response (not a last word or position) that must be undergone and even to some extent acted out [or repeated] if certain problems are to be understood empathetically and worked through [or repeated with significant variation or change]" *Writing History, Writing Trauma* (Baltimore: Johns Hopkins University Press, 2001), n. 8.). Despite his generally favorable response to Paul Ricoeur's work, Hayden White sees Ricoeur as simply excluding the sublime and the hyperbolic, a charge he has leveled against others, notably historians: "I once commended *Time and Narrative* to Norman O. Brown who, having looked it over in his way, said to me, 'What's wrong with Paul Ricoeur? Paul Ricoeur never goes *too far*!' Brown would have probably thought the same about *Memory, Forgetting:* not *messianic* enough. That is true." "Guilty of History: The *Longue Durée* of Paul Ricoeur" [an essay-review of Paul Ricoeur's *Memory, History, Forgetting*], *History and Theory* 46 (2007): 233–51 at 249.

the film or its maker the sentiments of negative sublimity and sacredness that have at times surrounded the Holocaust or other extreme, traumatic events (something that I think occurs in Shoshana Felman's as well as in other treatments of the film and its confusingly hallowed maker, including at times by Lanzmann himself). Lanzmann saw his film as a work of art, what he termed "a fiction of the real,"[22] and "not a documentary... not at all representational"[23]—a self-understanding that many commentators have accepted at face value and followed. Yet such a reading or interpretation does not entirely accord with Lanzmann's vicarious relation to the victim and his desire to reclaim a traumatic experience that he seems to envision melancholically as a lost object and to seek to transmit to the viewer. The latter tendencies lead him to question intrusively, manipulate the victim, and insist on the reliving of a traumatic past—an approach most evident in the sequence in the barbershop with Abraham Bomba. How can this scene be interpreted in purely or even primarily aesthetic terms, sublime or otherwise? In what sense is there a staging of a "fiction of the real" with Bomba simply "playing himself" when the former barber at Treblinka breaks down and cannot go on but, after an excruciating pause, does go on, as Lanzmann, in a pronounced gesture of projective identification, insists "we" must go on?[24] Is not the reliving of a traumatic experience precisely the point at which the aesthetic frame itself breaks down and the distinction between life and art, or the documentary and the aesthetic/fictive, does so as well?[25]

Here one may raise the question of the relation of the sublime to horror, which Gary Weissman, in a critical analysis that partially converges with my own, believes is the affect that representations of the Holocaust attempt to convey in the most powerful and at times immediate form possible.[26] He does not seem interested in the prevalent idea that a source of fascination with the Holocaust is a voyeuristic frisson produced by representations of

22. Claude Lanzmann, "Le lieu et la parole," in *Au suject de "Shoah": Le film de Claude Lanzmann,* ed. Michel Deguy (Paris: Belin, 1990), 301.

23. Lanzmann, "Seminar with Claude Lanzmann, April 11, 1990, *Yale French Studies* 79 (1991): 96–97.

24. *"Shoah": The Complete Text of the Acclaimed Holocaust Film* (New York: Da Capo, 1995), 108.

25. See my discussion of Lanzmann's *Shoah* (as well as various treatments of it) in *History and Memory after Auschwitz* (Ithaca: Cornell University Press, 1998), chap. 4. See also Stuart Liebman, ed., *Claude Lanzmann's "Shoah": Key Essays* (New York: Oxford University Press, 2007).

26. Gary Weissman, *Fantasies of Witnessing: Postwar Efforts to Experience the Holocaust* (Ithaca: Cornell University Press, 2004). See also Caroline Joan (Kay) S. Picart and David A. Frank, *Frames of Evil: The Holocaust as Horror in American Film,* foreword Dominick LaCapra, intro. Edward J. Ingebretsen (Carbondale: Southern Illinois University Press, 2006).

horror from which one, as a viewer, is safely insulated. Instead, he postulates that a desire to get experientially as close as possible to the horror of the Shoah and in some vicarious sense to reexperience that horror is both general in the recent past and particularly marked in the secondary witness, whose goal is to identify with the victim and to appropriate trauma. One may take issue with Weissman's insistent and at times excessive focus on horror but agree with his general point about the function of the Holocaust (along with other foundational traumas), which he makes with reference to Alfred Kazin's appropriative use of Elie Wiesel (the self-proclaimed and widely acknowledged witness par excellence) as a Job-like, existentially rebellious Jew: "The Holocaust serves as that site where our own identity crises can gain dramatic intensity and be lent profound meaning" (39). (Or, as he puts it in even more forceful terms in a later discussion: "Many nonwitnesses *desire* the rendezvous with hell" [121].) One may also agree with Weissman's reasons for questioning the notion of the secondary witness in light of its invocation to underwrite phantasmatic investments and forms of identification but nonetheless note that he does not provide insight into transferential processes that may induce more or less unconscious identification and "haunting" or even "possession" by the past and its victims. Nor does he explicitly inquire into the need to engage and work though one's differential implication in an emotionally charged past one did not live through oneself. However much open to criticism as a text in the public sphere, Binjamin Wilkomirski's fraudulent 1996 memoir, *Fragments: Memories of a Wartime Childhood,* which Weissman discusses in the concluding pages of his book, indicates the need for such inquiry, especially if one thinks, as Weissman does, that "it now seems probable that [Wilkomirski] has come to believe that he is a child survivor of the Holocaust" (213). Weissman provides little insight into the question of how a Wilkomirski is both psychically and socioculturally possible.

Still, Weissman is justified in criticizing gullible or indiscriminately valorizing appreciations of Wilkomirski's book, facilitated by the way it seems to validate questionable theories of deep memory and traumatic recall. And a desire for experiential closeness to horror and trauma is certainly possible. Weissman discusses many cases in which he thinks this desire is active, focusing on Elie Wiesel, Lawrence Langer, Steven Spielberg, and Claude Lanzmann. He refers to the U.S. Holocaust Memorial Museum and, quoting from one of its official publications of 1994, asserts that the museum "consciously attempts to create such an experience for the broad public within the space of its permanent exhibition by 'personalizing' the horror, 'bring[ing] home the tragic reality of the Holocaust and mak[ing] it not a distant historic event but an immediate experience with great personal meaning'" (211–12). Weissman, whose unknown distant relative and namesake died in the Holocaust (14), himself evidently experiences the desire for closeness and wants to counteract if not exorcise its unearned appeal, to the point of rejecting notions of secondary witnessing and referring only to the nonwitness in cases where one has not lived through the Holocaust oneself. But it may be questionable to generalize the desire for closeness to horror as well as to overreact to it. Indeed the subject position the generalization seems to assume is that of someone who feels deficient in affect and desires to make up for what is presumably missing or lacking by coming closer to the Holocaust and especially the victim's experience of it. Such a view itself bears witness to a possible and perhaps more or less prevalent subject position. But what may be experienced as deficient is in most cases probably empathy, and horror arises as an object of desire when empathy is conflated with identification and horror itself is positioned as the actual or perhaps appropriate experience of victims and of those who identify with them.

For Weissman, horror combines "fear, shock, and disgust" (211). He does not address the question of the sublime and its relation to horror. The sublime would seem to be a more "elevated" feeling that may include (or attempt to sublimate) horror, but even in an accentuatedly negative form, the sublime would not be reducible to horror or to the visceral in general. Sublimity involves awe and some ecstatic dimension, even a form of elation well indicated in the German term *das Erhabene.* Hence one has the temptation to link the sublime and the sacred, especially in its transcendent form. In Kant the sublime is related to "higher" faculties. To see horror as the key to the sublime would appear reductive and—at times perhaps usefully—deflationary or desublimating. (It is noteworthy that Weissman quotes Langer, whom he criticizes for fixating on, and identifying with, inconsolably despairing victimhood, as asserting that "it has been exhilarating for me, the discovery that you can bring alive such a memory" of irremediable victimhood, traumatization, "the inexpressible," and "the unimaginable" [124].)[27]

27. See also my discussion of Langer in *Representing the Holocaust: History, Theory, Trauma* (Ithaca: Cornell University Press, 1994), 194–200. A question here is the extent to which one might see an artifact treating the Holocaust in terms of horror or the sublime, say, as a horror film (a template that has arguably served in many popular films treating the Holocaust). Weissman attempts to relate both Spielberg's *Schindler's List* and Lanzmann's *Shoah* to the experience of horror in at times pointed ways, bringing out that there are indeed images referring to the annihilation in *Shoah,* for example, the throat-cutting gesture or the use, in illustrating the testimony of Sonderkommado Filip Müller, of Mieczyslaw Stobierski's graphic model of an Auschwitz-Birkenau crematorium, "complete with miniature SS men, dogs, and victims"

Without pursuing further the question of horror and the sublime, I shall turn to the complex, contestable problems and processes I have touched on as they apply to the perpetrator, the victim, and the commentator. The latter roles may be combined in an expanded version of Primo Levi's gray zone, but they also may at times be sufficiently distinct.[28]

I doubt whether a victim of an abusive, traumatic experience figures it as sublime or sacred when it is occurring. This figuration or even experience during traumatic events (say, killing operations) is probably the province of the perpetrator or, in more equivocal form, the perpetrator-victim or at times the bystander or spectator. For the victim in situations of extreme abuse, the experience is typically one of confusion, numbness, and dissociation (perhaps at times a certain uncanniness as well).[29] And a crucial problem, which deserves more inquiry than it has thus far received, is the difficult, perhaps never fully successful, movement from victim to survivor and sociopolitical agent. Insofar as the victim lives on but remains a victim, he or she exists in the melancholic aftermath of trauma and is haunted or possessed by the traumatic experience, as if reliving it time and again. It may at times color and addle later experience in the manner Lawrence Langer, among many others, describes in *Holocaust Testimonies.*[30] But it is possible, I think, for the victim not only to live on, caught in a crushingly oppressive past, but also to survive, even if that survival never, with respect to extremely traumatic experiences, fully overcomes depression or melancholia and fully

(199). And Weissman indicates, as others have, that Lanzmann's allusive, indirect effects depend on the knowledge, the expectation, and at times even the evocation of the images and archival materials he intentionally excludes. But Weissman may overstate his case in concluding that "*Shoah* whets the appetite for a film like *Schindler's List*" (206), situating Lanzmann's film as a kind of horror- or trauma-tease. It is equally likely that *Shoah* may generate disgust, if not horror, at the more manipulative techniques of Spielberg's film, as evidenced in Lanzmann's well-known reaction itself. In any event, the more general—including the critical—response has been to see Lanzmann's *Shoah* as sublime and to find whatever traces of the horror film there may be in it as dissonant or demeaning to its iconic status. I doubt whether achieving closeness to horror is the principal point of what I have analyzed as Lanzmann's identificatory relation to Abraham Bomba and Bomba's reliving of trauma.

28. On the figure of the victim in recent discourse, see Fatima Naqvi, *The Literary and Cultural Rhetoric of Victimhood: Western Europe, 1970–2005* (New York: Palgrave Macmillan, 2007).

29. Being attacked by a long-time neighbor or friend you thought you knew well can be uncanny but would probably not be experienced as sublime. Here one has the problem of the relations between the sublime and the uncanny, which are at times conflated, approximated, or at least associated (or "linked") in uncritical ways, including in discourse about the *Muselmann* and that figure's putative relation to the living dead.

30. Langer, *Holocaust Testimonies: The Ruins of Memory* (New Haven: Yale University Press, 1991).

heals traumatic wounds. The ability to give testimony is itself one important component of survival. It requires a certain distance from a past that nonetheless remains all too pressing, painful, and at times unbearable. Still, despite the forms of breakdown, bewilderment, and seeming recapture by the past that mark many testimonies, giving testimony is an indication that one is not simply bearing witness to trauma by reliving the past and being consumed by its aftereffects. It is also performative in that it helps to provide some space in which one may gather oneself, engage the present, and attempt to open viable possibilities. Testimony is also and importantly a social and perhaps a political relation in that it requires the actual or virtual presence of others to whom one tells one's story or gives one's account. It may take many forms, and perhaps we have been too prone to privilege narrative, indeed narrative conceived in a very conventional way. Without denigrating the role of narrative or the interest of its analysis, one may recognize that testimony may come in many forms, for example, the essay, the poem, the joke, song, and dance as well as less conventional forms of narrative. And it may be bound up with complex processes of mourning and working-through in general. The hold of the conventional narrative is of course very strong and has influenced Spielberg, for example, in his insistence that the Holocaust narratives collected under his auspices conclude with a family reunion or even some analog of a Hollywood ending, a desire that shapes the conclusion of *Schindler's List* (1993).[31] I also think this straining for the happy ending affects Benigni's unsurprisingly successful and award-winning *Life Is Beautiful* (1998), which can be criticized not for its appeal to humor but for its overly benign, rather conventional form of humor—a form of

31. In the wake of Spielberg's film on Schindler, the atypical rescuer of Jews, we have had two films focusing on Claus Schenk Graf von Stauffenberg, the would-be assassin of Hitler. Jo Baier's 2004 award-winning German TV movie was followed by Brian Singer's 2008 *Valkyrie* (*Walküre* in the German version), starring Tom Cruise as Stauffenberg. Cruise's role in the film provoked controversy because of his affiliation with Scientology, although the focus of the film on an altogether exceptional hero, reinforced by Cruise's star status, might be the more significant issue insofar as it could be seen as furthering questionable processes of "normalization." Without placing Spielberg in the same category, I would note a response that I would not see in terms of working-through but—if not meant ironically—of disavowal. Concerning the newly constructed Contemporary Jewish Museum in San Francisco, Sue Fishkoff writes: "It's a museum that could only have been built in California, says Mitchell Schwarzer, an art history professor at the Bay Area's California College of the Arts. It fits a community that is highly innovative, largely unaffiliated and has not experienced the discrimination Jews have felt elsewhere. 'This is a place of life and celebration and moving forward,' he says. 'It's not a place of reflection on tragedy, because the Jewish experience in California has not been a tragic one.'" "Starting the Conversation," in *Discover the New Contemporary Jewish Museum*, a supplement to *The Jewish News Weekly*, June 6, 2008, p. 2b.

humor that, I think, is simply not up to the level of the catastrophic events and experiences to which it responds.

Recently historians and others have turned to the study of perpetrators.[32] Here I would simply observe that I think it is important for perpetrators to have forums to present and represent their suffering and loss but not to render them in equivocal, self-serving, or book-balancing terms. If such forums are not available in the public sphere, one may preclude even the small chance that perpetrators will be able to work through the past and not simply keep it encrypted or melancholically interred within themselves, with the possibility that the repressed or disavowed will recur once the occasion arises. Thus it is important for perpetrators to be able to bear witness or give testimony other than in trials or in situations leading to adjudication and punishment. One need not accept or validate the results, and one may be hard pressed to come up with convincing empirical cases of former perpetrators making nonapologetic, self-critical, other-than-evasive attempts to address an embarrassing or guilt-ridden past.[33] In any event, the opportunity to represent losses is necessary, and it is possible to do so in a way that, to some extent, indicates that a genuine attempt is being made to work through the past and arrive at different forms of self-understanding and activity. The Germans, for example, did suffer losses on the eastern front and in the bombing of Dresden and other cities.[34] But everything hinges on how the presentation of such losses proceeds and the larger framework in which it takes place, including the sociopolitical implications it may be argued to have.[35]

32. Two principal reference points are Christopher Browning, *Ordinary Men: Reserve Police Battalion 101 and the Final Solution in Poland* (New York: HarperCollins, 1992), and Daniel Jonah Goldhagen, *Hitler's Willing Executioners: Ordinary Germans and the Holocaust* (New York: Alfred A. Knopf, 1996). See also my discussion in *Writing History, Writing Trauma,* chap. 4, and Saul Friedländer, *Nazi Germany and the Jews 1939–1945,* vol. 2, *The Years of Extermination* (New York: HarperCollins, 2007).

33. Arguably, one might in this respect refer to at least certain efforts made over a twenty-year period in Spandau prison by Albert Speer. See the account in Gitta Sereny, *Albert Speer: His Battle with Truth* (New York: Alfred A. Knopf, 1995).

34. Recently attention has turned to the nature of the postwar Allied occupation in general. For a study of the often harsh practices in different zones (including widespread rapes), exacerbated by Allied reactions to the extent of Nazi atrocities, see Giles MacDonogh, *After the Reich: The Brutal History of the Allied Occupation* (New York: Basic Books, 2007). Unfortunately, the story MacDonogh tells does not seem atypical with respect to other occupations following conflict that itself was "brutal," and in this case it went to genocidal extremes. In MacDonogh's account, Lucius B. Clay, commander in chief of the American zone from the spring of 1947, comes in for special praise, especially in light of his belief that Germans should be allowed to govern themselves. MacDonogh's "prize" for crass cynicism probably goes to Stalin.

35. This question arises with respect to W. G. Sebald's *On the Natural History of Destruction,* trans. Anthea Bell (1999; New York: Modern Library, 2004). Sebald provides a compelling

It is also important to recognize both that the perpetrator may be traumatized by extreme acts and that he or she may transfigure trauma into the sublime, the regenerative, or the sacred. Certain ideologies or aesthetics may even function to enact or facilitate such transformation or transfiguration. Nazi discourse, or even fascist discourse in general, is perhaps prototypical in this regard, even though many military or terrorist organizations may lend themselves to such procedures and rhetoric. Ernst Jünger drew back from the Nazis, whom he found vulgar, but his own writings facilitated a transfiguration of the traumatic into the sublime, with the so-called *Fronterlebnis,* or experience of fighting on the front and engaging in repeatedly violent, traumatic scenes, as the occasion for a regenerative enactment of sublime exaltation. Sections of Himmler's infamous 1943 Posen speech seem to indicate that for Himmler and his acolytes there was a sublime dimension in annihilating Jews, and there are many documents in the book *"The Good Old*

---

analysis of the devastating role of the aerial bombing of German cities by Allied forces during World War II with often caustic observations on the manner in which this question has been avoided or treated in aestheticizing terms. I quote but one of his arresting critical observations, reminiscent of passages in Adorno: "The construction of aesthetic or pseudo-aesthetic effects from the ruins of an annihilated world is a process depriving literature of its right to exist" (53). Sebald carefully avoids not only aestheticization but the dubious book-balancing approach, which insists that one not speak of the Holocaust unless one also speaks of the bombings of German cities or the Russian invasion on the eastern front. But, at least at certain moments, his essay seems to move in uncoordinated, even contradictory, directions. On the one hand, he associates sober description and painstaking documentary precision on the level of details with conceptual nebulousness at the points his text amalgamates Allied aerial bombings of German cities with allusions to killing actions or events in concentration and death camps via categories such as "the catastrophe," "annihilation," and (at times naturalized) "destruction," along with the generalized idea of postwar disavowal or suspiciously defective memory. This approach may indeed render the experience of Sebald and others living in the wake of genocide and of devastating bombings that might appear subjectively to level the victims of "destruction" to a common mass of abject beings or "bodies in pain." But the amalgamation is open to question on more historical, analytic, and critical levels. On the other hand, in the analytic and rhetorical crescendo concluding his essay on aerial bombings, in discussing letters sent to him after its initial presentation as "Zürich lectures," and bringing to a close a trenchant discussion of Nazi behavior and what he sees as related phenomena in German culture (including Fritz Lang's films *Dr. Mabuse, the Gambler* [1922] and *Kriemhild's Revenge* [1924]), he goes so far (perhaps too far) as to state that "we [Germans under the Nazis?] actually provoked the annihilation of the cities in which we once lived" (103)—a compensatory sentiment that may continue to overgeneralize in its use of the "we." I think Sebald's approach would be less problematic—and perhaps less absorbing—if he distinguished his subject position, along with those comparable to it, from that of Jewish or other victims of the Third Reich and circumscribed it in terms of a German "born later," who is in a certain sense "victimized" by having to live in the melancholic aftermath of genocidal crimes in which he did not participate but for which he is constrained to assume the legacy and even a limited liability, indeed for which he even seems to feel an indeterminate "guilt."

*Days"* that would also lend themselves to such a reading.[36] It is arguable that Nazi practice, in eliminating from the *Volksgemeinschaft* what was figured as a polluting or contaminating presence, even had for certain perpetrators quasi-sacrificial and redemptive dimensions.[37]

Still, Himmler's own stomach cramps and the nocturnal fits of screaming of his close ally, Erich von dem Bach-Zelewski, indicate that perpetrators may be traumatized and that, even when it is available, a more or less strategically numbing and/or elated discourse of sublimity, as well as a quasi-sacrificial (even at times robotic) practice, may not always function to ward off "unsublimated" posttraumatic symptoms. And these sometimes overdetermined symptoms may be bewilderingly close to those of the victim. But this psychic proximity of course does not mean that the perpetrator and the victim are invariably accomplices in the same indistinct gray zone. The difference between them is social, ethical, and political, and even the traumatized perpetrator is not a victim in the pertinent ethical and political sense. The gray zone of perpetrator-victims cannot simply be generalized to apply to everybody. For Primo Levi it was occupied by people, such as *Sonderkommando* ("special" units of Nazi death camp prisoners constrained to assist in the killing process) and certain kapos or members of Jewish councils, who themselves were often put in double binds or impossible situations as a facet of Nazi practice in the attempt to confuse issues and make accomplices of victims. The category of perpetrator-victim itself requires further differentiations in the difficult but altogether necessary effort to discern various situationally variable shades of gray on gray (which is one of the important but dismal tasks of contemporary comparative history).[38]

36. Ernst Klee, Willi Dressen, and Volker Riess, eds., *"The Good Old Days": The Holocaust as Seen by Its Perpetrators and Bystanders,* foreword Hugh Trevor-Roper (1988; New York: The Free Press, 1991). *Die Schöne Zeiten* (The good old days) was the name Kurt Franz gave to his picture album commemorating his time as the last commandant of Treblinka.

37. See the discussion of "redemptive anti-Semitism" in Saul Friedländer, *Nazi Germany and the Jews,* vol. 1, *The Years of Persecution, 1933–1939* (New York: HarperCollins, 1997), chap. 3.

38. Levi's "gray zone," while seen as of great significance, is not extended by him, as it is by Giorgio Agamben (*Remnants of Auschwitz: The Witness and the Archive,* trans. Daniel Heller-Roazen [New York: Zone Books, 1999]), in a rashly generalized, gray-on-gray fashion to obliterate all distinctions, including distinctions between incumbents of sufficiently distinct roles such as victim and commentator or filmmaker. (See my discussion of Agamben in *History in Transit,* chap. 4.) There may be perpetrators who are not victims in any relevant sense, and there may be victims who are not perpetrators, although there is also typically a variable gray zone, or heterogeneous gray zones, of differing intensities with respect to often quite different historical situations and agents. Recently prominent is the plight of conscripted child soldiers who are often kidnapped and forced to kill and commit atrocities, at times against

In the case of victims who may in retrospect "sublimate" earlier traumatic experience or even construe it as, in some sense, sacred, I intimated that a commentator such as myself on a very basic level does not have a viable subject position from which to make pertinent critical observations. The case of the *hibakusha* in Japan is obviously significant here. How could one possibly be inclined to tell victims of Hiroshima or Nagasaki that they should not enshrine or even sacralize traumatic experiences? Of course that is not the only thing they have done, and their role in antinuclear and other protest movements has been noteworthy. Still, with respect to the public sphere, when organizations or movements take up sacralized or sublimated traumas and use them for political or other ends, then critical commentary may indeed be warranted. Here one may mention Peter Novick's *The Holocaust in American Life,* a book that details some questionable uses and abuses of the Holocaust on the part of Jewish organizations.[39] (One may also mention Tom Segev's *The Seventh Million,* on manipulative uses of the Holocaust in Israeli politics, which was written before Novick's book and serves as a kind of implicit template for it.)[40] Analyses that stress the role of identity politics or the dubious uses of trauma and victim status as symbolic capital are at times warranted. But they should not ignore the way such use and abuse is not specific to any one people or group. They should also not deny the force and extent of traumatic experience or its aftermath. Here one has the intricate issue of the intergenerational transmission of trauma or its symptoms to intimates of trauma victims, something I (unlike Novick) think may occur even in America. Moreover, such transmission may be addressed in a way that is not self-serving but instead careful, moving, and self-critical, as I think occurs, for example, in Art Spiegelman's *Maus* or, to give a French case, Henri

---

fellow villagers if not family members. Victimized even as perpetrators, child soldiers are beginning to testify to devastating experiences and attempts to work through them, as in the narrative of Ismael Beah of Sierra Leone, *A Long Way Gone: Memoirs of a Boy Soldier* (New York: Farrar, Straus and Giroux, 2007).

39. Boston: Houghton Mifflin, 1999. See also my discussion of this book in *History in Transit,* 93–95.

40. Segev, *The Seventh Million: The Israelis and the Holocaust,* trans. Haim Watzman (1991; New York: Hill and Wang, 1993). Novick does not refer to Segev's book. On longer-term tendencies and their bearing on Israeli-Palestinian relations, see Elliott Horowitz's *Reckless Rites: Purim and the Legacy of Jewish Violence* (Princeton: Princeton University Press, 2006). Horowitz points out that there were "traditional" justifications among some Jews (including the American-born Lubavitch teacher and mystic Rabbi Yitzchak Ginsburgh) for Baruch Goldstein's shooting early Purim morning 1994, at a large crowd of kneeling, praying Muslims in a mosque in Hebron, which killed twenty-nine people and wounded many others. His supporters saw Goldstein (also American-born) as a hero fulfilling the commandment to destroy Amalek, with whom some settlers and their sympathizers equate the Palestinians.

Raczymow's novel, *Writing the Book of Esther.*[41] I would add that my caveat, concerning the lack of a viable subject position for pertinent commentary on what victims do with traumatic experience in order to be able to cope or live with it, does not apply to their representation of it in the public sphere or to their role as commentators on phenomena such as films and novels. The fact that survivors respond positively to (or "like") *Schindler's List* or *Life Is Beautiful* may help alert other commentators to features of these films that they might otherwise miss. But, whatever the therapeutic value of certain responses for survivors, it would be questionable to posit a taboo against nondismissive criticisms of their commentaries.[42]

I would like to return to the complex, much debated figure of the secondary witness. Not only have testimonies achieved a prominent status. So has the secondary witness, who in some problematic, contestable sense also bears witness or testifies. In the best of circumstances, the secondary witness bears witness to (not for) the witness and attempts to go beyond reporting or facts in acknowledging, affirming, and exploring the nature of responsive understanding involving affect—what I have referred to as empathic unsettlement, a form of compassion that, as I intimated, resists identification or incorporation and respects differences—at times very important differences—with respect to the witness and survivor. I have noted that there has been an important testimonial dimension, including various forms of secondary witnessing, in many fields, including literature and art. At times secondary witnessing has been very problematic. Wieviorka herself

41. Art Spiegelman, *Maus: A Survivor's Tale* (New York: Pantheon Books, 1986) and *Maus II: A Survivor's Tale and Here My Trouble Begins* (New York: Pantheon Books, 1991), as well as my discussion in *History and Memory after Auschwitz,* 139–79. See also my discussion in *History in Transit,* 114 and 130. On the intergenerational transmission of trauma, see also Nicolas Abraham and Maria Torok, *The Shell and the Kernel,* ed. and trans. Nicholas Rand (1987; Chicago: University of Chicago Press, 1994), vol. 1, esp. part 5. Also relevant is Toni Morrison's *Beloved* (New York: Alfred A. Knopf, 1987) as well as David L. Eng and Shinhee Han, "A Dialogue on Racial Melancholia," in *Loss,* ed. David Eng and David Kazanjian, afterword Judith Butler (Berkeley: University of California Press, 2003), esp. 354–56. In *Writing the Book of Esther,* trans. Dori Katz (1985; New York: Holmes and Meier, 1995), Henri Raczymow provides an extreme case of identification with the victim. He tells the story of a young woman who, in an *imitatio* of an aunt who died at Auschwitz, starves herself, shaves her head, dresses in prison garb, and finally commits suicide by gassing herself. (The original French title of the novel is *Un cri sans voix.* In view of its controversial history in terms of its seeming justification of genocidal violence by Jews, the choice of the Book of Esther in the translation of the title, which makes reference to the protagonist's name but is not further explained, is at best problematic.) On the Book of Esther and its vexed history, see Elliott Horowitz, *Reckless Rites,* part 1.

42. I think Larry David implicitly makes this point in the *Seinfeld* episode in which Jerry's parents are horrified by Jerry and his girlfriend "necking" during the showing of *Schindler's List.*

is concerned and upset by the way historians in France have been called on at trials not simply to provide information but, somehow and however oxymoronically, to bear witness to history. I have intimated that figures such as Claude Lanzmann and, in another register, W. G. Sebald have not only been, deservedly, objects of intense interest but, more questionably, construed as models to be emulated by commentators, especially with respect to the issue of how authentically to bear witness and, in addition, to be open to psychoanalytic commentary. This witnessing stresses inconsolable melancholy or impossible mourning, and the type of psychoanalysis it almost invites is a certain variant of trauma theory that often comes with a discourse of the sublime or even sacralization and at times a longing for messianic or miraculous interventions. Here the work of Shoshana Felman on Lanzmann and of Eric Santner on Sebald may perhaps be taken as paradigmatic.[43]

This work contains many valuable insights, sensitive close readings, and even moving passages. Melancholy may have a critical or at least cautionary dimension, especially when its attachment to lost others places in question a context in which there is a pronounced inclination to forget or objectionably airbrush a disconcerting past and the fate of its victims. There may even be a sociopolitical potential in the mobilization of melancholy in the creation of "communities of loss."[44] Inconsolable melancholy, impossible mourning,

43. See Felman's contributions to Felman and Laub's, *Testimony*. See also Cathy Caruth, *Unclaimed Experience: Trauma, Narrative, and History* (Baltimore: Johns Hopkins University Press, 1996). On the question of *Trauer* (mourning) and melancholy in Sebald, see Mary Cosgrove, "Melancholy Competitions: W. G. Sebald reads Günher Grass and Wolfgang Hildesheimer," *German Life and Letters* 59 (2006): 217–32. Cosgrove argues that "melancholy resignation is the only 'Trauer' discourse deemed suitable [by Sebald] for discussing the Jewish victims of the Holocaust. . . . Sebald's enormous success ensures that his subjectively valid position on the past has gained currency in some academic discourses, not always as an intriguing phenomenon within a specific context of taboos and prohibitions, but as a context-creating discourse in itself. It is this tendency to extrapolate from a single perspective on the past which should be critiqued, for it is highly problematic when applied to general interpretative frameworks, and invites undiscerning forms of identification" (232).

44. See the essays in *Loss*. This collection is thought-provoking and well worth serious attention. But, notably in the editors' introduction, melancholia is very broadly conceived in largely unqualified, somewhat idealized terms. The presumably counterintuitive strategy employed is one of reversal with reference to a "normative" hierarchy that privileges a stereotypical, simplistic idea of mourning and dubiously pathologizes melancholy—but the reversal threatens to remain within a binaristic frame of reference that both induces questionable readings of other perspectives and may limit intellectual and sociopolitical options. A pronounced gesture supplementing reversal is the tendency to blur or collapse distinctions (such as that between melancholia and mourning) without raising the question of how to reformulate problematized distinctions and assess their relative strength or weakness in fact and in right. Indeed the problem of alternative normativities is not broached, and normativity in general tends to be collapsed into normalization. What may emerge (as in dimensions of the early

and endless lament may be the only possible responses for those in dire circumstances in which the only relief is afforded by momentary or evanescent occurrences. And one may acknowledge and affirm the often unpredictable role of what is to come (*l'à-venir* in Derrida's locution) as an implication of the deconstruction of closed systems and absolute foundations without becoming fixated on messianicity or conceiving it as a sufficient basis for an ethics or politics. Indeed, when melancholia paradoxically becomes critical and creative, for example in group formation or even in political action, one may suspect that the paradox itself is not absolute and that at some level a process of working-through is being engaged in counteracting but not simply transcending less-enabling forms of repetition, but that process may be disavowed because of anxiety over possible betrayal or infidelity to the lost or dead.

Still, the danger in the insufficiently qualified valorization of melancholy (or its "manic" and miraculous or messianic accompaniments) is to remain gridlocked, that is to say, locked within the grid of victimization—the grid involving perpetrator, victim, survivor, bystander, gray zone, rescuer, and so forth, to which we must now add secondary witness, including the secondary witness with sacralizing, sublimating, or messianic inclinations. This frame of reference may be empirically necessary in analyzing certain situations, but it is excessively limiting, possibly even disempowering, in its ethical and political effects. For it may restrict ethics and politics to the horizon of the witness to abjection, however much charged with melancholic pathos and transfigured into the putative vehicle of miraculous epiphanies, sublime revelations, or even limited opportunities in forming communities. Whatever passages to "new possibilities of collective life" (in the phrase of Eric Santner)[45] may be opened by an attentiveness to stranded objects and slight yet saving modifications of subjective disposition, something may nonetheless be amiss when one is restricted to the mutually reinforcing extremes

Benjamin) is a displacement of a radical sectarian, at times antinomian, Christian perspective in which melancholia is valorized while mourning (as working-through, even in a complex, never totalized or exclusionary form) is adamantly resisted. Melancholia may even be detached from earlier historical associations as either masculine (in the melancholic or even mad "genius") or feminine (in the traditional inconsolable mourner) and now recoded (especially in response to the AIDS pandemic) as "queer." In addition, one may perhaps argue that "queer" or "gay" melancholy functions largely as a redefined trope signifying limited empowerment, critique, ethical responsibility, and a call for group mobilization (especially in the face of AIDS and its widespread mainstream neglect as a serious concern) and having at most a problematic relation to clinical forms of melancholia, including the debilitating effects of depression.

45. *On Creaturely Life,* 133. I would suggest that the form of abjection that Santner discusses as creaturely life—and would like to transform, however evanescently—is close to what early modern Calvinists referred to as the "worm-feeling."

of valorized melancholia or loss, on the one hand, and, on the other, invocations of enchantment, events of grace, messianic longings, chance happenings, or, at best, "communities of loss" and, more dubiously, some opaque combination of putatively divine (or pure) violence and neighborly love. Such an approach may contribute little to an understanding of politics that insistently raises the question of how to get beyond the entire grid of victimization (along with the belief that society requires, or even is founded on, sacrificial victimization) by working through problems in a way that could never dissolve all melancholy, heal all wounds, or lay all ghosts to rest but that does open up the possibility of significantly different social and political relations, including specific institutional changes.

I wish to emphasize the point that working-through, in the sense I am invoking, varies with different subject positions and contexts. I have been trying both in this work and in others to elaborate a more complex, critical concept of working-through that is neither the simple binary opposite of acting-out or the repetition compulsion nor a total transcendence or disavowal of the traumas and losses of the past that continue to haunt or even possess the present. I would reiterate that I envision working-through as a mode of immanent critique (involving aspects of deconstruction) that engages both personal and collective problems, including posttraumatic symptoms. In working-through one does not totally transcend but rather attempt to generate counterforces to melancholia and compulsive repetition, both through psychic "work" on the self and through engagement in social and political practice with others, from mourning (which may have a political valence) to more directly sociopolitical forms of action directed toward institutional change and what might be termed the situational transcendence of unjust or incapacitating structures and contexts. Work here should not be opposed to play, and the carnivalesque has a crucial role both in certain types of mourning and in sociopolitical processes in general that contest unjust institutions and policies. The carnivalesque, along with the comic and the grotesque in general, is also a significant counterpart to the sublime, which helps to question it and bring it down to earth.

To the limited extent one may generalize, one may suggest that working-through—not as a panacea but as an ethically, politically, and psychically pertinent process—implies the possibility of agency that does not disavow vulnerability but rather affirms it in the attempt to undercut the projective tendency to scapegoat and victimize others. (A crucial aspect of scapegoating is the denial or disavowal of one's own vulnerability.) Working-through implies the affirmation of a vulnerable agency in counteracting compulsive repetition, disempowerment, and gridlock. In any event, I think there is no viable politics, or ethics relevant to such a politics, without some attempt to work through, without simply forgetting, the past—in a word, some attempt at psychoanalytically and historically informed immanent critique—in the interest of elaborating more desirable practices and institutions in the present and future.

Postscript: one may note in criticism and theory a tendency to approximate, if not amalgamate, the sublime and the uncanny.[46] It is noteworthy that, in his landmark essay on the uncanny, Freud himself does not mention the sublime and may even seem to imply that it is not germane to his discussion, although certain of his remarks may nonetheless be taken to raise the question of their tangled relations.[47] Sublimation in Freud might be understood as an "immanent" form of the sublime that, notably in art, may produce various sublime effects, but its relation to the uncanny is problematic even though sublimation itself is not disembodiment but a more or less uncanny return of the erotic in the "spiritual" or elevated (a relation explored ironically in Thomas Mann's novella *Death in Venice*). The sublime and the uncanny may more generally be taken as postsecular experiences that unsettle certainties about secularization as an overcoming—instead of an intricate problematic displacement—of the religious or the sacred. Freud himself refers narrowly to animism and the primitive, which he thinks reality testing may perhaps overcome (154). But he finds childhood complexes, which uncannily and at times traumatically return as the repressed, to be more intractable, and he at least indicates the significance of formal questions in the study of literature by presenting the aesthetic in general as posing special or supplementary problems for analysis that his approach may not entirely resolve in spite of the fact that he has taken a literary text (E. T. A. Hoffmann's "The Sandman") as a primary "specimen" for his analysis (155). He notes, for example, that the one exception to the parallel between the uncanny in literature and

46. For example, Neil Hertz's widely read, thought-provoking *The End of the Line* (New York: Columbia University Press, 1985) treats the uncanny in a book devoted primarily to the sublime without exploring the complex relations between the two. See esp. chap. 6 on "Freud and the Sandman." David Ellison's *Ethics and Aesthetics in European Modernist Literature: From the Sublime to the Uncanny* (Cambridge: Cambridge University Press, 2001) came to my attention only after the completion of the present book. It contains many interesting readings of texts but encompasses them in a dubious "from/to" schema that inhibits a more pertinent analysis of the interaction between the uncanny and the sublime. (The latter has hardly disappeared or even diminished as a reference point.)

47. See "The Uncanny" in *The Uncanny* [1919 with later revisions; New York: Penguin Books, 2003], trans. and preface David McClintock, intro. Hugh Haughton. In many ways Haughton's introduction parallels Hertz's analysis.

in life, which is especially forceful in the case of possibly traumatic childhood experiences, is the way a reader may not identify with a figure in the grip of the uncanny but with some other figure less compulsively taken by it (in "The Sandman" the sober Klara, say, instead of the undecidably "mad"/ fantastic-enchanted Nathanael)—or the reader may even, I would add, resist unmediated identifications. The narrator may also ironize the uncanny or subject it to critical scrutiny (as the narrator does at times in "The Sandman." See "The Uncanny," 157–58.)

Freud proceeds to blur the distinction he initially posits between the putatively primitive and the return of childhood experience, even exclaiming: "Since nearly all of us still think no differently from savages on this subject, it is not surprising that the primitive fear [*Angst*] of the dead is still so potent in us and ready to manifest itself if given encouragement" (149). (Throughout, *Angst* and its cognates are [mis]translated in terms of fear rather than anxiety.) Freud adds that "we do not feel entirely secure in these new convictions [that we have "*surmounted*" such "primitive" modes of thought]: the old ones live on in us, on the look-out for confirmation" (154). For Freud the uncanny (*Das Unheimliche*), related to the repetition compulsion, is indeed active in everyone, although Freud suspiciously maintains (as he does, in *Civilization and Its Discontents,* with respect to the not unrelated, womblike "oceanic feeling") that "it is a long time since he experienced or became acquainted with anything that conveyed the impression of the uncanny" (124). Working on "The Uncanny" at about the same time as *Beyond the Pleasure Principle* (1920), he discusses such phenomena as haunting, projective identification, déjà vu, the root ambivalence of words (*heimlich/unheimlich*), childhood trauma, feelings of helplessness, terroristic doubles, anxiety about threats experienced as coming from others (the "evil eye" and "demonic" possession, for example), uncertainty about boundaries between the animate and the inanimate (where one might situate the "living dead"), and in general apprehension concerning death and the dead (phenomena not usually associated with the sublime).[48] In more delimited terms, he notes that a marginalized meaning is the repressed

48. Yet in "[Dream]" Georges Bataille figures in a sublime fashion what would seem to be his childhood traumatic abuse at his father's hands: "Kind of ambivalence between the most horrible and the most magnificent. . . . I see him spread his obscene hands over me with a bitter and blind smile. This memory seems to me the most terrible of all. One day returning from vacation I find him again showing me the same affection. . . . I'm something like three years old my legs naked on my father's knees and my penis bloody like the sun. . . . My father slaps me and I see the sun." *Visions of Excess, Selected Writings, 1927–1939,* ed. and intro. Allan Stoekl, trans. Allan Stoekl with Carl R. Lovitt and Donald M. Leslie Jr. (Minneapolis: University of Minnesota Press, 1995), 4. See also my discussion of Bataille in chapter 4.

component of a word's dominant sense that joins or even merges with it, and he arrestingly concludes a seeming "collection of examples" of the uncanny with what he uncannily terms "the most pleasing [*die schönste*] example of our conception of the uncanny"—the sense that "neurotic men" have "that there is something uncanny about the female genitals." Freud sees this as an ultimate confirmation that the uncanny or *unheimlich* is the repression and disguised or distorted return of the familiar, "cosily" intimate, homelike, or *heimlich,* concluding that the prefix "un" is the indication or token [*die Marke*] of repression and that "love is a longing for home"—a nostalgia [*Heimweh*] for the "mother's genitals or her womb," once everyone's home (151). (One might add that, in questionably gendered terms, the phallus is often figured as sublime or transcendent rather than uncanny.)

Freud's neoromantic analysis of the uncanny as the defamiliarization of the once familiar, which is more disorienting than reductive and even familiarizing appeals to the castration complex (with which it may be associated but from which it need not be derived), epitomizes the argument that the *heimlich* and the *unheimlich,* while in one sense antonyms, also in an important (incestuous?) sense merge in meaning with one another, especially with respect to the *heimlich* as the secret, private, or hidden, and the *unheimlich* as the strangely disconcerting disclosure or entry into the open of what should have remained secret or concealed (notably including the private parts). (Here one has Freud's uncanny analog of the play between the concealed and the disclosed or "the open" in Heidegger.) In Hoffmann's story, it does not seem to be "the sight of [Coppelius's—the "bad" father and presumed double of Coppola] approach that brought on Nathanael's fit of madness," as Freud asserts ("The Uncanny," 138), but rather Nathanael's sight of his fiancée Klara standing in front of Coppola's spyglass, as Nathanael tries to see from the tower what Klara observes as "that strange little grey bush... that seems to be coming towards us"—a grey bush that apparently is conflated with Klara herself, in a textual moment on which Freud curiously does not comment and which would point more to the uncanniness of *Heimweh* than of castration anxiety and a death wish toward the father. Moreover, after he does not succeed in his frenzied attempt to throw Klara from the tower, Nathanael's subsequent suicidal jump, which does coincide with his catching sight of Coppelius below, would seem to be both a psychoanalytic and a formal requirement (or *mise en abîme*)—a way for a posttraumatic symptom to be sacrificially acted out and a way for the narrator to get rid of the uncanny Nathanael (in a sense, his own double) and put a stop to his compulsively repetitive, uncontrollably delirious, and finally violent life. Freud himself briefly associates the *heimlich/unheimlich* interplay with problems concerning the sacred, the magical, the occult, and the holy, especially in his reflection on dictionary definitions and examples at the beginning of his essay, but he does not extend further his reflections concerning these associations. (Freud's choice of "The Sandman" may account for his discussion of the uncanny with respect to the destabilization of the human-automaton, rather than the human-animal, relation, an issue that might be raised with reference to other literary works, including Hoffmann's *Kater Murr.* Kafka and others such as Sebald, where the human-animal relation in its uncanniness is insistent, tend to be prominent in more recent analyses.)

I would conclude by observing that, while the uncanny and the sublime gravitate (sometimes as debris) in the orbit of the postsecular (perhaps a reason for their frequent, often unproblematized conjunction), as my preceding discussion intimates they may represent in important ways different or even divergent vectors. At least in one of its important forms, the sublime tends in the direction of transcendence (including the seeming movement beyond the repetition compulsion [and the uncanny] through a radical break, utopian leap, decisive cut, unmediated vision, affirmation of autonomy, or creation ex nihilo, that may be related to hopes or anxieties about full secular enlightenment, emancipation, or transcendence with respect to the sacred and the "superstitious"). In seeming contrast, the uncanny involves immanence, including a necessary implication in the repetition compulsion (hence Freud's association of it with the "primitive" and the "animistic" that we do not fully "outgrow"). As intimated earlier, the uncanny would seem closer to immanent forms of the sublime, notably sublimation (with the erotic repeated, displaced, and even disguised in the "higher" and "spiritual"). The uncanny and the sublime also have differing relations to trauma. There have been pronounced attempts to transfigure the traumatic into the sublime, while the uncanny would seem less prone to "traumatropic" transfiguration, although it may serve as either cause or effect of trauma and its symptoms (as in the case of Nathanael and his childhood trauma). In a related manner, one might suggest that the sublime could be seen as a disguised displacement (upward) or uncanny repetition of the repressed, suppressed, or disavowed sacred. Moreover, the sublime itself may have uncanny effects (for example, vertigo and the blurring of distinctions), and the uncanny may induce an attempt to seek transcendence or release from its compulsively repetitive involvements, perhaps through decisive violence, which may be figured as sublime (or divine). The repeated return to the sublime, including the textual sublime of the aporia or *mise en abîme,* may seem uncanny or at least compulsive. The complex, variable connections between the sublime and the uncanny, including their possible relations to displacements of the sacred as well as to (quasi)sacrificial and scapegoating processes (notably in the attempt to get rid of and redemptively transcend the uncanny and the "contaminating" other or threatening double on whom one projects one's own anxieties), would require extended treatment, as would their relation to limited processes of working through ensuing entanglements. It is arguable that an extremely risk-laden openness to the "totally other" (including a notion of "autoimmune" self-destruction or *mise en abîme*), which Derrida emphasized in his later work and even saw, contestably, as a (if not *the*) crux of "democracy," could be construed as an uncanny form of the sublime (for example, as the return of a repressed or disavowed possibility of total annihilation). I would add that the totally other may be construed as sublime but not, at least initially, as uncanny. But someone or something you find totally other (or a sheer impossibility with respect to yourself) that you realize is like or within you, as well as someone or something you think you know well that comes to seem totally other, may give rise to an experience of the uncanny.

# CHAPTER 4

# Toward a Critique of Violence

> One can understand why Surrealism was not afraid to make for itself a tenet of total revolt, complete insubordination, of sabotage according to rule, and why it still expects nothing save from violence. The simplest Surrealist act consists of dashing down into the street, pistol in hand, and firing blindly, as fast as you can pull the trigger, into the crowd. Anyone who, at least once in his life, has not dreamed of thus putting an end to the petty system of debasement and cretinization in effect has a well-defined place in that crowd, with his belly at barrel level. The justification of such an act is, to my mind, in no way incompatible with the belief in that gleam of light that Surrealism seeks to detect deep within us.
>
> —André Breton, "Second Manifesto of Surrealism," 1930

Among the many far-fetched aspects of my famous or infamous epigraph is the inchoate idea (could it be called instrumental?) that it is somehow a mark of distinction, if not elevating or even redemptive, to "dream" that random acts of violence may cause the downfall of a "debased" sociopolitical and cultural system.[1] Another startling aspect of the statement is the conjunction of traumatizing violence and a sublimely abyssal "gleam of light... deep within us." While the relation between the *passage à l'acte* and fantasy or dream is left indeterminate or perhaps simply muddled, Breton expresses the fascination with figurations of violence that have played a prominent but differential role in the more or less symptomatic dimensions of the thought of noteworthy modern Western thinkers.[2] I would like to inquire critically into these figurations and, in so doing, signal the questionable manner in which violence has been valorized and presented in foundational, sacralized, sublime, or redemptive terms.

1. André Breton, *Mainfestoes of Surrealism,* trans. Richard Seaver and Helen R. Lane (Ann Arbor: University of Michigan Press, 1969), 125.

2. See the suggestive cross-disciplinary engagement with the problem of violence and visual culture in Martin Jay, *Refractions of Violence* (New York: Routledge, 2003).

A crucial problem is that such figurations of violence tend to free it from normative limits and associate it with excess. It is important, both analytically and critically, to understand the ideological and practical appeal of violence rendered sacred or sublime. It is equally important to appreciate the countervailing normative role of orientations that seek alternatives to—or at least attempt to place limits on—violence even when it is directed toward seemingly "emancipatory" ends. An end, whose ostensible role is to limit violence, may itself become so abstract and ill defined that it does not limit but in fact promotes or even justifies the excessive use of violence, especially in the context of advanced technology and more or less covert interests (such as a quest for geopolitical dominance) that facilitate massive, if not unlimited, destruction and death. The violent pursuit of invasively expansive, utterly utopian ends (limitless conquest, total victory, uncompromisingly "radical" yet unrepresentable transformation, even fighting terror and supposedly spreading freedom or equality) may fail systematically to work in strategic or tactical ways and be tantamount to, or at least have the same excessive effects as, a sacralization or rendering sublime of violence. Conversely, the valorization of violence may itself serve to endow such extreme, phantasmatic ends with an aura of legitimacy and possibly be one of their disavowed motivations.

Violence both poses questions that cut across disciplines and is closely related to other significant cross-disciplinary problems. It is, for example, difficult to see how one could discuss trauma, which has become an increasingly widespread concern, without relating it to violent processes of various kinds, from the experience of physical assault to the symptom-inducing imaginary identification with the victim of violence.[3] Indeed, violence is the typical manner of breaking the psyche's protective shield or forcefully transgressing

3. Debarati Sanyal, in *The Violence of Modernity: Baudelaire, Irony, and the Politics of Form* (Baltimore: Johns Hopkins University Press, 2006), tries to dichotomize violence and trauma in the interest of stressing political agency, which she associates with a focus on violence. But, in the course of her interesting book, the dichotomy breaks down and it becomes evident that concern with violence and with trauma need not be mutually exclusive. The literature on trauma is itself enormous and goes in various directions, not all of which are narrowly psychological. Still, much remains to be done in historiography, in relating an informed, nonreductive approach to trauma and political, social, and more generally contextual analyses of violence. See the fruitful initiatives in Nancy Wood, *Vectors of Memory: Legacies of Trauma in Postwar Europe* (Oxford: Berg, 1999); Lawrence Douglas, *The Memory of Judgment: Making Law and History in the Trials of the Holocaust* (New Haven: Yale University Press, 2001); and Mark S. Micale and Paul Lerner, eds., *Traumatic Pasts: History, Psychiatry, and Trauma in the Modern Age, 1870–1930,* (Cambridge: Cambridge University Press, 2001). My own contributions include *Representing the Holocaust: History, Theory, Trauma* (Ithaca: Cornell University Press, 1994), *History and Memory after Auschwitz* (Ithaca: Cornell University Press, 1998), *Writing History, Writing Trauma* (Baltimore: Johns Hopkins University Press, 2001), *History in Transit: Experience, Identity, Critical Theory*

normative limits and thereby causing traumatization. Terrorism may be seen at least in part as the systematic traumatization of a subject population whether by a government or by nongovernmental groups. And traumatizing violence, including sacrificial violence, may be theorized and turned to in a deceptive effort to break through what is experienced as a deadly compulsive cycle of repetition in the pursuit of hoped-for purification, regeneration, or redemption—but with effects that instead intensify that cycle's vicious force. Indeed, the compulsive repetition of scenes of violence, which constitutes the clearest form of Freud's so-called death drive and was situated by him beyond the pleasure principle, is a "reign of terror" that typically ensues upon the unqualified quest for a redemptive breakthrough to an utterly transformed world. Moreover, the enumeration of formal analogies between trauma and the sublime may not extend analysis far enough.[4] Certain theorists (at times taking a formalistic or aestheticizing turn) may even conjoin trauma and violence conceptually and evaluatively in a manner that construes them as ecstatic experiences of the sublime or as sacralizing, salvific, or foundational forces.[5]

A tendency to transfigure trauma into the sublime is especially prevalent in apocalyptic and postapocalyptic thinking where violent, traumatizing action is understood as marking a radical, even total, rupture with the past—a kind of creation ex nihilo, conversion experience or primal leap (origin as *Ursprung*) that is taken to be the necessary condition for a breakthrough into a typically blank or unknowable utopian future. This is one significant way in which violence may be glorified and made into an object of desire. The figuration of violence has been replete with sacrificial or sublime motifs and presented as a redemptive or regenerative force for the individual and the group.[6] The foundation of a polity as well as of a personality is often

(Ithaca: Cornell University Press, 2004), and "Tropisms of Intellectual History," *Rethinking History* 8 (2004): 499–529, a version of which is included here as chapter 7.

4. See Frank Ankersmit, "The Sublime Dissociation of the Past: Or How to Be(come) What One Is No Longer," *History and Theory* 40 (2001): 295–323.

5. Aestheticizing sublimation, along with participatory exhilaration (what Kant termed *Schwärmerei*), was evident in Karlheinz Stockhausen's immediate response to the September 11, 2001, suicide bombing of the World Trade Center as "the greatest work of art imaginable for the whole cosmos." His entire comment, which he subsequently retracted, may be found at http://www.osborne-conant.org/documentation_stockhausen.htm. A sacralizing or sublime valorization of violence goes beyond aesthetic shock effects when it motivates or legitimates action, and it may well impede more specific forms of political and ideological analysis, including a critical inquiry into sacralizing, sacrificial, and sublime motifs in the thought and practice of historical agents.

6. For the American colonial context and the frontier experience involving warfare against Indians, see Richard Slotkin's controversial classical study, *Regeneration through Violence: The*

traced to some violent, traumatic, transgressive, often sacralized or "sublimated," event that is presumed to mark a turning point or rupture in history and the instauration of a new era. Among such events, often mythologized or merging religious and political history, one may list the killing of Laius by Oedipus, the killing of Remus by Romulus, the killing of Abel by Cain, the intended sacrifice of Isaac by Abraham, the crucifixion of Christ (readable either as the self-immolation of the deity or the killing of the son abandoned by the father), the beheading of Louis XVI during the French Revolution (a regicide that was also a deicide), and the more abstract idea of the death of God who, as Nietzsche contends, was killed by us as the inaugural moment of modernity. Perhaps one might add the Nazi genocide against the Jews as well as other genocides or excessive, violent events, at least when they are construed in certain ways or function as foundational traumas and reference points or templates for later events and actions, often becoming constraining frames of reference. For example, the phantasm of the Nazis returns time and again—in Baader-Meinhoff for the German government, in the German government for Baader-Meinhoff, in the Arabs for certain Israelis, in the Israelis for certain Arabs, and so forth.[7] It is also interesting to note that, about the time Nietzsche was announcing the death of God,[8] the Catholic Church declared the infallibility of the Pope[9]—something it is tempting to see as a contested, anxious, anthropocentric gesture denying the possibly traumatizing recognition that the place of the "big Other" might indeed be vacant or a void.

There is a broad intellectual and cultural current in modernity that is not restricted to the idea of the foundational trauma and encompasses some extremely problematic components. With varying degrees of critical distance on the intricate nexus linking violence, trauma, victimization, sacrifice, the sacred, and the sublime, this current includes many different historical figures and movements that in a more extended treatment would require greater differential analysis.[10] What I would underline here is the dimension, coming

---

*Mythology of the American Frontier, 1600–1800* (1973; New York: Harper Perennial, 1996). See also my discussion of the founding or foundational trauma in *Writing History, Writing Trauma*, chap. 2.

7. On these problems, see Jeremy Varon, *Bringing the War Home: The Weather Underground, the Red Army Faction, and Revolutionary Violence in the Sixties and Seventies* (Berkeley: University of California Press, 2004), and Tom Segev, *The Seventh Million: The Israelis and the Holocaust*, trans. Haim Watzman (1991; New York: Hill and Wang, 1993).

8. Section 108 of *The Gay Science* first published in 1882.

9. The First Vatican Council of 1870.

10. The relations between the sacred and the sublime may also be approached in terms of the religious and the secular, especially the aesthetic. These often ill-defined and labile relations

into prominence in the twentieth century, wherein critical distance drops to a minimum or disappears and violence is understood as definitive of antagonistic human relations (as in social Darwinism) and valorized, justified, or even glorified as a transformative, regenerative, or originary/foundational force. In this sense violence is not seen as significantly varied in its forms, as always problematic, and as at best only partially justifiable in terms of the context and the ends toward which it is directed (which is close to my own view, as well as, I think, to an important dimension of Marx's thought, despite the latter's own apocalyptic-messianic aspects). From the perspective I am analyzing critically, violence is postulated as legitimate in unqualified or even absolute terms, whether by an appeal to God, the sovereign state, natural law, the terroristic threat of an elusive enemy, the maintenance of an imperial order, or the good, even the transcendence, of the human with respect to the animal.[11] Violence is not explicitly seen as having only a contestable claim to legitimacy that is subject to argument in given circumstances. And an attempt is not made to disengage the sacred and the sublime (as well as the gift) from sacrificialism involving victimization and to subject the latter to sustained critique. Instead, the sacred or the sublime is indiscriminately or tendentiously validated (say, as foundational, radically transcendent, or beyond ethical judgment), and violence, including traumatization, is figured or experienced as something that runs counter to or even transcends instrumental reason, perhaps all reason, and constitutes an excessive, apocalyptic,

---

are not restricted to Romanticism. Still, see the analysis in M. H. Abrams, *Naturalism Supernaturalism: Tradition and Revolution in Romantic Literature* (New York: W. W. Norton, 1971). He quotes T. E. Hulme's provocative comment: "Romanticism, then, and this is the best definition I can give of it, is spilt religion" (quoted, 68). For a more recent discussion of figures such as Walter Benjamin, Émile Durkheim, Matthew Arnold, and Virginia Woolf, see Vincent P. Pecora, *Secularization and Cultural Criticism: Religion, Nation, and Modernity* (Chicago: University of Chicago Press, 2006).

11. An opposed view, amounting to a strategy of reversal, would postulate nonviolence as an absolute value related to the sanctity of life, and it would defend violence only as a "fall" or diversion from this value made necessary by contingencies. (I have heard Simon Critchley eloquently defend this opposed view in a lecture at Cornell on April 12, 2008, where he associated it with anarchism and even presented it, I think implausibly, as the nonviolent meaning of Benjamin's notion of "divine violence.") I do not agree with this view, which obviates the need for a critical assessment of types and conditions of violence and in effect leaves its application to "judgment calls" that may be arbitrary. The idea of the sanctity of life would have to be approached cautiously for many reasons, but its absolutization is questionable and would seem to rule out voluntary assisted suicide (or "death with dignity") as well as some or possibly all forms of abortion. One might speculate that the notion of the sanctity of life has been tenacious both because of the horrors related to the Nazi notion of "life unworthy of life" and because of the more general relativization of values in "modernity," which seems to leave life as the residual repository of absolute value and "sanctity."

redemptive power. It may even be seen as a decisive way to break through a compulsively repetitive, oppressive, monotonous life that grips a society or an individual. Hence violence, from the latter perspective, is indeed sacred or sacralizing or, in more secular terms, a glorious or sublime bearer and giver of an exhilarating, unrepresentable, ineffable, even "born again," experience presumably beyond experience and transcendently out of this world.[12]

This process of sacralization even occurs in unlikely places, for example, toward the end of Temple Grandin's interesting book, *Thinking in Pictures and Other Reports from My Life with Autism,* where the slaughterhouse and the killing of animals in it are sacralized. The danger in this gesture is that it may seem to sanctify or glorify violence and killing rather than to limit and counteract their uncontrolled, invidious effects, including effects of victimization (such as extreme disempowerment and disorientation).[13] Grandin states that one-third of the cattle and hogs in the United States are handled in equipment she has designed, which she has tried to build on humane principles (20). Her technique is to empathize or even identify with the animal on the apparatus that takes it to slaughter. She attempts to experience, from the perspective of the animal, the path, or rather the forced and often abusive preliminaries, to being slaughtered. Yet she also sacralizes the slaughterhouse, which I doubt is the animal's perspective. But she does so in a very subdued manner, apparently because she believes, in however untimely a fashion, that

12. While recognizing the importance of René Girard's work, I find questionable the categorical ideas that the sacred may be reduced to the sacralization of violence or that mimetic rivalry, the scapegoat mechanism, and violent sacrificial ritual (however great their importance may indeed be) are at the root of all culture, at least until the coming of Christ that creates a putative Christian exceptionalism. The figures and phenomena I discuss nonetheless raise the problem of specific articulations of violence and the sacred and render more credible Girard's view that, in the absence of formal rituals that, however problematically, establish institutional limits (an absence or deficit common in "modernity"), sacrificial (or quasi-sacrificial) violence tends to become excessive and goes to the extreme of generalized crisis, cycles of destruction, and, at times, "states of exception." I return to Girard in a note in chapter 6. Here I would observe that, in the gospel from which Girard takes the title of what is arguably his summa, *Things Hidden since the Foundation of the World,* trans. Stephen Bann and Michael Metteer, research undertaken in collaboration with Jean-Michel Oughourlian and Guy Lefort (1978; Stanford: Stanford University Press, 1987), the haunting phrase concerning immemorial hidden things appears (Matthew 13:35) in a series of statements about the parable, which is specified (in terms so important for Kierkegaard) as Christ's sole mode of (indirect) communication with the multitude. Girard does not comment on the textual setting of his title in Matthew or engage the problem of the parable, which is always subject to multiple readings. Instead he puts forth a lapidary reductive explanatory "hypothesis" on mimeticism and its putative derivatives (including sacrifice and scapegoating).

13. Grandin, *Thinking in Pictures and Other Reports from My Life with Autism,* foreword Oliver Sacks (New York: Random House, 1995).

it is only through the sacralizing role of ritual that some limits can be placed on the often objectionable way animals are handled or mishandled on their way to death.[14]

It would be worth exploring the extent to which there are links between violence and the sublime, or even the sacred, in Burke, Kant, and the aesthetic of the sublime in general, including a dubious tendency for the sublime to function as a criterion of the transcendence, superiority, and sovereignty of humans over other animals and the rest of nature—at times over groups of abjected humans as well. In other words, there is a need to rethink the aesthetic of the sublime in a differential and neither dismissive nor indiscriminately participatory way—to rethink it carefully neither as a categorical debunker nor as an unqualified enthusiast, especially when the sublime is linked not only to excess but also to trauma and violence and becomes a force for foundation, transfiguration, or putative redemption.

To specify further the concerns I am evoking, I shall mention some significant texts that warrant further analysis.[15] I discuss them in a selective fashion that brings out aspects that are problematic and warrant critical reflection, even if these problematic aspects may not typify the entire thought or even a specific text of a given figure, for the latter issues could be addressed only in a much more extended treatment.

One finds an insufficiently guarded apology for violence in Georges Sorel's *Reflections on Violence* (first published in book form in 1915 but in periodicals as early as 1906 and 1908), a work that Zeev Sternhell has seen as significant for fascists despite its affirmed "leftist" anarcho-syndicalism and proletarian leanings.[16] Even if one disagrees with Sternhell in important ways, one may at the very least see Sorel's perspective as symptomatic of broader currents in the early twentieth century and modernity more generally, currents exacerbated but not caused by World War I and the Great Depression as well as

14. Her concluding words are: "I believe that the place where an animal dies is a sacred one. There is a need to bring ritual into the conventional slaughter plants and use it as a means to shape people's behavior. It would help prevent people from becoming numbed, callous, or cruel. The ritual could be something very simple, such as a moment of silence. In addition to developing better designs and making equipment to insure the humane treatment of all animals, that would be my contribution. No words. Just one pure moment of silence. I can picture it perfectly" (206). It may be more difficult to picture that a "pure" moment of silence is sufficient to have the desired effect.

15. See also the discussion in *History in Transit,* 263–70.

16. Sorel, *Reflections on Violence,* trans. T. E. Hulme (1915; New York: Peter Smith, 1941); Sternhell, *Neither Right nor Left: Fascist Ideology in France,* trans. David Meisel (1983; Berkeley: University of California Press, 1986). It is noteworthy that Hulme was motivated to translate Sorel's book.

linked to forms of colonial and imperial violence. One should take seriously Sorel's engagement with marxism and his elaboration of a revisionist version of it that stressed its bearing on anarcho-syndicalism. But the crucial point for my account is that Sorel's apology focuses on violence as a regenerative or redemptive force that will transfigure civilization, mark the return of heroic values, and end the reign of despised bourgeois complacency and instrumental or calculative rationality. Its vehicle, the proletarian general strike, is termed a "complete catastrophe" (147) and is left utterly void of content. The general strike signals the possible coming of what might be termed a blank utopia—a utopia about which one can say nothing and which marks a radical break or disjunction with the past, an end to the "burden" of history and the inauguration of a brave new era. Proletarian violence is the good object in contrast to bourgeois violence, typified in the Terror during the French Revolution, which represents the bad object. In the modern world, however, the opposition between good and bad violence may tend to collapse, since Sorel sees violence as a regenerative force for both the bourgeoisie and the proletariat in a presumably reinvigorated class struggle. It is unclear how such renewed struggle relates to cycles of violence and endlessly repeated traumatizing scenes. With special reference to proletarian violence, the book's final words are: "It is to violence that Socialism owes those high ethical values by means of which it brings *salvation* to the modern world" (295). Here one has the link between violence, seemingly sublime ethical values, and salvation—with violence itself invoked as a largely abstract concept that brings in its train a host of uncontrolled and unqualified connotations.

Sorel was quite important for the early Walter Benjamin of the "Critique of Violence" (1920–21), which is a critique only in the most problematic of senses and conveys a rather uncritical, quasi-religious apology for a certain sort of violence or force.[17] (*Gewalt* in German, meaning both violence and force, remains equivocal in Benjamin's text, yet often seems to mean violence.)

Active in Benjamin's essay is the binary opposition between mythical state representational violence, which is bad, and divine, absolute, pure redemptive violence (arguably linked at least implicitly to the revolutionary

17. "Critique of Violence," in Walter Benjamin, *Reflections: Essays, Aphorisms, Autobiographical Writings,* ed. and intro. Peter Demetz, trans. Edmund Jephcott (New York: Harcourt Brace Jovanovich, 1978), 277–300. Despite—or perhaps because of—its complex, allusive, and at times bewildering nature, this essay has become a touchstone of much recent commentary, in part because of Derrida's discussion of it.

proletarian general strike), which is good. Good, or more precisely, pure, immediate, sovereign, divine violence (in a sense, inaugural, originary, or foundational violence situated beyond good and evil—analogous, I think, to the intended divinely commanded violence of Abraham's sacrifice) is, for Benjamin, unrepresentable and performatively undermines the entire system of representation. Divine violence, with its invisible expiatory power, is even equated with what Benjamin terms bloodless but lethal annihilation (297). Although Benjamin does not explicitly say as much in his extremely allusive essay, it is conceivable that for him divine violence will be the ultimate anarchic, somehow expiatory and educative, force that decisively breaks the "mythical" cycle of endless violence and inaugurates an unimaginable new age. In his final paragraph, he affirms that "on the breaking of this cycle [of law-creating and law-preserving violence], maintained by mythical forms of law; on the suspension of law with all the forces on which it depends as they depend on it, finally therefore on the abolition of state power, a new historical epoch is founded." In his concluding, cryptic words, he invokes divine violence as sovereign: "Divine violence, which is the sign and seal but never the means of sacred execution, may be called sovereign violence" (300).

This is not the place for a more extended analysis of Benjamin's tangled discussion, but it may be noted that Derrida in "The Force of Law" provides a treatment of it that manifests a kind of Freudian *fort-da* attraction and repulsion with respect to Benjamin's line of thought, sympathetic if not emulative at points (notably with respect to an originary, revolutionary *coup de force,* a concept that Derrida seems to accept), and then drawing back, especially when extrapolations are made (at least in addenda) to Nazism and the "final solution."[18] Derrida's own text provides a complex, partially participatory reading of Benjamin's essay that is as intricate and open to diverse readings as the "Critique of Violence" itself, both prompting the mention of these texts in the series of discourses on violence I am exploring and making any clear-cut determinations of their status or import contestable.

18. Derrida, "The Force of Law: The 'Mystical' Foundation of Authority," *Cardozo Law Review* 11 (1990): 920–1045. It is also included in Drucilla Cornell et al., eds., *Deconstruction and the Possibility of Justice* (New York: Routledge, 1992). See also my commentary on Derrida's essay as it was presented at a conference at Cardozo Law School, "Violence, Justice, and the Force of Law," *Cardozo Law Review* 11 (1990): 1065–78. The translation that served as the basis of my commentary was somewhat faulty (the original French version was not made available to me), and Derrida's essay did not as yet include the footnotes and "Post-scriptum" on Nazism and the "final solution" (973–74 and 1040–45). (I saw these addenda for the first time only in the published and corrected version of Derrida's essay in the *Cardozo Law Review.*)

Without claiming that it dominates the entire argument, I would single out as especially problematic a passage in the principal text of Derrida's "Force of Law" in which violence and force seem to assume an originary, performative role, with interpretation and, presumably, discourse (including normative discourse) having a derivative or at least secondary status.

> [Justice's] very moment of foundation or institution (which in any case is never a moment inscribed in the homogeneous tissue of a history, since it is ripped apart with one decision [*il le déchire d'une décision*]), the operation that consists of founding, inaugurating, justifying law [*droit*], making law, would consist of a *coup de force*, of a performative and therefore interpretive violence that in itself is neither just nor unjust and that no justice and no previous law with its founding anterior moment could guarantee or contradict or invalidate. No justificatory discourse could or should insure the role of metalanguage in relation to the performativity of institutive language or to its dominant interpretation. (941–43)

Continuing to write in a kind of discursive middle voice or participatory, free indirect style, Derrida goes on to call this foundational, performative violent power "the mystical." He asserts that "silence is walled up in the violent structure of the founding act" (943), and his stress moves to the *coup de force* and the performative, at least creating the impression that they transcend any "always already" situatedness or supplementarity and alone institute or found justice and law. Revolution as *coup de force* would seem to be cut off from its construction, in terms of a rethinking of historical temporality, as a radical modality of *différance* on the model of trauma, which would combine repetition with a decisive break or disjunction. Indeed, "performative and therefore interpretive violence" is dissociated from history (itself construed in reductively homogeneous, seemingly non-Derridean terms) and given a transcendental status as an *actus purus* creation ex nihilo, perhaps an opening to the *tout autre* (totally other), or, at the very least, a foundational trauma.[19] (As in many other contestable contemporary discourses, the radically constructivist formula seems to be: All power to the performative!)

Here one might object that in any historical situation, for example, the French Revolution, the *coup de force* is intimately bound up with legitimating

19. Derrida's analysis may be compared with Alain Badiou's in *Saint Paul: The Foundation of Universalism*, trans. Ray Brassier (1997; Stanford: Stanford University Press, 2003) and with comparable gestures in the work of Slavoj Žižek.

or justificatory discourse that should not be understood as a metalanguage but that is not simply derivative either—discourse that appeals to past discourses (Rousseau's, for example, or, on another level, both classical texts and Christian sacrificial and redemptive discourse) and informs the violent or forceful act or imbricates it with "immanent" sociopolitical and ethical considerations, however misguided.[20] Yet one might counter this objection with an exegesis of Derrida's own discourse whereby it is interpreted not as isolating the *coup de force* but as analytically distinguishing it (however abstractly) and postulating at best a quasi-transcendental status for it that, in its performativity, situates it not as totally other than, but as irreducible to, prior situations or contexts. Such an exegesis would accord with Derrida's thought in other texts concerning *différance,* supplementarity, and a rethought historicity, but one might nonetheless be left with the impression that, in this text, Derrida's discourse is not as clear as it might be on the status of the *coup de force* and, notably in its occasional appeal to violence (whereby history is "ripped apart by one decision"), might seem to be lending greater force to the performative *coup de force* than would be desirable (or than my suggested exegesis would allow). And the notion of violence is used in different registers, from interpretation to revolution, in a possibly bewildering and insufficiently regulated way (something that may be a constitutive problem in a discursive middle voice or participatory style that may perhaps be seen as enacting a transferential relation to the other—in this case, Benjamin's text and elsewhere, about the same time, Paul de Man and his World War II journalism).[21]

It is nonetheless significant that Derrida's treatment of divine violence, while it may be open to question as an exegesis of Benjamin, tries insistently to resist taking that violence as authorizing what is permissible in human action,

20. For a study of sacrificialism with respect to the French Revolution and such figures as Joseph de Maistre, Georges Sorel, and Georges Bataille, see Jesse Goldhammer, *The Headless Republic: Sacrificial Violence in Modern French Thought* (Ithaca: Cornell University Press, 2005). Despite differences in emphasis and interpretation, Goldhammer's analysis partially converges with my own. (I think he downplays the role of excess or, at times, indifference in apologies for violence, however abstractly conceived or formulated, notably in the mythologizing Sorel, for whom the actual number of victims of violence in the proletarian general strike might—or possibly might not—be small.) Problems concerning sacrificial and sacralized violence extend well beyond the figures and the French contexts he treats. But Goldhammer tellingly highlights the often tangled and complex interactions of valorizations of sacrificial violence across the political spectrum.

21. On Derrida's treatment of de Man's World War II journalism, see my *Representing the Holocaust,* chap. 4.

thus countering the sacralization of human violence.[22] I would also recall that in the "Post-scriptum," added (to the best of my knowledge) after the initial presentation of his text at a conference at the Cardozo Law School (and in what I am tempted to see as a belated recognition that resonates with the concerns I am putting forward), Derrida saw, as dubiously symptomatic, crucial aspects of Benjamin's "Critique of Violence" and took critical distance from it in a manner that, despite certain hesitations (*vide* the enigmatic parenthetical insertions of "perhaps, almost" and "perhaps, perhaps"), is more pronounced than anything to be found in the principal text of "The Force of Law":

> What I find, in conclusion, the most redoubtable, indeed (perhaps, almost) intolerable in this text, even beyond the affinities it maintains with the worst (the critique of *Aufklärung,* the theory of the fall and of originary authenticity, the polarity between originary language and fallen language, the critique of representation and of parliamentary democracy, etc.), is a temptation that it would leave open, and leave open notably to the survivors or the victims of the final solution, to its past, present or potential victims. Which temptation? The temptation to think the holocaust as an uninterpretable manifestation of divine violence insofar as this divine violence would be at the same time nihilating, expiatory and bloodless, says Benjamin, a divine violence that would destroy current law through a bloodless process that strikes and causes to expiate.... When one thinks of the gas chambers and the cremation ovens, this allusion to an extermination that would be expiatory because bloodless must cause one to shudder. One is terrified at the idea of an interpretation that would make of the holocaust an expiation and an indecipherable signature of the just and violent anger of God.
>
> It is at that point that this text, despite all its polysemic mobility and all its resources for reversal, seems to me finally to resemble too closely, to the point of specular fascination and vertigo, the very thing against which one must act and think, do and speak, that with which one must break (perhaps, perhaps). This text, like many others by Benjamin, is still too Heideggerian, too messianico-marxist or archeo-eschatological for me. (1044–45)

22. "The Force of Law," 1033–35. In contrast to Derrida's reading, which develops an aporia with respect to Benjamin's concluding passage on divine violence, I would argue that the passage more plausibly is read as advocating violent, putatively revolutionary, action in uncertainty about whether or not it is divinely sanctioned. See my "Violence, Justice, and the Force of Law," 1074–76.

In these passages Derrida seems to oscillate between extremely decisive judgment and the kind of undecidability that is difficult to distinguish from more ordinary indecision and equivocation, perhaps attesting to his intense, not quite worked-through relation to Benjamin and his text. In any event, Derrida's treatment of both Benjamin and violence in "The Force of Law" is fraught and invites at best problematic analysis.

Less self-questioning and hesitant are the sacralization and rendering sublime of violence that are at times quite forceful in the work of Georges Bataille. Still, Bataille explicitly yet tortuously engaged the problem of the relation between fascism and his own apology for violence in the traumatic context of sacrifice, unproductive or useless expenditure (*dépense*), and the uncompromising critique of instrumental rationality (including for a time a seeming defense of what was seen as *surfascisme* or the escalating appeal to fascist procedures, including violence, in presumably opposing fascism—an instance of the presumed antidote becoming excessive and possibly as bad as the disease, or an autoimmune system creating a surfeit of antibodies that may turn on and destroy itself).[23] He hoped for a union of workers and the lumpen proletariat—the "dregs" or most abject groups in society who, unlike Marx, he did not see as most prone to mobilization by the far right. Instead, in the late 1930s, he drew an opposition between this desired (fantasized?) united front and fascism. He even seemed to construe class conflict or war as a modern

23. As Allan Stoekl (ed. and intro.) notes, in his appropriately entitled collection of Bataille's writings, *Visions of Excess: Selected Writings, 1927–1939,* trans. Allan Stoekl with Carl R. Lovitt and Donald M. Leslie Jr. (Minneapolis: University of Minnesota Press, 1985): "The reader will note in the speech ("Popular Front in the Street"), given by Bataille at a Contre-Attaque meeting in November 1935, the emphasis placed on force, agitation, and violence, to the exclusion of boring political and doctrinal debates. By the time this speech was published in May 1936, Breton's surrealist contingent was already disclaiming any association with Contre-Attaque, labeling it "sur-fasciste." Bataille himself in later years did not deny that in this group, among Bataille's friends and even in himself, there was a certain "paradoxical fascist tendency." (xviii)

One may add that, in "Popular Front in the Street," Bataille looks to direct action in the streets as the redemptive site of confrontation between "the fascists and the people" (168) and affirms "that strength [that] results less from strategy than from collective exaltation, and exaltation can come only from words that touch not the reason but the passions of the masses" (167). Indeed, he concludes his essay by declaring that "only this ocean of men in revolt can save the world from the nightmare of impotence and carnage in which it sinks!" (168). At this point the two primary "sacred" spaces for Bataille appear to be the street and the locked bedroom, the latter at times pictured as a kind of Sadean torture chamber. In what seemed like a war between enemy brothers, Bataille earlier wrote of the quote from Breton that serves as my epigraph: "M. Breton did not hesitate to make himself ridiculous.... That such an image should present itself so insistently to his view proves decisively the importance in his pathology of castration reflexes: such an extreme provocation seeks to draw immediate and brutal punishment." "The 'Old Mole' and the Prefix *Sur*" (first published in 1968 but probably dating from 1929–30), in *Visions of Excess,* 39.

analog of destructive, possibly apocalyptic, potlatch, misleadingly construing potlatch as the very prototype of gift exchange in traditional (or what he termed "archaic") societies.[24] Within the larger notion of the heterogeneous, Bataille associated *dépense* not only with ambivalent affect involving attraction and repulsion but also with "violence, excess, delirium, madness" and "extreme emotions" more generally.[25] Indeed, class conflict would enable the workers to destroy the bourgeois order in "the grandest form of social expenditure" that "threatens the very existence of the masters."[26]

Bataille's thought, both in its own workings and in its insights into modern social experience, points to "postsecular," often covert or unconscious, permutations (or even *disjecta membra*) of the sacred and the sacrificial after the "death of God." In this context, he put forward the notions of sacrificial communities of loss and of unity or communion "through rents or wounds."[27] For a linkage of trauma, the sublime, and *jouissance,* one might also refer to Bataille's ecstatic essay on the aftermath of the atomic bombing of Hiroshima discussed with reference to "a core of darkness [that] remains untouchable" (221), "a boundless suffering that is joy, or a joy that is infinite suffering" (232), and sovereign *dépense* beyond agency and politics (here there is no difference between natural disasters and bombings for Bataille—between the dropping of an atomic bomb and, say, a tsunami).[28] In effect, Hiroshima and its victims are seen in terms of a masochistic sublime that might be related to the transhistorical traumatic "real" (somewhat like Agamben's dubious figuration of the *Muselmann,* the most abject—starved, exhausted, resigned, and apathetic—victim in the camps, in *Remnants of Auschwitz*).[29] This correlation between the most abject or low, including the victim, even the victim of torture, and the ecstatic, sublime, or sacred is both commonplace in certain forms

24. See "The Notion of Expenditure" (first published in January 1933 and included in *Visions of Excess*) in which he asserts that "the archaic form of exchange has been identified by Mauss under the name of *potlatch* borrowed from the Northwestern American Indians who provided such a remarkable example of it. Institutions analogous to the Indian *potlatch,* or their traces, have been very widely found" (121). Potlatch becomes in Bataille not an extreme, even relatively exceptional, form but the very model or prototype of exchange as excessive, wasteful expenditure, tantamount to sovereignty in his particular sense of the term (related, I think, to his understanding of the Nietzschean *Übermensch*).

25. "The Psychological Structure of Fascism" (1933–34), in *Visions of Excess,* 142.

26. "The Notion of Expenditure," in *Visions of Excess,* 126.

27. "The College of Sociology" [presented on July 4, 1939], in *Visions of Excess,* 251.

28. "Concerning the Accounts Given by the Residents of Hiroshima," in *Trauma: Explorations in Memory,* ed. and intro. Cathy Caruth (Baltimore: Johns Hopkins University Press, 1995), 221–35. Bataille's essay, first published in 1947, takes the form of an extremely participatory reading of John Hersey's *Hiroshima* (1946; New York; Bantam, 1985).

29. I discuss this aspect of Agamben's thought in *History in Transit,* chap. 4.

of thought and extremely dubious. (It is, for example, taken to an extreme in Mel Gibson's film *The Passion of the Christ.*) Bataille himself was fascinated, even obsessed, by 1905 photographs of a Chinese torture victim.[30] He described his response in terms that suggest mystical, if not pure and idealized, masochistic identification:

> The young and seductive Chinese man of whom I have spoken, left to the work of the executioner—I loved him with a love in which the sadistic instinct played no part: he communicated his pain to me or perhaps the excessive nature of his pain, and it was precisely that which I was seeking, not so as to take pleasure in it, but in order to ruin in me that which is opposed to ruin.[31]

Whatever one makes of the exoticized and eroticized aestheticization of the torture victim as *beau désastre,* or of the extreme gesture of ruining what is opposed to ruin, as well as of the figurations of sublimity or ecstasy such reversed ruination may induce (I fear they may contribute to a prevalent sense of abject but more or less enlightened or theorized disempowerment), one may acknowledge the importance of Bataille in bringing out both the limitations of instrumental rationality or economism and the persistent role of sacralizing and sacrificial forces, including their often encrypted appeal in modernity. He was especially probing in detecting the covert, perhaps

30. Bataille, *The Tears of Eros,* trans. Peter Connor (San Francisco: City Lights Books, 1989), 206. Certain of Bataille's early writings, notably "[Dream]" and "The Solar Anus" of 1927 (*Visions of Excess,* 3–9), suggest posttraumatic response to child abuse at the hands of his blind, paralytic, syphilitic father—a response rendered in haunting, transfigured, and at times ecstatically glorified imagery. Or was it Oedipal and related obsessions that brought about a fantasy of child abuse? In his monumental *Georges Bataille: An Intellectual Biography,* trans. Krzysztof Fijalkowski and Michael Richardson (1992; London: Verso, 2002), Michel Surya treats these (as well as many other) questions with studied indirection and participatory allusiveness. Existing evidence may not allow for a clear answer concerning the nature of the "horror" in his early childhood that preoccupied Bataille for his entire life.

31. Bataille, *Inner Experience,* trans. Leslie Anne Boldt (Albany: SUNY Press, 1988), 120. One may find the incredible photographs of the so-called torture of a Hundred Pieces in Michel Surya's *Georges Bataille.* Surya notes: "The torture victim was Fu Chou Li, guilty of murdering Prince Ao Han Ouan. The emperor's leniency (!) granted that he should not be burned as decreed, but cut to pieces, into a hundred pieces: cut up alive" (93). Surya further notes: "These photographs obsessed [Bataille]. He often spoke of them, and always kept them" (94). Bataille's response, in emphasizing what he termed "a fundamental connection between religious ecstasy and eroticism," actually oscillated between an emphasis on masochism and on sadism (94). The torture of a Hundred Pieces revealed to Bataille that the "crucifixion was little more than a 'happy' torture" and that "only horror when it is laid bare" is truly sacred as a measure of "divine ecstasy" (94–95). In Bataille's words, "What I suddenly saw . . . was the identity of these perfect contraries, divine ecstasy and its opposite, extreme horror" (quoted, 95).

unconscious, role of sacrificial forces in seemingly secular experience, for example, in mutilation and self-mutilation.[32] He also emphatically insisted on the value of spending the self without expecting a return on one's "investment." And his approach to the sacred and sacrifice stressed the role of voluntary victims not scapegoated outsiders (except perhaps in the case of the bourgeoisie—not a subordinate or oppressed group but one bearing the brunt of Bataille's polemical animus as boring, unheroic, and productive).[33] Moreover, Bataille's elated or effervescent rereading of Durkheim and Marcel Mauss, influenced in part by both surrealism and his reading of Nietzsche, tended to reverse the emphasis of Durkheim and Mauss on the role of legitimate limits as resistances to transgression and excess in order to formulate an influential view of social existence that stressed the value of excess, including violent and sacrificial excess, in which limits threatened to become little more than pretexts or inducements to transgression. I have intimated that a primary bearer of this excess and the vehicle of base materialism, stressing the dirty, ugly, repressed sides of being, was an anarchistic proletariat, prominently including the lumpen proletariat, that would not create a new order, as desired by Sorel, but would rather be an acephalic, self-dispossessing, disempowered, but nonetheless virile and ecstatic, force for heterogeneity in which the role of recurrent violent sacrifice either seemed to be a necessary revitalizing force or at best remained equivocal. Except for destructive, useless expenditure, the goal of action remained vague and was addressed by Bataille only in resoundingly rhetorical, often violent, phrases such as the idea of life as a "virile unity" that has "the simplicity of an ax blow."[34] A significant absence in Bataille's extensive reflection on sacrifice was the perspective of the victimized themselves. One might argue that a difficulty in Bataille is that he so internalized both conceptions of social constraint and modern

32. See especially the powerful analysis in "Sacrificial Mutilation and the Severed Ear of Vincent Van Gogh" [1930], in *Visions of Excess,* 61–72.

33. Of course the animal could not cogently be seen as a voluntary victim. It was evident that a principal object of Bataille's animus was safe, restrained (or restricted) bourgeois economic activity, typified by the family firm prominent at his time in France. Even in this context, Bataille pays scant attention to the excesses of colonialism. One may ask whether there could be a Bataillian account or even defense of the inversion of potlatch in excessive, unregulated, destructive, at times evanagelical, capitalism that does not play it safe but is coordinated with a war economy and involves assertions of power, takeovers, extreme risk, and the possibility of loss, while promoting unlimited wasteful expenditure, including "sacrificed" lives (both "at home" and abroad, in business enterprises, slaughterhouses, and the battlefield) and environmental devastation (nuclear waste, oil spills, depredation of the rain forest, elimination of species, and so forth).

34. "The Sorcerer's Apprentice" [1938], in *Visions of Excess,* 227.

atomistic individualism that he was unable to see any way around them other than through violent, sacrificial self-shattering, involving projective identification with the victim.[35]

Bataille had a pronounced performative, participatory sense of the often encrypted role of the sacred and the sacrificial in modernity and was important in bringing a set of considerations into postwar French thought and modern thought more generally, not only for René Girard but for many others (including Michel Foucault, particularly in the abstract paean to both Bataille and transgression offered in his "Preface to Transgression").[36] How

35. I think the inability to distinguish the question of victimization was a consequence of Bataille's anthropocentric, projectively identificatory approach in which there was not sufficient critical distance to allow for raising the problem of the victim and its relation to the gift and useless expenditure. Bataille often treats sacrifice as if the sacrificer is always somehow at one with the victim. One may further note that Bataille underscored the significance of laughter as a disorienting response to the Hegelian dialectic—one of Derrida's focal points in his early essay on Bataille. Indeed laughter and sacrifice, which may of course be combined (for example, in certain variants of carnival and the carnivalesque), seemed to be two key ways in which Bataille envisioned a response to the heterogeneous—what did not fit in or could not be integrated into an existing (perhaps any) order. (One may nonetheless ask whether in Bataille, in contrast with Derrida, laughter remains humorless if not hysterical, and whether Bataille, even at his most disconcertingly ludicrous, has any sense of self-directed irony or parody.)

36. Michèle Richman simply reads Durkheim through Bataille's pineal eye and makes Durkheim a one-sided theorist of the excess of "collective effervescence." See Michèle Richman, *Sacred Revolutions: Durkheim and the Collège de Sociologie* (Minneapolis: University of Minnesota Press, 2002). A more critical procedure would bring out the significant tensions between Durkheim as well as Mauss, on the one hand, and Bataille, on the other, notably with respect to the issues of violence, sacrifice, potlatch, excess, limits, and desirable social change. Durkheim and Mauss explored the interaction of limits and excess, with a stress on the role of legitimate limits requiring socioeconomic restructuring, while Bataille tended to polarize the two, notably in his conception of a generalized as opposed to a restricted economy, with a pronounced emphasis on excess, destruction, useless expenditure, loss, the excremental, and the heterogeneous. Mauss valorized the role of "amiable rivalry," which did not overwhelm the other and was compatible with mutual respect. He saw the potlatch not as the prototype but as the "monster child" of the gift system. See Mauss, *The Gift: Form and Functions of Exchange in Archaic Societies,* trans. Ian Cunnison, intro. E. E. Evans-Pritchard (1925; New York: Norton, 1967), as well as my discussion in *Emile Durkheim: Sociologist and Philosopher* (1972; Aurora, Colo.: Davies Group, 2001, 98–102). Mauss, like Durkheim, wanted to combine social science and ethicopolitical critique. He sought to "discover those motives of action still remembered by many societies and classes: the joy of giving in public, the delight in generous artistic expenditure, the pleasure of hospitality in the public or private feast. Social insurance, solicitude in mutuality or co-operation, in the professional group and all those moral persons called Friendly Societies, are better than the mere personal security guaranteed by the nobleman to his tenant, better than the mean life afforded by the daily wage handed out by managements, and better even than the uncertainty of capitalist savings" (67). The overall goal was to arrive at "the supreme art" of "conscious direction" of "the common life"—"politics in the Socratic sense of the word" (81). See also Ivan Strenski, *Contesting Sacrifice: Religion, Nationalism, and Social Thought in France* (Chicago: University of Chicago Press, 2002). Strenski stresses the extreme, "darker" side of sacrifice and focuses on the willing victim of self-sacrifice, having little

to arrive at an overall appreciation of Bataille, including the role of violence in his thought, is a complex task that has too often been met with rather uncritical celebration (as in the studies of Michèle Richman or Michel Surya), an occlusion of political questions (as in the early essays of Foucault and Derrida), or an overly summary, even dismissive, conception of Bataille's "left fascism."[37]

---

to say about unwilling victims or those who sacrifice others and seek regeneration through sacrificial violence. He traces what he sees as "the classic definition of sacrifice as a cosmic drama involving self-annihilation and expiation" (4) to seventeenth-century French Catholic thought and emphasizes the role of the sacrificial in both religious and secular thought and practice in France, including the French Revolution, the Dreyfus affair, and the writing of such figures as Maistre, Durkheim, Hubert, Mauss, Girard, and Bataille. Although he ends his book by praising the valiant if inadequate effort of Durkheimians to validate social life and self-sacrifice while contesting more extreme versions of sacrifice, he nonetheless terms their approach "moderate," "prudent," or even "bourgeois." At points he seems to favor "extreme thinkers like Georges Bataille." In rather unqualified terms, he asserts of Bataille: "Far from shunning the perversity of sacrifice as unbridled self-destruction and violence, Bataille revels in it. Taking cues from Sade, 'cruelty,' essential at least to the ritual act of animal sacrifice, is for Bataille a virtue. All this trafficking in the extremism of total giving serves the goal of transcending our bourgeois humanist natures and ascending to the sacred" (176). Unable to develop certain lines of thought evident in Durkheim and Mauss themselves, Strenski apparently cannot envision a nonsacrificial critique of "bourgeois" humanism in which a sense of legitimate limits is both validated and related to desirable institutions and institutional transformation, while justice is supplemented by gift giving but not indentured to the excesses of violence, victimization, and self-immolation.

37. Michel Foucault, "A Preface to Transgression," in *Language, Counter-Memory, Practice,* trans. Donald F. Bouchard and Sherry Simon (1963; Ithaca: Cornell University Press, 1977), 29–52; Jacques Derrida, "From a Restricted to a General Economy: A Hegelianism without Reserve," in *Writing and Difference,* trans. Alan Bass (1967; Chicago: University of Chicago Press, 1978), 251–77. It is perhaps the height of mimetic rivalry that René Girard does not even mention Bataille in *Things Hidden since the Foundation of the World* and refers to him only rarely in other works. On an analytic level, Michel Surya's *Georges Bataille* (like much of Bataille's own writing) valorizes incompletion and is perhaps intentionally frustrating. Surya's style courts identification with the *monstre sacré* that is its glorified object of study but, understandably, rarely attains the evocative imagery and surrealistic power of suggestion of Bataille at his most disturbingly provocative. For a markedly unsympathetic analysis in terms of "left fascism," see Richard Wolin, *The Seduction of Unreason: The Intellectual Romance with Fascism from Nietzsche to Postmodernism* (Princeton: Princeton University Press, 2004), 153–86. For a comparison of Bataille and Carl Schmitt, see Martin Jay, *Force Fields: Between Intellectual History and Cultural Critique* (New York: Routledge, 1993), 49–60. While one may debate its weight in the context of his thought, including postwar essays such as that on John Hersey's *Hiroshima,* in which nuclear devastation seems to become a sublime form of *dépense,* one should nonetheless note Bataille's attempts at self-qualification once he saw the nature of fascism in power. The designation of "left fascist," which might apply to Pierre Drieu la Rochelle, does not seem suitable for Bataille, whose labile thought is not readily adapted to left/right political oppositions, even though he is often a believer in the "all or nothing" approach and could write in 1936 that "existence is not only an agitated void, it is a dance that forces one to dance with fanaticism" ("The Sacred Conspiracy," in *Visions of Excess,* 179). Still, in important ways, Sartre may not have been altogether wrong in his early appreciation of Bataille as a "new

The dubious sides of excess, transgression, and the apology for "sublime" violence were indeed manifest in their role in fascism and Nazism, which one should take seriously as dimensions of modern thought and practice. If one makes selective use of it, Klaus Theweleit's *Male Fantasies* provides valuable analyses of the cult of violence, including misogynistic and antisemitic fantasies, of the Freikorps, notably in the writings of such important figures as Ernst Jünger and Ernst von Salomon.[38] For Jünger and Salomon, the *Fronterlebnis* (or experience of fighting at the front in World War I) was itself an ecstatic existential peak that had sacrificial and regenerative force. It would be desirable to carry analyses such as Theweleit's forward into the discussion of fascists and Nazis, as well as to situate the latter with respect to earlier phenomena, including the cult of violence, World War I, colonialism, and imperialism. Such an approach is needed especially in light of the overly

---

mystic," however ironically this designation was intended. Jean-Paul Sartre, *Situations I* (1943; Paris: Gallimard, 1947), 133–74. One may also contrast Derrida's early treatment of Bataille on *dépense* and the excessive gift with his discussion of Mauss and the gift in *Given Time: 1. Counterfeit Money,* trans. Peggy Kamuf (Chicago: University of Chicago Press, 1992). In the latter work Derrida does not invoke a from/to format that privileges excess. Instead he sets up countervailing stresses on the excessive, asymmetrical generosity (and possibly overwhelming and destructive power) of the gift and the role of limits or moderation, even asserting: "What is recommended [by Mauss] is not just any compromise; it is the good one, the right one. Now, from his reflection and his inquiry into the gift, Mauss has learned that the *pure* gift or the gift that is *too good,* the excess of generosity of the gift—in which the pure and good gift would consist—turns into the bad; it is even the worst. The best become the worst. It is because he has understood this turnabout to be the law of the gift that the anthropologist tends toward this wisdom, this policy, this morality of the *mediocritas* and of the happy medium" (64–65). Rather than see the compromise formation that Mauss recommends as a plea for mediocrity and an Aristotelean happy medium or golden mean, I think it is better understood in terms of a tense, problematic, variable interaction between excess and legitimate limits or, in Derridean terms, as a supplementary relation that, as Derrida notes, cannot itself be perfectly realized but nonetheless functions as a kind of regulative ideal. More broadly, one might argue for the desirability of a mutual interaction between asymmetircial generosity (or the gift) and justice, requiring (in my judgment) normative limits and reciprocity (however imperfect) that should not be understood only in a purely prudential or instrumental manner. See also Derrida's related discussion in *Cosmopolitanism and Forgiveness,* trans. Mark Dooley and Michael Hughes, preface Simon Critchley and Richard Kearney (1997; London: Routledge, 2001). In this work, instead of seeing justice in terms of normative limits and a warranted demand for reciprocity (as I have understood it), Derrida presents it as a negotiation between unconditional, infinite, or asymmetrical forgiveness (an act of grace or pure gift or sorts) and a conditional, prudential, instrumental rationale for reciprocity and reconciliation. Derrida's absolutist orientation toward the pure gift and pure forgiveness (along with impossible mourning), which is frequent in his later work, may be contrasted with his own appreciation of Mauss's affirmation of the "good" gift and what might be seen as the desirable compromise formation.

38. Theweleit, *Male Fantasies,* 2 vols., trans. Erica Carter and Chris Turner with Stephen Conway, foreword Anson Rabinbach and Jessica Benjamin (1978; Minneapolis: University of Minnesota Press, 1987, 1989).

restricted, even tendentious, inclination to see the Holocaust predominantly if not exclusively in terms of instrumental (or means-ends) rationality, technology and modernization, the machinery of destruction, and industrialized mass murder or, more recently, biopolitics and mere naked life or *homo sacer* (in Giorgio Agamben—but the general tendency in which Agamben may be situated is found in very different figures, including Raul Hilberg, Omer Bartov, Zygmunt Bauman, and Philippe Lacoue-Labarthe as well as in a crucial dimension of Horkheimer and Adorno's *Dialectic of Enlightenment*). This entire perspective on the Holocaust, stressing its modernizing, bureaucratizing, industrial, technological, biopolitical, analytically reductive aspects is indeed important, but it is also one-sided and insufficient.[39] One effect of a focus on bureaucratic structures as well as the everyday life and "ordinary" motivations of Germans in the Third Reich (one sense of the "banality of evil," at least for historians) is that, despite its partial validity, it may turn attention too much away from the group of committed Nazi militants and their ideological, at times quasi-sacrificial and "sublime," incentive that was bound up with the "everyday" yet extreme violence inflicted on victims. This shift of focus is one problem in Claudia Koonz's otherwise excellent *Nazi Conscience* as well as in the important work of Christopher Browning.[40]

39. In comparison with Bataille's notion of the ambivalent attraction-repulsion of the sacred, which Agamben rejects, the latter's *homo sacer* would itself amount to an analytically reduced concept that would apply to the one-dimensional limit case of the accursed outlaw or outcast. Note, moreover, that the term "biopolitical" is subject to multiple, at times indeterminate, meanings. In Michael Hardt and Antonio Negri's *Multitude: War and Democracy in the Age of Empire* (New York: Penguin, 2004) it has a broadly encompassing meaning with respect to existential concerns and sociocultural forms of life. Roberto Esposito has attempted to disengage a "positive" notion of biopolitics from a "negative" biopower and elaborated the idea of an "autoimmune aporia" and crisis, whereby attempts to protect a community against threats (alien others, terror) become excessive and self-defeating. He applies these notions not only to contemporary phenomena, such as the "war on terror," but also to an analysis of the Holocaust and a critique of Agamben. While it is often thought-provoking, his level of discourse remains ultrathreoretical and does not engage historical problems and the historical literature on them in their specificity, at times making his critical dialogue with Agamben seem like an internal dialogue or an intramural debate. See the special issue of *Diacritics* 36 (2006), ed. Timothy Campbell, dedicated to Esposito's work. For example, in his own contribution to the *Diacritics* special issue, "The Immunization Paradigm" (23–48), there is a reference to Paul Friedländer's book on Plato but none to Saul Friedländer's work on the Holocaust. In addition to insufficient engagement with historical research, Esposito does not attempt to relate his provocative ideas about immunity to quasi-ritual and sacrificial processes, thereby threatening to replicate in his own discourse both the analytically reductive biologistic paradigms and the self-consuming autoimmune excesses that he criticizes.

40. Claudia Koonz, *The Nazi Conscience* (Cambridge: Harvard University Press, 2003); Christopher Browning, *Ordinary Men: Reserve Police Battalion 101 and the Final Solution in Poland* (New York: HarperCollins, 1992). I would note that Theodor Adorno and Max Horkheimer's

In a different and at times dubious register, the American-born Jonathan Littell's prize-winning, massive historical novel, *Les Bienveillantes,* is also worth mentioning.[41] Its often normalizing first-person, at times retrospective, narrative offers an "it could happen to anyone" rendition of an SS officer's experience during the Holocaust and the campaign on the eastern front, and familiar and copious, if at times disconcertingly gruesome, documentary material is downloaded and reprocessed with occasionally salacious twists (including the stereotyped figuration of the narrator-protagonist as having a phantasmatic and, in early life, actual incestuous relation to a sister with whom anal sex and identification induce in him a "passive" homosexual orientation). The title itself, which is gendered feminine, ostensibly refers to the (pacified) Furies and perhaps as well to the narrator-protagonist himself as well as his well-meaning homoerotic fellow SS officers who at one point are confusingly construed as being in basic human solidarity with the victims they torture and kill (142). The often leveling "machinery of destruction" seems to sweep up, mangle, and render choiceless even the lives of SS officers. Yet the narrator-protagonist, who starts his *Bildungsreise* with literary and philosophical ambitions and ends it escaping punishment through a ruse and then directing a lace-making factory, occasionally has reflections of an other-than-normalizing sort:

> Since childhood I was haunted by the passion of the absolute and the transcendence of limits; now this passion had led me to the edge of common graves in the Ukraine [where Jews were shot and dumped during "killing" actions]. I always wanted my thinking to be radical; well the State, the Nation also chose the radical and the absolute; how could I, at this very moment, turn my back and say no, ultimately preferring the comfort of bourgeois laws and the mediocre assurance of the social contract? That was obviously impossible. And if radicality was the radicality of the abyss, and if the absolute revealed itself as the bad absolute, it was nonetheless necessary—I was intimately persuaded—to follow them to the very end, with my eyes wide open.... (95)
>
> The killing of the Jews at bottom serves no purpose.... It has no economic or political utility, no practical goal. On the contrary it is a

influential *Dialectic of Enlightenment* (1947; New York: Seabury, 1972) is marked by a possibly fruitful but unthematized tension between seeing Western history, culminating in the Nazi regime, as marked both by instrumental rationality gone awry and by sacrificialism and scapegoating, whose violence is not reducible to an instrumental means-ends schema and whose role is especially emphasized by them in the chapter on "Elements of Anti-Semitism."

41. Paris: Gallimard, 2006.

rupture with the world of economics and politics. It is waste, pure loss. That's all. And thus what is happening can have only one meaning: that of a definitive sacrifice, which definitively binds us together and prevents us, once and for all, from turning back. (137; my translations)

The comments of Littell's narrator-protagonist suggest the ways even a Himmler was neither a monstrous anomaly nor a banal "everyman" but an extreme and singular instance of more prevalent tendencies. Himmler took these tendencies in directions that were both entirely unacceptable and nonetheless construed or even experienced in ways that had resonances elsewhere, notably with respect to a variant of the aesthetic of the sublime oriented to violence and lived in an extremely disconcerting kind of aporetic sensibility. The true Nazi, for Himmler, held together or was able to bear (*durchstehen*), in authentic hardness and self-possession, an aporia that joined the antinomies of existence: decency and the seemingly sublime ability to behold mass slaughter (with the occlusion of the fact that the aesthetic spectators or bystanders in this case were also among the perpetrators).

I am of course alluding to a section of Himmler's now famous or infamous Posen speech of October 1943.[42] It gives some sense of the meaning of genocidal violence (as well as its relation to achieving psychic hardness) for the Reichsführer and the Nazi upper-level SS officers to whom the speech was addressed—making the speech a kind of touchstone in this respect. Himmler's Posen speech was not propaganda for the public but a communication by an insider to insiders, which of course does not mean that everything in it was true or even believed to be true by Himmler or his audience, for example, confidence about winning the war, especially after Stalingrad and losses in North Africa. But one may suggest that in important respects what Himmler asserted in the speech was performatively to be held as true, if not self-evident, by the committed Nazi elite, and anxiety about a possible or even likely loss of the war against the Allies might heighten the significance, as well as the sacrificial and self-sacrificial quality, of a "victory" in the "war" against the Jews. In any case, evident in the speech is at least one way Nazi violence was not simply, and perhaps not primarily, a question of instrumental rationality, however self-defeating or unbalanced.[43]

42. In *A Holocaust Reader,* ed. and trans. Lucy Dawidowicz (West Orange, N.J.: Behrman House, 1976), 132–33.

43. For an empirically based archival study that provides evidence for the role of what he terms Nazi "redemptive anti-Semitism," see Saul Friedländer, *Nazi Germany and the Jews,* vol. 1, *The Years of Persecution 1933–1939* (New York: HarperCollins, 1997).

There are important lines of inquiry under way that examine the hypothesis that the Nazi genocide may have displaced or at least paralleled practices prevalent and, for many, acceptable in the colonies when applied to people of color.[44] There are indications of this view in the work of Frantz Fanon, although there is also the questionable tendency to dichotomize good and bad violence and to justify anticolonial violence undertaken by people of color not simply strategically but as therapeutic and transfigurative in terms at times uncomfortably close to the views of Sorel or the early Benjamin. To quote but three statements that follow closely on one another near the beginning of *The Wretched of the Earth:* "Decolonization is truly the creation of new men.... Its definition can, if we want to describe it accurately, be summed up in the well-known words: 'The last shall be first.'... The last can be first only after a murderous and decisive confrontation between the two protagonists."[45] In brief, at times for Fanon, the cathartic decolonization of the psyche, the overcoming of posttraumatic symptoms, and the achievement of virility and dignity required anticolonial violence on the part of the oppressed. But it is important both historically and critically to understand the way colonial violence of the sort Fanon counterattacked was sometimes of genocidal proportions and may well have been analogous to, or even one basis for, later initiatives that have been seen, in too unqualified a form and too much within an exclusively Eurocentric context, as unique, totally unexpected, and unprecedented. I would note as well that Hannah Arendt in *On Violence* argues that Sartre, notably in his preface to Fanon's *Wretched of the Earth,* is much less qualified than Fanon himself in his apology for, if not glorification and rendering sublime of, violence.[46] Indeed Sartre, in bringing

44. See Sven Lindqvist's suggestive *"Exterminate All the Brutes,"* trans. Joan Tate (1992; New York: New Press, 1996). In *Absolute Destruction: Military Culture and the Practices of War in Imperial Germany* (Ithaca: Cornell University Press, 2005) Isabel V. Hull states, at least with respect to German colonial violence, which attained extreme or even genocidal proportions: "The continuities between colonial and European warfare are not due, as I thought at the beginning of this project, to Europeans learning evil lessons in the colonies and then applying them at home (though many an evil lesson was doubtless learned). Rather, Germans approached colonial wars from inside frames of their military culture as it had developed in Europe. The colonial situation merely provided the opportunity to practice on Africans [the Herero in 1904–7 and the Maji-Maji in 1905–7] or Chinese [the German intervention in 1901] what the military experts took to be the immutable precepts of warfare" (3). These comments run counter to the view of Aimé Césaire and Frantz Fanon, as formulated by Robert Young, that "Fascism was simply colonialism brought home to Europe." *White Mythologies: Writing History and the West* (London: Routledge, 1990), 125. I shall return to more general features of Hull's analysis.

45. Fanon, *The Wretched of the Earth,* trans. Richard Philcox, foreword Homi Bhabha, preface Jean-Paul Sartre, (1961; New York: Grove Press, 2004), 2–3.

46. Arendt, *On Violence* (New York: Harcourt Brace and Company, 1969).

his flamboyant preface to a close, asserts that "violence, like Achilles' spear, can heal the wounds it has inflicted."[47] But the prevalence of such sentiments, especially on the far left and the far right, may be more significant than their appearance in this or that figure. Even Maurice Blanchot, in one of his less edifying, right-wing antisemitic and fire-breathing journalistic pieces of the 1930s (this one appeared in the July 7, 1936, issue of *Combat*), could write the following:

> It is necessary that there be a revolution because one does not modify a regime that controls everything, that has its roots everywhere. One removes it, one strikes it down. It is necessary that that revolution be violent because one does not tap a people as enervated as our own for the strength and passions appropriate to a regeneration of decency, but through a series of bloody shocks, a storm that will overwhelm—and thus awaken—it.... That is why terrorism at present appears to us as a method of public salvation.[48]

In this quotation the phantasm of the totally pervasive and omnipotent system appears in a stark form, and it functions as a force for degeneration or enervation. Violence and terrorism are advocated as a kind of traumatizing shock therapy to regenerate and redeem a decadent, enervated (for André Breton, debased and cretinized) people—a perspective that seems light years away from the postwar Blanchot.

It may be apt to discuss briefly the analysis of violence in its relation to ideology and practice in the work of two prominent historians, to whom I have already referred. Zeev Sternhell and Isabel V. Hull may be seen as both converging and radically diverging in their insistent and at times one-sided emphases.[49] Both dichotomize ideology and practice, with Sternhell emphasizing the former and Hull the latter. Hull's orientation may be more prevalent in the historical profession, and that orientation has received much less sustained critical scrutiny than Sternhell's.[50]

47. Preface to *The Wretched of the Earth*, lxii.

48. "Terrorisme comme méthode de salut publique," *Combat* 1 no. 7 (July 7, 1936). My translation.

49. I thank Samuel Moyn for bringing this point to my attention.

50. As I intimated in chapter 2, Gabrielle Spiegel, in her introduction to *Practicing History: New Directions in Historical Writing after the Linguistic Turn* (New York: Routledge, 2005), may be seen as trying to provide the loosely formulated theory related to Hull's practice—what Spiegel oxymoronically terms "Practice Theory." V. R. Berghahn commends Hull for "an introduction [to *Absolute Destruction*] that is striking for its concise statement of her purposes and unencumbered by lengthy methodological and historiographical discussions." *American Historical Review* 110 (2005): 1269.

Indeed Sternhell has been criticized on numerous grounds: his exaggeration not only of the role of ideology in general but of France in particular in the genesis and functioning of fascism; his idea that France had a special status with respect to the "essence" of fascism because it presumably existed in that country in its ideological purity and was not compromised in practice through embodiment in a regime; the insufficiently defined and qualified role he attributes to Sorel; his overemphasis on the slippage from the left to the right in the interwar period; his underemphasis of the phenomenon of rightists staying on the right, supporting or not resisting fascism, believing they could manipulate it, and at times becoming radicalized in a fascist or *fascisant* direction. Despite the validity of these criticisms, one may nonetheless argue that Sternhell (like his teacher George Mosse, who also was a reference point for Hull) recognized and extensively analyzed the role of ideology even though he tended to see it in decontextualized if not Platonic terms and attributed to it an excessively causal role. Here the point would be that one should supplement and contest his account with an analysis of the complex relations of ideology to practice (movement, regime, and so forth)—ideology not simply as systematic philosophy but as often vaguely articulated assumption or even prejudice that may be especially forceful in the formation of subjects, including fascist or *fascisant* subjects.

Instead of providing an account of the sustained interaction of ideology and practice, Hull in *Absolute Destruction* defines ideology narrowly and dismisses its relevance. She focuses exclusively on practice, which she even identifies with "culture"—at least with respect to German military culture. Yet, like Sternhell, she may also be seen as stressing particularity, indeed as developing another version of the German *Sonderweg* thesis that provides a new twist in construing the "special path" in terms of German military practice at home and in the colonies. But she reverses the more common "postcolonial" conception of the direction of influence in that she stresses the way the colonies provided a field of deployment for "beastly" practices first developed on the Continent: "The point, at least for this study, is not that Europeans learned beastliness from their imperial encounters but that they could try out abroad the techniques, assumptions, doctrines, and scripts they carried with them, in an atmosphere relatively unlimited by law and conducive to the application of more force when the first allotment failed to achieve the goal" (333). Hull notes that what distinguishes the Third Reich from the earlier period, in which she believes excessive violence may be explained through "bureaucratic functioning," standard operating procedures, and means-ends rationality, all gone awry, was the importance of "Nazi ideology as interpreted by Hitler" (326). But, despite her expansive reference to "techniques, assumptions, doctrines, and scripts," she elaborates a restrictive notion of practice and contends that "the 'cult of violence' that epitomized National Socialism was simply the reification of practices and behavior (that is, action templates) that had become severed from the old Imperial military culture... [and] easily harnessed for the ideological ends of even greater mass destruction and death" (333). Thus, with respect to the pre-Nazi period, the key for Hull is the role of a historically specific German military culture existing almost exclusively on the level of practice. It would be unfair to see Hull as isolating and exaggerating the role of Hitler in an ideologically tendentious manner. But, even with respect to the Nazi period, she does present a "cult of violence" as the reification of "action templates" that are somehow "harnessed" to "ideological ends" in what seems to remain an exclusive framework of means-end rationality. This framework may be analytically insufficient to account for the valorization and excessive enactment of violence, especially in the quasi-sacrificial context of a "cult."

One may argue that the broader problem is to analyze the interaction between ideology and practice in a wide-angled, yet differentiated, understanding of violence in particular and "culture" in general. One may also note that there is no need, as Hull at one point seems to assume, to confine explanatory or interpretive options to two extremes: the unmediated attempt to account for historical phenomena (à la Žižek) by appealing to a transhistorical "death drive" or traumatic real, on the one hand, and "ordinary organizational dynamics" or "practice" in which violence has an inertial force unless countered by institutional limits, on the other (331). One may certainly recognize the genuine significance of what Hull amply demonstrates: the importance of military culture and institutional dynamics, including limits they may create. But one need not exclude the more general role of ideology, which is at times related to practice. Ideology in this sense is not restricted to "a highly structured belief system"—the concept of ideology Hull invokes in order to downplay its role in pre-Nazi Germany (329). As I have intimated, ideology may be understood in terms of more encompassing processes of subject formation, involving assumptions, prejudices, and (at times phobic or quasi-ritual) affect and fantasy, directed, for example, at other "races" in ways that may enable or valorize violence, destruction, and death, or even render them "sublime." And attempts to interpret experience and practice can be divorced from ideology only insofar as behavior is robotic or compulsive (behavior that may nonetheless be legitimated ideologically, for example, in terms of hardness and imaginary body armor). (In reading *Absolute Destruction,* one may wonder what experiential and subject-forming processes, involving thought and feeling—or possibly the resistance to them—are touched on in the letters and other documentation left by Lt. Gen. Lothar von Trotha [the German commanding officer during the genocidal massacre of the Herero] to which Hull had access.) The question is whether ideology in a more comprehensive and historically pertinent sense played a significant role even in the historical phenomena Hull so usefully describes and analyzes.[51] Indeed a prominent realization one derives from her extensively researched and documented book is how she joins others in recognizing the overall importance of analyzing closely the interactions between domestic, foreign, and colonial policy, notably in terms of mutually reinforcing processes. And, even if one stresses the need to understand complex processes involving the variable interaction of forces, one may construe in ideal-typical fashion and recognize the value of both Sternhell's and Hull's approaches if they are seen in dialogic terms as thought-provoking interventions that prompt further thought, argument, and conceptual refinement in the historical profession, notably with respect to the broad-gauged analysis of the nature and functioning of violence.[52]

51. In a relatively uncontested dimension of his influential *Orientalism* (2003; New York: Random House, 1978), for example, Edward Said wrote that ideology did play a significant enabling and not only ex post facto rationalizing role with respect to English and French colonialism, which (Hull contends) was at times quite violent but did not go to the same genocidal extreme as the German. For criticisms of Said, see the discussions in Young, *White Mythologies,* and in Robert J. C. Young, *Postcolonialism: An Historical Introduction* (Oxford: Blackwells, 2001). (Hull's view of the nature and extent of French colonial violence may be contrasted with that of Olivier Le Cour Grandmaison discussed in the following note.) The larger question here is whether there were significant differences in colonial practices, ideologies, and their interaction (or noninteraction), notably including such ideologies as racism, social Darwinism, "*pro patria mori*" sacrificialism, and an aesthetic of the sublime, along with the way they were experienced affectively or "lived" over time and place.

52. For a quasi-sacrificial, sublime, almost mystical sense of violence in French colonialism, see the testimonial early twentieth-century work of Ernest Psichari (1883–1914), especially *Les voix qui crient dans le désert* (1920; Paris: Librairie Jacques Lambert, 1948; reprinted Editions L'Harmattan, Les Introuvables, n.d.). Psichari was the grandson of Ernest Renan. He joined the army and served first in the Congo and then in Mauritania. Psichari writes: "There is not in me a more determined will, a stronger intention, than to go now across the world, concentrated within myself, determined to conquer myself by violence. I shall not, as an amateur, traverse the earth with all its virtues; rather I shall demand of it, at all times, force, rectitude, purity of heart, nobility, and candor. Because I know that great things are done by Africa, I can demand everything of her, and, through her, I can demand everything of myself. Because she is the figuration of eternity, I demand of her that she give me the true, the good, the beautiful, and nothing less" (110–11; my translation). (I thank Benjamin Brower for referring me to the work of Psichari.) For an ambitious cross-disciplinary study of French colonialism, see Olivier Le Cour Grandmaison, *Coloniser. Exterminer: Sur la guerre et l'État colonial* (Paris: Fayard, 2005). Having some of the perhaps inevitable limitations of a sweeping, analytic narrative over the *longue durée* (such as limited attention to the internal complexities and self-contestations of texts and discourses), the book effectively brings out the extremes to which colonial violence was taken. Le Cour Grandmaison does not elucidate the forces touched on by Psichari or the significance of the affective and the phantasmatic in general. But he convincingly argues for

One could discuss still other, at times significantly different, historical figures and processes in the terms I have offered, for example, F. T. Marinetti and Carl Schmitt or, in another register, Antonin Artaud and Heidegger. (I think Heidegger's attraction to the Nazis was in part related to his initial understanding of them as the possible bearers of a regenerative force that would end inauthentic modern civilization and, in an originary act or *Ursprung,* creatively repeat the so-called Greek miracle.)[53] And one detects an echo of Sorel's penchant for abstract, sensationalist assertion when one reads Žižek in his "Plea for Ethical Violence" concluding that "authentic revolutionary liberation is much more directly identified with violence [than with a use of violence to establish a nonviolent harmony]. It is violence as such (the violent gesture of discarding, of establishing a difference, or drawing a line of separation) that liberates."[54] These resounding words, with their heads-must-roll connotations, are immediately preceded by a reference to Che Guevara's putative conception of "revolutionary violence as a 'work of love'" (88). (There is an element of projection at work here, since the quotation from Che that Žižek provides does not itself mention violence but refers to "the true revolutionary" as "guided by strong feelings of love.") In any case, one cannot infer from Žižek's heady peroration that his article seems to be primarily a defense of a strong, censuring Bartleby-the-scrivener–type superego that goes against the permissive grain of avoiding harsh confrontational judgment, not so much by prohibiting enjoyment as by permitting nonenjoyment. One might even see Žižek as advocating a Bartleby-type passive resistance or even disengagement

---

important mutual implications of practice and ideology in its discursive (but not necessarily systematic) dimensions. He links colonial violence to developments in Europe, including its role in preparing the ground for later genocides, especially the Holocaust. He also notes that, for many in France, including such important figures as Tocqueville, Lamartine, and Renan, there was a close connection between colonialism and domestic sociopolitical issues. Colonialism was seen as assuring social peace and averting socialism by providing a place to ship "turbulent and dangerous" elements and by offering France its own "California to exploit" (14–15). Le Cour Grandmaison even presents colonial violence, not World War I or its aftermath, as providing the origins of total war and allowing for the invocation of a "state of permanent exception" as well as the use of "unconventional" procedures such as devastating raids (*razzias*), torture, mutilation, and profanation. He makes the arresting statement: "When the other becomes totally other [*tout autre*], whether in terms of savagery or barbarism (it matters little) and opposes the conquering ambitions of whites, everything once again becomes permissible" (194; my translation). In light of Le Cour Grandmaison's analysis, the practices of Germany in southwest Africa may not seem all that exceptional.

53. See my discussion in *Representing the Holocaust,* chap. 5. See also chapter 5 of this book.

54. "A Plea for Ethical Violence," *Umbr(a): A Journal of the Unconscious* (2004): 89. See also the version of this essay, "Neighbors and Other Monsters: A Plea for Ethical Violence," in Slavoj Žižek, Eric L. Santner, and Kenneth Reinhard, *The Neighbor: Three Inquiries in Political Theology* (Chicago: University of Chicago Press, 2005), 134–90.

combined with an ecstatically apocalyptic dream of violence close to Breton's. Moreover, Žižek, in his typical gesture of taking it to the limit every time and seeing others as insufficiently radical (the assertion of a need for a "more radical" level, claim, or position appears three times on one page alone [87]), asserts that what is missing in Judith Butler as well as in Adorno and Emmanuel Levinas (but presumably not in Lacan or himself) is a recognition of the "radical, 'inhuman' otherness" of "a terrifying excess... inherent to being human" (86). Rather predictably, Žižek, like Agamben, locates this excess in the *Muselmann* ("the 'living dead' of the concentration camps"—but is this allusion to the vampire preceded by a reference to Stephen King really apt?). One might just as readily see a fascination with "inhuman," "terrifying excess" in Himmler and those in attunement with his Posen speech, and some discrimination between modalities and contexts of "terrifying excess" might well seem desirable. Moreover, one may acknowledge this "terrifying excess," and the threat it harbors for oneself as well as others, but still question certain approaches that compulsively return to it time and again or fixate on its sublimity or its relation to an iridescent if abstract and insufficiently specified figuration of violence. Or, to vary the formulation, one may affirm that there is a "totally other" or enigmatic, excessive dimension in every other but not therefore conclude that every other is totally other or reducible to a terrifying excess.[55]

I would conclude by observing that there have been powerful, substantive critiques of violence, at times from the same figures in whom there is

55. One should, however, be wary of any generalized, unqualified "critique" of violence, in particular the dubious co-optation of a prevalent animus against violence and, especially, terrorism to refer indiscriminately to activists who generally employ legal procedures and turn to civil disobedience or breaking the law in extreme circumstances that do not involve violence against persons. The branding as terroristic of environmental and animal-rights activists, who infringe existing property rights by spilling paint on high-priced fur coats or by setting free animals used for experimentation or confined in unacceptable factory-farm conditions, is a reminder of the way a critique of violence can be invoked for contestable purposes. According to a report in *The Chronicle of Higher Education,* Steven Best, a professor of philosophy at the University of Texas at El Paso who supports the Animal Liberation Front, was banned from traveling to Great Britain on the grounds that he was considered (in the words of an official with the Home Office) as "fomenting and justifying terrorist violence and seeking to provoke others to terrorist acts and fomenting other serious criminal activity." The grounds for this judgment were apparently comments Best had made at a conference and quoted in a British newspaper: "We are not terrorists, but we are a threat. We are a threat both economically and philosophically. Our power is not in the right to vote but the power to stop production. We will break the law and destroy property until we win." Responding to the decision of the Home Office, Best argued that his comments at the conference were taken out of context: "I argued that I didn't mean anything violent, that we'll wipe these guys off the face of the earth through legal means, through boycotts." *Chronicle of Higher Education* 52 (3) August 9, 2005: A10.

a tendency to become fascinated with it if not render it sacred or sublime. These critiques deserve sustained attention, for example, in dimensions of Arendt, Camus, Durkheim, Fanon, Heidegger, and Derrida. Without being able to provide that sustained attention in the present context, I would simply stress the point that in Arendt, while violence is recognized as sometimes necessary, political action is contrasted with violence or the imposition of will and bound up with deliberative judgment or *phronesis* arrived at through dialogic relations between and within selves—relations requiring open discussion, debate, institutionalized limits, and attempts at establishing validity through persuasion.[56] With respect to Camus, *L'homme révolté* (1951) could be reread beyond the cold war polemics in which it was understood by Sartre and others in order to elicit the basic conception of the need for an ethic of violence in politics itself, an ethic setting limits to the use of violence that are not simply tactical or strategic. In a similar vein, the thought of Durkheim could be interpreted in the light of his insistence on an institutionally and normatively grounded sense of legitimate limits that could serve as a basis of desirable social transformation and interact forcefully with transgressive and even anomic initiatives.

Heidegger's *Gelassenheit* (or letting Being be) and his critique of the conversion of the world, including all others, into a stock of raw material for

56. See the helpful discussions of Arendt in Dana Villa, ed., *The Cambridge Companion to Hannah Arendt* (Cambridge: Cambridge University Press, 2000). As Villa notes in his introduction: "*The Human Condition* mines ancient Greek poetry, drama, and philosophy in order to show how, in its original understanding, political action was viewed as the very opposite of violence, coercion or rule. It was, in Arendt's rendering, the 'sharing of words and deeds' by diverse equals, whose 'acting together' generated a power quite different from the forceful ability to 'impose one's will' which we normally identify with political power" (12). In commenting on Arendt's understanding of phronesis and practical judgment in politics, Maurizio Passerin d'Entrèves states: "In matters of opinion, but not in matters of truth, 'our thinking is truly discursive, running, as it were, from place to place, from one part of the world to another, through all kinds of conflicting views, until it finally ascends from these particularities to some impartial generality.'... Arendt always stressed that the formation of valid opinions requires a pubic space where individuals can test and purify their views through a process of mutual debate and enlightenment. She was, however, quite opposed to the idea that opinions should be measured by the standard of truth, or that debate should be conducted according to strict scientific standards of validity. In her view, truth belongs to the realm of cognition, the realm of logic, mathematics and the strict sciences, and carries always an element of coercion, since it precludes debate and must be accepted by every individual in possession of her rational faculties.... In this respect, truth is anti-political, since by eliminating debate and diversity it eliminates the very principles of political life" (254–55). From an Arendtian perspective, a basic question would be the relation of politics and ethics, including its bearing on the limited use of violence. Moreover, the concepts of truth and "strict scientific standards" invoked in the above quote are idealized and subject to debate, even with respect to logic, mathematics, and "the strict sciences."

narrowly human exploitation (or even endowment with meaning) might lead to a broadly ecological vision of existence that would counteract the violence of certain forms of human assertion, including interpretive ones (although there are certainly difficulties with Heidegger's views about nonhuman animals).[57] With respect to Derrida, I would stress the point that one of the principal implications of deconstruction is the undoing or unsettlement of sharp, decisive binary oppositions that are essential for the *coup de force* that expels threatening alterity (including animality) from the self and projectively constitutes a violent scapegoat mechanism. This dimension of deconstruction is one of its principal ethical and political contributions.[58] From a Lacanian perspective, Žižek too provides a forceful critique of the projective nature of scapegoating, which forecloses an encounter with the traumatic "real" in those who resort to scapegoating. And in Fanon, one might emphasize the fruitful tension or internal self-contestation between the notion of violence as a therapeutic, if not an apocalyptic, redemptive force for the oppressed person of color and the discussion in *Wretched of the Earth* itself of what Fanon terms "*troubles mentaux*" that colonialism engendered in the oppressed—mental dislocations that often seemed exacerbated rather than cured or redeemed by acts of violence.[59] In other words, the violent catharsis, if there was one, did not invariably regenerate; it might just as well undermine if not drastically disempower the self, making the "new men" prone to prolonged depression, nightmares, and other posttraumatic symptoms, including much-feared sexual impotence. (Here a pertinent question would be the traumatization of one committing acts of violence, traumatization at times forceful enough to break through the protective shield provided by redemptive, self-justifying ideologies as well as militaristic discipline.)

57. On Durkheim, see my *Emile Durkheim: Sociologist and Philosopher.* On Heidegger, see chapter 5 of the present book.

58. For an ambitious yet problematic combination of Benjamin and Derrida that affirms Derrida's later texts as "revolving around two central questions: politics and technology" and defends his "aporetic work of mourning that, so to speak, succeeds most when it fails, which is to say when it cannot be resolved," see Alessia Ricciardi, *The Ends of Mourning: Psychoanalysis, Literature, Film* (Stanford: Stanford University Press, 2003), 12.

59. I thank Emma Kuby for her observations about the possibly traumatizing effects of presumably therapeutic violence in Fanon. For a discussion of the "ethical turn" in French thought after the events of 1968, including various reconsiderations of the role of violence, see Julian Bourg, *From Revolution to Ethics: May 1968 and Contemporary French Thought* (Montreal and Kingston: McGill-Queen's University Press, 2007). Bourg brings out the importance of attempts to link ethical concerns to sociopolitical practice, institutions, and associational activities. For a study of comparable attempts in the early Third Republic, focusing on the way masculine sexuality was crucial in the making of republican citizenship, see Judith Surkis, *Sexing the Citizen: Morality and Masculinity in France, 1870–1920* (Ithaca: Cornell University Press, 2006).

The foregoing observations indicate the necessity to keep in mind the limits and the limitations of my analyses both of the series of figures or ideological currents I have referenced and of the treatment of the problem of violence and trauma. While I think it is credible to discuss them together and raise the problem of the relationship among figures or movements I have discussed, it would be worse than a performative contradiction to conflate or amalgamate them. Each of the figures I mentioned (as well as others who might be mentioned) requires extensive, differential, and specific historical analysis with respect to their contexts and possibly to the intricacy of their thought in responding to those contexts, including in particular the role of violence in the political, economic, and social systems to which they were responding. As Homi Bhabha has noted:

> Fanon forged his thinking on violence and counterviolence in . . . conditions of dire extremity, when everyday interactions were turned into exigent events of life and death—incendiary relations between colonizer and colonized [Bhabha refers to particularly brutal aspects of the French policy of *regroupement* involving the killing and camplike internment of Algerian peasants], internecine feuds between revolutionary brotherhoods [here he refers to the 1957 bloodbath at Melouza in which the FLN slaughtered males over fifteen of the opposing Algerian political group, the MNA (Mouvement Nationaliste Algérien), even ordering FLN operatives to "exterminate this vermin"], [and] terrorist attacks in Paris and Algiers by the ultra right-wing OAS (Organisation [de l']Armée Secrète) and their *pieds noirs* supporters (European settlers in Algeria). As a locus classicus of political resistance and the rhetoric of retributive violence, *The Wretched of the Earth* captures the tone of those apocalyptic times.[60]

As Martin Jay has reminded us in his *Refractions of Violence,* the entire question of the position, role, and response to violence offers a way of both rereading intellectual traditions and shaping one important approach to sociopolitical, economic, and cultural criticism.[61] One obvious implication of

60. Foreword to Fanon, *The Wretched of the Earth,* xxxiv–xxxv.

61. While it has obvious relations to the problem of trauma, this approach should not be limited to genocide and other extreme events, however important they may be in history and however much other forms of violence may at times induce or even lead to them. But one cannot equate trauma and history. On the contrary, one should devote sustained attention to less spectacular forms of "structural violence" discussed, for example, by Paul Farmer in his *Pathologies of Power: Health, Human Rights, and the New War on the Poor* (Berkeley: University of California Press, 2003). Farmer relies heavily on the crucial concept of "structural violence"

my discussion is that there is no inherently Nazi or fascist form of violence but rather, in their nonetheless distinct cases (one should not simply conflate Nazism and all forms of fascism), an assimilation and usage of prevalent motifs in a particular political context and in an accentuatedly virulent manner. Without oversimplifying the sociopolitical and religious complexities of Islamic fundamentalism and suicide bombings, it should be more than obvious that violence, including terrorism, with sacralizing, sacrificial, or sublime significations is not something that can be projected outside the West and localized in some "Oriental," Arab, or Muslim other. It is very much an "other" within, functioning as a constitutive outside, at times going beyond what is projected outside and deceptively localized in the other. It is important to distinguish, insofar as possible, limited or qualified, strategic and contextual justifications of violence, notably by the oppressed, from figurations of violence as sacred, sublime, or redemptive. Seen in the broadest sense, these considerations indicate that a key problem for contemporary critical thinking is to attend to various forms, modalities, and constructions of violence as well as to the forces in history that may help to limit if not avert the occurrence and to counteract the effects of at least certain forms of violence, notably those involving sacralizing or redemptive valorization, the establishment of oppressive power differentials, and attendant forms of victimization.

---

wherein certain groups, notably the poor, are, because of their social position, subject to greater risks of violence and of largely untreated but treatable diseases such as AIDS. Indeed their very conditions of life are in a nontrivial sense violent even if they are not subject to direct assault or massive injury, as they nonetheless too often are.

# CHAPTER 5

# Heidegger, Violence, and the Origin of the Work of Art

A seeking, a searching.
To seek whither?
To search the land, to seek the origin,
To seek out the base, to search out the unknown,
To seek out the *atua* [spirit].
May it be effectual.

—A Maori diviner's spell (quoted in Émile Durkheim, *The Elementary Forms of the Religious Life*)

I begin with an invocation or incantation that has always seemed to me to resonate with the thought of Heidegger, especially after the so-called *Kehre* or turn, when the intimate relation between poetry and philosophy and the orientation of thought in seemingly sacral directions became more prominent. Heidegger is a notoriously difficult, yet at times deceptively simple, thinker who tries to rethink problems on a very fundamental level. He seeks a different use of language that regenerates submerged aspects of the Western tradition and may make contact with tendencies more prominent in other traditions or cultures. He writes from an uncertain interregnum, a "no longer and not yet" after the departure of the old gods and before the hoped-for coming of the new. In an interview with the important German magazine *Der Spiegel* toward the end of his life, he made the seemingly shocking statement that only a god can save us. At least through a belated recognition, one may see this statement as a not altogether unprepared "postsecular" addendum to his thought. Particularly in his later texts, he seems to use language in an evocative, even incantatory, way to lure the gods back into the deserted temples. In a sense his thought is both pre- and postapocalyptic—paradoxically waiting for some "big bang" in culture and existing after it, especially after what Nietzsche famously called the death of God.

In the 1935 essay "The Origin of the Work of Art," my primary focus, Heidegger tells us that "at bottom, the ordinary is not ordinary; it is extraordinary, uncanny" (54).[1] One may read this statement in many registers. Aesthetically, it might be taken as in one sense a "desublimating" gesture, either to displace a concern with the sublime in the direction of the uncanny or to indicate that the sublime is not situated in a transcendent realm but is a telling yet subtle modification of the everyday. Religiously, it might be read as an affirmation of the immanence or this-worldliness of the sacred and a questioning of a notion of radical transcendence in the sense of "the totally other" or Hidden God. There is a pronounced sense of transcendence (or being beyond) in Heidegger, but one may doubt whether it goes to the extreme limit of "the totally other"—the *ganz anders* or *tout autre.* Or perhaps one might say that for Heidegger every other is paradoxically strange and familiar—totally other and totally close. In "The Origin of the Work of Art" there is a notion of creation ex nihilo in art itself, but it applies to art's uncanny swerve in relation to the ordinary from which it may not be derived or to which it may not be reduced. Instead, art invites us to recognize how the ordinary is itself extraordinary—a recognition that may be construed, or perhaps misconstrued, in terms of art's performative or improvisational impetus. Art is not creation ex nihilo insofar as it repeats or recaptures in its own distinctive manner the "withheld vocation" of the past, what Heidegger elsewhere refers to philosophically as thinking the unthought of tradition (76). In a different but related register one might also refer to Walter Benjamin's notion of historiography as returning to unrealized possibilities of the past that are worth reactivating in the present. With respect to Heidegger's own writing, one may notice a painstaking reworking of ordinary language until it becomes uncanny, an attempt that often calls upon, and at times tries, the patience of the reader in following his explorations and excavations.

Here one may also recall Freud's notion of the uncanny as the return of what was once familiar but has been defamiliarized through repression or perhaps disavowal. Heidegger may not have explicit and developed notions of repression or disavowal related to the role of the unconscious. But these notions supplement his thinking and respond to places in it where they seem at least to be suggested. Indeed, his overall project was in one sense to return

1. Heidegger, "The Origin of the Work of Art," in *Poetry, Language, Thought,* trans. Albert Hofstadter (New York: Harper and Row, 1971), 15–87. It is noteworthy that in the introduction to the texts he translates in this collection, including "The Origin of the Work of Art," Hofstadter, like many other commentators, stays entirely within Heidegger's mode of thought, making no allusion whatsoever to the problem of his Nazi context or his implication in it.

to the repressed or disavowed—the unthought or "withheld vocation" of the West—and to think it through in a way that would enable its return. In the context of contemporary conditions, this return would be traumatic and even catastrophic—an upheaval of apocalyptic proportions. What its political and social implications would be, especially in terms of institutions and practices, was never clear or even adumbrated in Heidegger's thought, except insofar as it finds a contestable place in his writings during his overt affiliation with the Nazis, especially in 1933–34. One of the crucial questions in reading Heidegger is one's understanding of the possible political and social implications of his thought in relation to his own understanding of them in terms of "synchronization" (*Gleichschaltung*) with the Nazis. For, while Heidegger's thought in many crucial ways seems to move in a nonviolent direction, the Nazi regime went to extremes in its violent ideology and its practices, some of which were in evidence as early as 1933.[2]

One critical and self-critical limitation in Heidegger is that he does not make the sustained attempt to contextualize his own thought in order to investigate the extent to which it might, however blindly, be reinscribing or repeating the terms and moves of contemporaneous ideologies, most notably that of conservative revolutionaries in Germany, many of whose motifs were taken up and given a distinctive spin by Nazis.[3] Conservative revolutionaries wanted to go back to an idealized, mythical past, a kind of golden age, in order to radically change or revolutionize the present. Despite his evocations of the pre-Socratics (or perhaps in keeping with them insofar as so little is known about their thought), Heidegger's own initiative often moves on such a basic foundational (or profoundly antifoundational) level that it seems to situate questions of context, institution, and sociopolitical process on a deceptively superficial level where they almost become *infra dignitatem* or irrelevant with respect to the authentic mission of thought. Heidegger may well be convincing in arguing that art or thought in general may not be reduced to contextual constraints, sociopolitical applications, or even putative implications. But he is not convincing when he seems to ignore or trivialize such constraints, which may at times affect his own thinking in relatively uncontrolled and insufficiently contested ways. It is important to recall that "The Origin of

2. See, for example, Enzo Traverso, *The Origins of Nazi Violence*, trans. Janet Lloyd (2002; New York: The New Press, 2003). For a discussion of the complex relations between the uncanny and the sublime, which are very much at issue in Heidegger's thought, see the postscript to chapter 3 of the present book.

3. For a rather reductive analysis of Heidegger in terms of his relation to the ideology of conservative revolution, see Pierre Bourdieu, *L'ontologie de Martin Heidegger* (Paris: Editions de Minuit, 1988).

the Work of Art" was itself presented in 1935, just after the brief period during which he was rector at Freiburg under Nazi auspices and his series of at times politically misguided articles or pieces aligning the university with the Nazi regime. (Some pieces even ended with "Heil Hitler!")[4]

The context Heidegger took as most pertinent to his own effort was that constituted by the works of major thinkers and poets of the West. His thought involves a continual dialogue and often an internally dialogized relation with major thinkers and their unthought possibilities—Plato, Aristotle, Hegel, Kierkegaard, Nietzsche, Husserl, and Sartre, to mention only the most obvious in philosophy. There are also poets such as Friedrich Hölderlin and Georg Trakl with whom Heidegger was in an especially intimate vis-à-vis in his later thought. The "dialogue" in question is itself a creative strife or questioning and self-questioning agon, contest, or "deep play" that both questions and renews traditions, often by bringing out their more submerged or repressed sides. Thought in this respect is what Heidegger calls *das andenkende Denken*—thinking that responds or recalls. It tries to think the unthought of tradition and to enable that unthought to contest orientations that are dominant in the modern world. From this perspective, the world is dominated by what Heidegger terms a technological *Gestell* or framework, not so much technology in any narrow sense but rather a technological set of deeply embedded, unexamined assumptions that prefigure the approach that reduces all problems to puzzles and then seeks "technical" solutions to them. This puzzle-solving approach becomes uncomfortable with thought that investigates problems that may be explored but not solved, that result in nothing remotely resembling a satisfying demonstration or QED effect, indeed problems that may ultimately turn out to be riddles or enigmas—a crucial point that, I think, may apply to certain basic—not all—levels of thought. As Heidegger puts it somewhat dismissively in "The Thinker as Poet," "few are experienced in the difference between an object of scholarship and a matter thought" (5).[5] Elsewhere Heidegger refers to Nietzsche as the West's last metaphysician—the last figure who explored problems rather than seeking solutions to puzzles but who remained within assumptions that had to be thought through and beyond.

The technological framework dominating modernity is, for Heidegger, heavily indebted to traditional philosophy or metaphysics. In this sense modern man displays an unself-questioning reliance on nearly exhausted

4. See the pieces translated in the valuable collection *The Heidegger Controversy: A Critical Reader,* ed. Richard Wolin (New York: Columbia University Press, 1991), part 1.

5. Included in *Poetry, Language, Thought,* 1–14.

traditional forms that seem efficient in producing results, for example, concepts such as form and content or matter and spirit. The technological framework is itself the modern and perhaps the ultimate form of Western philosophy. It seeks mastery over the analytically reduced other—the thing, the person, the problem—and may construe the other as mere raw material or a human resource adapted to truncated or restricted anthropocentric purposes. In his "Letter on Humanism" Heidegger criticizes Sartre's idea of human freedom and consciousness, and Heidegger's entire approach involves a departure from Husserl's attempt to center philosophy on the intentional consciousness of the putatively meaning-generating, radically constructivist ego or subject.[6] Increasingly, the problem for Heidegger is to understand human being in relation to Being and not vice versa. In the "Letter on Humanism" he argues that the dignity of the human being is enhanced if it is seen within a larger relational network that is not unproblematically centered on human freedom or human interests.

In *Being and Time* (1927), which predates "The Origin of the Work of Art" (1935) as well as his Nazi commitment, most pronounced in 1933–34, Heidegger used the term *Dasein*—Being there—instead of human being or man.[7] As Derrida noted in "Les fins de l'homme," the translation of *Dasein* as human being or *réalité humaine* is already a questionable interpretation of it.[8] One might suggest that *Dasein* is not identical with human being yet it is not simply something other than human being. It is a term that indicates a lack of confidence in the name "man" or "human." We are *Dasein,* although *Dasein* is not simply us. Still, what else is or might be *Dasein* is an open question. Although for Heidegger other-than-human animals apparently did not qualify as *Dasein* and were poor in world (*weltarm*) or even worldless in their putative captivity to an environment (*Benommenheit*), it is at least conceivable that nonhumans are *Dasein.*

Heidegger saw *Dasein* as a being in question in its being. It was a being marked by language, being unto death, and an internally self-contestatory relation to world-disclosure (or the open). And *Dasein* was a site for an inquiry into Being as an open relational network (later evoked in Derrida's often misunderstood notion of a general text or trace-structure) in which

6. Heidegger, "Letter on Humanism," trans. Frank A. Capuzzi with J. Glenn Gray, in *Martin Heidegger: Basic Writings,* ed. and intro. David Farrell Krell (New York: Harper and Row, 1977), 189–242.

7. Heidegger, *Being and Time,* trans. John Macquerrie and Edward Robinson (1927; New York: Harper and Row, 1962).

8. Derrida, "The Ends of Man," in *Margins of Philosophy,* trans. and additional notes Alan Bass (1972; Chicago: University of Chicago Press, 1982), 109–36.

the being in question is always already implicated. *Dasein* questioned in a responsive way and, in questioning, placed itself in question. It could never be a purely objective, transcendental, God's-eye spectator or merely an object of knowledge, nor was its self-implicating relation to others simply one of objectification, including objectifying contextualization that does not implicate the inquirer.

In "The Origin of the Work of Art" Heidegger explicates a key term in *Being and Time*—*Entschlossenheit*. His gloss is of great interest whether or not it is entirely convincing as an explication of the earlier work. *Entschlossenheit* is generally translated as resoluteness or decision, indeed resolute decision (which seems to conjure up the image of a set jaw, a correspondingly determined will, and perhaps even a marching boot). For example, Richard Wolin depends on this translation in his harshly critical approach to Heidegger and his presumed "decisionism." Yet Heidegger counters this translation and readings based on it. He states: "The resoluteness intended in *Being and Time* is not the deliberate action of a subject, but the opening up of human being, out of its captivity, in that which is, to the openness of Being" (67). A footnote points out that *Entschlossenheit* literally means unclosedness. One might further note its relation to another key term in *Being and Time*, *Erschlossenheit*, which more patently means openness. Sartre translated the term into his own thought as *disponibilité*. And Agamben takes up the notion of the open in his own problematic way.[9] Yet there seem nonetheless to be dubious limits to openness in Heidegger.

In "The Origin of the Work of Art," Heidegger claims that the animal, like the plant, has no world (45). It has only—indeed is captive to—an environment. One crucial reason that Heidegger takes this turn is that he ostensibly believes language opens a world and that the animal has no language and perhaps no anxiety in "being towards death." Without trying to counter Heidegger on empirical grounds that would at least seem to raise questions about his differentiating terms (how open, constrained, or even compulsive are human worlds? how closed are the worlds of various animals?), one may nonetheless note that here Heidegger himself, in important respects, reverts to a rather traditional view—one that seeks a decisive criterion to separate the human from the animal, typically in the attempt to affirm the uniqueness of the human and to present the other-than-human animal as utterly subordinated to human interests and uses. One might infer that Heidegger would not draw the latter conclusion since the animal would at least benefit

9. See Agamben, *The Open: Man and Animal*, trans. Kevin Attell (2002; Stanford: Stanford University Press, 2004), as well as my discussion in chapter 6.

from his general critique of the anthropocentric reprocessing of all others in terms of human interests and uses. At least in retrospect (or as a belated recognition), one might argue that, along with resistances to such a move, elements in his thinking might allow its extension into a broader critique or deconstruction of the human/animal opposition (such as Derrida undertook in his later work, including a critical discussion of Heidegger on other-than-human animals). In any event, much in Heidegger seems to go in the direction of an ecological or environmental philosophy in which the relations between humans and other animals might be argued to have a crucial place. The entire orientation of his thinking places in question decisive criteria leading to binary oppositions that drastically cut into and close off the relational network in terms of which he tries to rethink problems. Indeed one may ask if nonhuman animals, whether or not they may question their being (and for Heidegger humans "proximally and for the most part" do not), nonetheless are closer to humans and have a significantly different place in a relational network than that intimated by the seemingly decisive notion that they are poor in world or captivated by their environment. The very German term for environment—*Umwelt*—might itself intimate a closer relation between other animals and having a world than would the English term "environment," although both terms indicate the world *around* us.

In *Being and Time* Heidegger criticized a conventional notion of time as a succession of now-points related to chronology. He also criticized a conception of history as either progress or mere change. Instead he saw historicity as a process that implicates *Dasein* as a historical being. One might say that, in psychoanalytic terms, he saw *Dasein* as involved in transferential relations with its objects of inquiry that only deceptively could be fully objectified. And, like Freud, he understood temporality in terms of processes of repetition, whether compulsive repetition or repetition coming with variation or change that opens possible futures and allows for projects. At least in *Being and Time* Heidegger saw his own project as making repetition explicit in a manner that enabled an explicit understanding of handing down to disclose both valuable aspects of tradition and unrealized aspects of the past that might be reactivated in the present. What Heidegger sought in thinking that recalls is not objective knowledge of tradition or an explanation of it. He sought a provocative and transformative understanding that might change the very questions we pose to the past and to ourselves as inquirers. On a "fundamental" or originary level—the level of origin as primal leap or *Ursprung*—this kind of questioning is a-critical, for it tries to avoid critical decision that cuts off subject from object and prevents an openness in the response to Being along with an attempt to let Being be (*Gelassenheit*). Heidegger is critical, at times excessively critical, of what he takes to be prevalent sociopolitical and cultural realities, for example, the role of public opinion or even the foundations of modernity in general (the technological *Gestell*). Yet he also seeks an a-critical mode of thinking that does not cut into things or make a violent assault on them. The sense of "originary" is that of an origin that repeats itself with variations each time a fundamental or essential question is posed, such as the question of art, and not an origin as an absolute beginning taking place at some empirical point in the past. One might make the same point, not entirely irrelevant to certain movements in Heidegger's thought, about original sin, which would be better termed originary sin whereby the Fall is repeated in every "sin" and *Dasein* may always be in free fall or erring. In *Being and Time,* however, the receptive process of repetition on an originary level at times slides into a more ordinary replication of contextual forces and ideological contexts. This is most notably the case with respect to Christianity and the thematic of originary *Gefallenheit* or fallenness, on the one hand, and conservative revolution and the attempt to radically transform, indeed find a redemptive alternative to, the degraded, unheroic present, on the other. There are also movements that could be argued to be coded in implicitly antisemitic ways, especially the vitriolic attack on *Gerede* or idle chatter in contrast to authenticity or *Eigentlichkeit.*

In discussing his thought after *Being and Time,* Heidegger himself referred to a *Kehre*—a turn or turning point. This was not a simple break or a speculatively dialectical progression to higher insight. It might be seen as a tangled web of compulsive repetition and the kind of explicit re-petitioning or asking again through which Heidegger rethought history itself. He sometimes referred to the step back that allowed one to ask or begin again and think further. Most ostensibly, the *Kehre* took Heidegger's primary attention from *Dasein* to *Sein* or Being that situated human being. As I intimated, it also led to a less traditionally philosophical or analytic discourse—a more manifestly poetic or figurative use of language that involved uncanny, at times opaque, turns of speech and movements of thought. It also came with a stress on etymology as itself returning to the origin of words and presumably helping to explore their deeply sedimented but still active, typically ambivalent, meanings. Indeed, etymology at times seemed to displace historical inquiry and to bypass the need for argument in making a point or directing discourse along one path or another. It also tended to obviate sustained investigation of changing contexts and uses over time that might overlay if not erode meanings that real or fictive etymologies might bring forward. "The Origin of the Work of Art" is itself written in an often evocative, disorienting style that at times approaches the incantatory.

Especially with reference to his thought after the so-called *Kehre* or turn, when he stressed the intimate relationship but not identity between philosophy and poetry, it is tempting to label or even dismiss Heidegger as a mystic, irrationalist, or reactionary. This temptation is increased when one addresses his political investments. But I think the summary and encompassing dismissal of Heidegger's work is unwarranted. There are questionable sides of his thought, notably with respect to an insufficient self-contextualization, a diminished sense of agency that is not only vulnerable but vanishing, a tendency to take the interplay between philosophy and poetry in the direction of an incantatory if not mesmeric style, a sense of significant problems so profound that it seems to render sociopolitical issues superficial if not irrelevant, and a desire for a transformation of the world so ultimate that it threatens to become a dangerous form of empty, abstract apocalyptic yearning open to the siren call of a political movement such as Nazism. But the problem of the relation of the questionable to the genuinely thought-provoking, question-worthy, and transformative sides of his thinking cannot be resolved in summary fashion.

The origin sought in "The Origin of the Work of Art" is in German *Ursprung*—primal leap. And, in this work, art is the primal leap or originary opening of a world that enables other ventures to take place. In one sense the title of the essay might well have been "Art and its Works as the Origin," for art is originary, and its great works bring about those movements in being that are both creations ex nihilo with respect to the ordinary (or routinized) and repetitions that recall a "withheld vocation," what is elsewhere the thought-provoking call of the unthought.[10] But art in this

10. One might, however, argue that, for Heidegger, myth (or *muthos*) is more originary than (or perhaps "equiprimordial" with) art as essential poetry. As he notes in his lectures on Parmenides: "It is *muthos* that reveals, discloses, and lets be seen; specifically, it lets be seen what shows itself in advance and in everything as that which presences in all 'presence.' Only where the essence of the word is founded in *aletheia,* hence among the Greeks, only where the word so grounded as pre-eminent legend pervades all poetry and thinking, hence among the Greeks, and only where poetry and thinking are the ground of the primordial relation to the concealed, hence among the Greeks, only there do we find what bears the Greek name *muthos,* myth." *Parmenides,* trans. André Schuwer and Richard Rojcewicz (Bloomington: Indiana University Press, 1992), 60. This notion of myth pervades "The Origin of the Work of Art" without being explicitly thematized in it. In a more general vein, Philippe Lacoue-Labarthe argues that in Heidegger "the essence of art is *Dichtung,* the essence of *Dichtung* is *Sprache* (both language and speech indissociably), the essence of *Sprache* is *Sage*—which is *muthos." Heidegger and the Politics of Poetry,* trans. Jeff Fort (Urbana: University of Illinois Press, 2007), 33. (I am indebted to Klas Molde for bringing these passages to my attention.) I would further note that, although Heidegger points to language, not to music, the basic structure of his argument concerning the relation between myth, art, and the "originary" is similar to Nietzsche's in *The Birth of Tragedy from the Spirit of Music* (trans. and commentary Walter Kaufmann; 1872, 1886; New York: Vintage

sense shares the problematic nature of Heidegger's quest in general in that it is rethought on such a seemingly primal, foundational, or originary level that such considerations as sociopolitical and cultural context and implications, including the role of commodification and cultural capital, seem to fade away. Yet their seeming elusiveness or even irrelevancy enables them to render Heidegger's thought, at least at certain points, symptomatic of those contextual forces that he does not address in a critically self-contextualizing manner.

I mentioned that the discourse of "The Origin of the Work of Art" itself enacts a tantalizing interplay between philosophy and poetry. It makes telling use of often indirect, allusive, or detoured approaches to problems. For example, the nature of equipment is approached not directly through an analysis of some piece of equipment, say a pair of shoes, but obliquely through the work of art, to wit, Van Gogh's painting of a pair of shoes. Moreover, the suitability of the painting for the analysis of equipment is placed in question by Heidegger's insistence that the painting is not representational but itself an opening to the originary. And while Heidegger manifestly privileges language as creating the opening or clearing in Being through which other things come to light, his two primary instances of art are, paradoxically, nonlinguistic: a painting and a temple. He does not address them in terms that make their disclosive power dependent on or derivative of language but seems to attribute to them a world-opening ability in closest proximity to the concealment or sheltering of Being.

One should also note with respect to indirection that Heidegger adds two paratexts to the principal text, an epilogue and an addendum. But neither of these clarifies the principal text; they insist on and even add to its complexities and undecidability. The epilogue begins with the warning: "The foregoing reflections are concerned with the riddle of art, the riddle that art itself is. They are far from claiming to solve the riddle. The task is to see the riddle" (79). The addendum seems to be intended to clarify certain points in the text, but the clarifications add to the difficulty of understanding them by repeating and expanding their complexity. And once again we are told that "what art may be is one of the questions to which no answers are given in this essay. What gives the impression of such an answer are directions for questioning" (86). In further elaborating these directions, Heidegger points to a "distressing difficulty, which has been clear to me since *Being and Time*

---

Books, 1967), even including the interplay between (Apollonian) limits and (Dionysian) excess via the notion of the fourfold interaction of concealment and disclosure among earth and world, men and gods.

and has since been expressed in a variety of versions"—the difficulty of "the relation of Being and human being," which was to preoccupy him increasingly in his later work (87). This notion of Being might have been less prepossessing, massive, abstract, and even godlike had Heidegger paid closer attention to other beings, their often intricate and "rich" worlds, and their relations with human beings, including the ways those relations were impoverished and distorted in good part because of their anthropocentric construction and insertion in a technological *Gestell.*

In the principal text of Heidegger's essay, the painting of the shoes might at first seem to be figurative or representational, but the temple gives no such impression.

> A building, a Greek temple, portrays nothing. It simply stands there in the middle of the rock-cleft valley. The building encloses the figure of the god, and in this concealment lets it stand out into the holy precinct through the open portico. By means of the temple, the god is present in the temple. This presence of the god is in itself the extension and delimitation of the precinct as a holy precinct. The temple and its precinct, however, do not fade away into the indefinite. It is the temple-work that first fits together and at the same time gathers around itself the unity of those paths and relations on which birth and death, disaster and blessing, victory and disgrace, endurance and decline acquire the shape of destiny for the human being. The all-governing expanse of this open relational context is the world of this historical people. Only from and in this expanse does the nation first return to itself for the fulfillment of its vocation. (41–42)

At first the temple seems almost like a free-standing nude, simply appearing there in the middle of the rock-cleft valley. Then the temple is clothed in a distinctive way by Heidegger's gloss. Not only is the god present in it, it is a site related to "the shape of destiny," "the world of this historical people," and "the fulfillment of [the nation's] vocation." The "open relational context" seems determined if not brought to closure in a rather particular way, and the phrases are at times somewhat ominous, especially if one compares them with analogous phrases addressed to Nazi Germany in Heidegger's own political writings and speeches of 1933–34. The historico-philosophical question here is whether the nonrepresentational temple that presumably sets the truth to work in a rather decontextualized and abstract fashion is nonetheless situated in history in a manner that places and contextualizes it with respect to other temples and monuments as well as the larger sociocultural and political matrix in which it is embedded. This question might even serve to bring closer together disclosive, worlding *Dasein* and the captive animal in its earthen *Umwelt*. And a closer attention to contextual constraints might provide a countervailing force to the free indirect discourse with which Heidegger gives voice to or clothes the temple in terms of his ontological concerns. These contextual constraints would not totally saturate or determine the meaning of the temple, but they would provide the specific historical terms with and against which its world-disclosing or world-concealing nature would have to work or play.

Heidegger's entire approach to the work of art is in terms of the question of truth and the manner in which art sets the truth to work. It is with respect to the question of truth that one seeks the origin of art—the primal leap that brings something into being as what it essentially is. This approach is not epistemological but seemingly ontological, although there are indications of how ontology itself, however fundamental, might not fully encompass Heidegger's mode of inquiry. Still, he is concerned with the being of art in its relation to truth. Anything more specifically or narrowly aesthetic is superficial from his perspective. It might not even be possible to speak of an aesthetic dimension but only (in the words of the epilogue) of the way "the beautiful belongs to the advent of truth, truth's taking of its place" (81).

The sacred is not irrelevant to the question of truth as it is posed in "The Origin of the Work of Art." The sacred is most patently at issue in the discussion of the temple, but it might be argued to inform the discourse in general. (Insofar as myth is the discourse of the sacred, the question of truth is simultaneously the question of myth.) As I noted earlier, in this essay the sacred is, in a nonreified, problematic sense, immanent in the world until the point the gods leave the temples and abandon the world of humans. But when the temple is the dwelling of the gods, the gods are "indwelling" in that they do indeed dwell or are present in the temple. And the statue of the god is the god. If one sees the sublime as a secular transfiguration or at least analog of the sacred, one might suggest that if there is a sense of the sublime in "The Origin of the Work of Art" it is not situated in some supersensible or noumenal realm that is out of this world. Nor is it a subjective projection of the human mind or spirit, however universal in ambition. To term it "totally other" would be at best problematic. It is rather a singular variation or inflection of the world itself, an iridescence of the ordinary that is epiphanous. The immanent sacred is the extra-ordinariness and alterity of the ordinary. It transcends the ordinary in that it transports or translates it toward the extra-ordinary or uncanny. Rather than being other-worldly, it seems implicated, however ecstatically, in the interplay of concealment, and unconcealment that the work of art enacts. In a possibly desublimating sense, art might even be termed a sacral, ontological striptease or dance of the seven veils.

It might also be worth noting that, while Heidegger does not use the term "play" but repeatedly refers to work, the notion of play and interplay might readily be used in ways that would not seem to distort his thought but rather to indicate the proximity of play and work in the way he employs the latter term. The work of Being would also seem to be the play of Being. And the "presencing" of Being in the work of art or the sacred would also seem to be a gift extended to beings, a gift that is never to be taken for granted but a gift nonetheless. Still, one very significant difference between Heidegger and Nietzsche is the explicit emphasis on play in the latter, as well as the ability to seriously play with his own ideas, indeed to parody and carnivalize himself in a manner that unsettles myth and all forms of uncontested high seriousness or piety. There is no *Ecce Homo* in Heidegger's works. And there is no disruptive, self-directed laughter. If there is any sense of humor at all, it comes in the form of subtle smiles that ripple with the movements of Being. Any irony is directed critically at others, not invoked as a frame to relativize or question one's own approach, however self-questioning, uncertain, or undecided that approach may be. Or perhaps one might say that the irony is constitutive of the approach in subdued and unobtrusive ways and somehow compatible with a sustained sense of piety and awe.

All language is ultimately poetic for Heidegger in the specific but non-generic sense that it opens a world and sets the truth to work, albeit in ways that may be deceptive, dissembling, or concealed. Even technology develops in a clearing inaugurated by poetic uses of language. Technology is the modern way in which Being discloses itself. But it is a harsh poem that may lead to destruction if it is not checked or countered within a different frame of reference. Heidegger employs two pairs of related terms constitutive of a kind of fourfold way in "The Origin of the Work of Art": earth and world, gods and men. The terms indicate that unconcealment or disclosure is intimately related to concealment, and folding to unfolding. The Greek term Heidegger invokes with respect to truth is of course *aletheia,* unconcealment, which itself includes or conceals *lethe,* forgetting. Earth (along with animals) seems to be on the side of concealment and world on that of disclosure, unconcealment, or unforgetting. But the terms are not one-dimensional. They are labile and interact in a kind of chiasmus. And their sometimes manifest gendering cannot be fixated. Earth thrusts but also seems feminine and motherly. Moreover, humans or men neither simply create gods, nor are they created by them. "Worlding" does not derive entirely from humans or human constructs. Earth, world, men, and gods coexist and seem to be, in the term Heidegger employed in *Being and Time,* equiprimordial, hence making relations a chicken-and-egg question or, more precisely, situating the terms in what I referred to earlier as an open relational network. In the modern world, the gods seem silent or have departed. And humans are often, if not typically, in the dark and confused, perhaps most decisively when they believe that they are on top of everything as anthropocentric generators or "endowers" of all meaning and value. *Dasein* may at times dispose, but *Sein* endows.

Heidegger tells us that he is concerned only with great art. But the opposition between fine or high and popular culture has no role in the essay. Both Van Gogh's painting and the anonymously "authored" temple are great art. Indeed the shoes might be seen as the displacement of the temple in the direction of the popular or lowly. They, even more than the painting of them, seem to have a sacral quality, at least as Heidegger discusses them, a feature of the text we shall soon come to. Yet the intimacy of things that belong together—art and truth, poetry and philosophy, earth and world, men and gods—is itself related to their difference. Here Heidegger employs the term *Riss*—rift. It unites seeming opposites like a joint. It marks the threshold that joins them, what Derrida plays out in the nonconcept of *différance.* The *Riss* does not simply dissociate but distinguishes while articulating, holding together while keeping apart in creative strife. As Heidegger puts it in Heraclitean terms that also appealed to Nietzsche, "the opposition of world and earth is a striving. But we would surely all too easily falsify its nature if we were to confound striving with discord and dispute, and thus see it only as disorder and destruction. In essential striving, the opponents raise each other into the self-assertion of their natures" (49). And "the work is the fighting of the battle in which the unconcealedness of beings as a whole, or truth, is won" (55). Hence it would be questionable at best to correlate strife in this essay with anything specifically political, unless one were to transform one's understanding of the political.

Heidegger insists at various points in the essay that the agonistic relations he discusses in art are nonviolent. He evokes "the feeling [that] violence has been long done to the thingly element of things and that thought has played a part in this violence, for which reason people disavow thought instead of taking pains to make it more thoughtful" (25), which would seem to imply more nonviolent. And he insists that the "thrusting" of the earth in his sense is nonviolent. Yet he also reaches a juncture where he notes that the circle in which he circles in tracing the intimate primal conflict of concealing and unconcealing, opening and closing, earth and world, truth and its simulacra, may also indicate the possibility of an abyss.

> What does the essential essence of something consist in? Presumably it lies in what the entity *is* in truth. The true essential nature of a thing is determined by way of its true being, by way of the truth of the given being. But we are now seeking not the truth of essential nature but the essential nature of truth. Thus there appears a curious tangle. Is it only a curiosity or even the empty sophistry of a conceptual game, or is it—an abyss. (50)

Heidegger's thought, in contrast to that of the early Wittgenstein at least on a manifest level, did not want "no more tangles." It sought to enter, explore, and wonder at the tangled, possibly abyssal web that ensnared and enchanted questions of art, truth, and being.[11]

I earlier alluded to the problem of Heidegger's Nazi turn and the question of the extent to which it is invited or resisted by his philosophy, a question that has received extensive attention since the late 1980s. In his pro-Nazi writings and speeches of 1933 and 1934 Heidegger himself tried to reread *Being and Time* and to construe some of its key concepts in terms that synchronized or coordinated them with Nazi ideology, including the text of the period with the most significant philosophical import: his 1933 rectoral address at the University of Freiburg, where "self-assertion" appears in the title, and the rather artless self-assertion of the German university is bound up with its *Gleichschaltung* or synchronization in the Nazi regime.[12] The issue for historical and critical analysis is whether and to what extent Heidegger, in turning his thought in a Nazi direction in 1933–34, was right in his self-understanding.[13] The Heidegger controversy, for which this question is crucial, itself has the quality of a returning repressed or resurfacing disavowed, since basic facts were known in the immediate postwar period, although the extent of Heidegger's investment in the Nazi phenomenon and some of his

11. The notion of the *Riss* as an abyss may allow too facile and possibly misleading an appeal to paradox in relating "abyssal" difference or distance to proximity, as I think occurs in Agamben's discussion of the human-animal relation.

12. "The Self-Assertion of the German University" [Die Selbstbehauptung der deutschen Universität], in *The Heidegger Controversy: A Critical Reader,* ed. Richard Wolin (New York: Columbia University Press, 1991), 29–39.

13. I have addressed this question, especially with respect to *Being and Time,* in a chapter of my book *Representing the Holocaust: History, Theory, Trauma* (Ithaca: Cornell University Press, 1994), chap. 5. I there try to provide a nuanced account that both indicates how tendencies in the text resist Heidegger's appropriation and how certain of them may invite it, notably the way dimensions of the text more or less blindly assimilate the views and the jargon of conservative revolutionaries such as Ernst Niekisch.

personally reprehensible acts in 1933–34 were not. Still, enough was known to raise the basic historical and critical issues I mention above.[14]

It was also known that, except for a few at best vague and equivocal comments, Heidegger after the mid-1930s said very little about his relation to the Nazis or about their genocidal treatment of Jews and violence toward other victims. While he was alive, there was the hope in some circles that he would say something substantive and to the point, if only in the guise of saying why he thought silence was the most appropriate response, for example, in terms of an inability or unwillingness to say anything that might be construed as an apology or a mitigation of his misguided commitment. Such a response was not forthcoming. On the contrary, he offered two posthumously published apologias, one of 1976 (the interview in *Der Spiegel*) and the other of 1985 ("The Rectorship 1933–34: Facts and Thoughts").[15] Heidegger questionably and even speciously tried to argue that he collaborated with the Nazis to preserve the autonomy of the university in the face of Nazi politicization. To put it crudely, he copped the plea that many other collaborators took in the postwar period, and he did this despite the fact that his writings and speeches alone attested to the way he explicitly tried to bring the university in line with the Nazi program of *Gleichschaltung.* The biography of Hugo Ott, reinforced by the largely derivative book of Victor Farias, brings out dimensions of Heidegger's personal behavior that by and large serve to reinforce

14. Translations of Heidegger's pro-Nazi writings as well as commentaries on them may be found in *The Heidegger Controversy,* and in Gunther Neske and Emil Kettering, eds. *Martin Heidegger and National Socialism: Questions and Answers,* intro. Karsten Harries (New York: Paragon House, 1990). For a fine-grained analysis of waves of Heidegger reception in France, see Ethan Kleinberg, *Generation Existential: Heidegger's Philosophy in France, 1927–1961* (Ithaca: Cornell University Press, 2005). Kleinberg delineates three basic, increasingly intense upsurges of the "Heidegger Affair," centering around the problem of Heidegger's Nazi affiliation and its implications (or lack of implications) for a reading of his work: 1946, 1968, and 1988. I focus on 1988 and its aftermath, which has been most important in the recent past. Treating many issues I do not discuss, Kleinberg brings out the importance of the relatively early, closely related responses to Heidegger's Nazism, along with the larger problem of the significance of the Shoah, in Maurice Blanchot (209–44) and Emmanuel Levinas (245–79). Their responses, which raise questions about Heidegger's thought with respect to his Nazi involvement, nonetheless tend to see the Shoah in transhistorical or even universal terms and might be subject to the type of criticism I address to Agamben and Žižek. Kleinberg observes: "Blanchot saw the Shoah as a singular and fundamentally ahistorical event, but also as the moment by which all history and meaning will now be understood" (225). See also my discussion of Blanchot in *Writing History, Writing Trauma* (Baltimore: Johns Hopkins University Press, 2001), 188–89n, and *History in Transit: Experience, Identity, Critical Theory* (Ithaca: Cornell University Press, 2004), 149. Neske and Kettering include Levinas's moving conversation with Philippe Nemo, "Admiration and Disappointment" (149–53), but neither they nor Wolin include anything from Blanchot.

15. Reprinted in *The Heidegger Controversy,* 29–39, and in *Martin Heidegger and National Socialism,* 5–13.

the argument that he was committed to the Nazi project as he knew it in 1933–34 and worked to make the university an integral part of the Nazi regime.[16] And his commitment may well have lasted long after the mid-1930s, at least in the sense that he remained a party member and may still have believed in the potential of the Nazis to bring about a desired radical change of Western civilization that would transform its technological imperative. He wanted to be the philosophical tutor, even to lead the leader of the Nazis and came to see them as not heeding his views. One should add that, conversely, the Nazis did not believe they could get much mileage out of Heidegger and even came to see his role as dispensable.

Heidegger did not publicly support racism and criticized biologism but was at least willing to make a commitment despite public knowledge that racism and antisemitism were components of Nazi ideology and policy. And one may detect traces of more traditional, nonbiological cultural antisemitism in his serious works, for example, the dismissal in *Being and Time* of *Gerede* or idle chatter, often coded as Jewish (as well as French) in discourses current at the time. In an unpublished but official letter of recommendation of 1929 he was, moreover, willing to write critically of the supposed "judification" (*Verjudung*) of the spiritual life of Germany. And he engaged in other personally reprehensible actions with respect to colleagues because of his willingness to support and even further Nazi policies, for example, by informing on colleagues he suspected of not having sufficiently pro-Nazi orientations.

What is more difficult to analyze is the relation of Nazi ideology to Heidegger's thought over time. For Habermas Heidegger's thought was thoroughly compromised by his Nazi affiliation, and Habermas takes a marked critical distance from it, starting with his own earliest writings.[17] He also is extremely critical of those he sees as close to Heidegger, for example, with respect to the intimate relation between philosophy and poetry or art (Derrida most significantly).[18] Adorno also was extremely critical of Heidegger whom he saw as a pied piper putting forth a wayward "jargon of authenticity."[19] The full-scale, relatively unmodulated indictment of Heidegger and those looking

16. Hugo Ott, *Martin Heidegger: Unterwegs zu seiner Biographie* (Frankfurt: Campus, 1988); Victor Farias, *Heidegger and Nazism*, ed. and foreword Joseph Margolis and Tom Rockmore, trans. Paul Burrell and Gabriel Ricci (Philadelphia: Temple University Press, 1989). Ott's important book was preceded by a series of articles.

17. Habermas, *Philosophical-Political Profiles*, trans. Frederick G. Lawrence (Cambridge: MIT Press, 1983). The sections on Heidegger were first published in 1953 and 1959.

18. See Jürgen Habermas, *The Philosophical Discourse of Modernity: Twelve Lectures*, trans. Frederick Lawrence (1985; Cambridge: MIT Press, 1987), esp. chaps. 6 and 7.

19. Theodor W. Adorno, *The Jargon of Authenticity*, trans. Knut Tarnowski and Frederic Will, foreword Trent Schroyer (1964; Evanston, Ill.: Northwestern University Press, 1973).

to him may be found in Richard Wolin, both in his book on Heidegger and his introduction to his collection of essays by and about him, and more recently in his *Seduction of Unreason*.[20] Many others, at least in the Continental tradition, have looked to Heidegger as a valuable thinker, indeed a figure who, in Derrida's term, was "incontournable" (someone who cannot be gotten around and must be taken into account). But until recently those who saw great value in Heidegger's thought paid too little attention to the problem of the relation of his Nazi commitment and writings to his important philosophical texts. Ott's biography and the works that followed in its wake made a more or less ostrichlike posture untenable, and they provoked others to confront the issues that Farias or Wolin resolved in a trenchant manner.

Both Derrida and Lacoue-Labarthe have been among those deriving much from Heidegger's thought. Their earlier writings are similar to those of others for whom the issue of Heidegger and the Nazis was basically not an issue.[21] But starting in the late 1980s, it does indeed become an issue for them.[22] What I would simply note in the present context is that both Derrida and Lacoue-Labarthe convincingly argue that complex philosophical texts are heterogeneous and that even the most thought-provoking ones like Heidegger's have their questionable aspects. I would translate this view into the more general idea that the goal of a historical and critical analysis is to explore, without necessarily resolving once and for all, the complex interaction among symptomatic, critical, and transformative dimensions of a text or a discourse. I have indicated that Heidegger's texts were insufficiently attentive to possibly symptomatic dimensions whereby they, whether unwittingly or consciously, inscribed crucial aspects of prevalent if not dominant contextual forces and ideological currents and may even have further legitimated them, most questionably those that became active in Nazi ideology and practice. This deficiency in self-critical contextualization impedes the critical and transformative potential of his texts, and it was exacerbated by an explicit quest for a profound or originary level of discourse that deceptively seemed to render contextual issues superficial if not irrelevant and to imply that the only truly desirable change was a well-nigh apocalyptic one that fundamentally transformed all of society and culture down to the roots of one's basic concepts and very being. In light of the foregoing considerations,

20. Wolin, *The Seduction of Unreason: The Intellectual Romance with Fascism from Nietzsche to Postmodernism* (Princeton: Princeton University Press, 2004).

21. This point applies to my own references to Heidegger in *Rethinking Intellectual History: Texts, Contexts, Language* (Ithaca: Cornell University Press, 1983).

22. As I intimate in footnote 10, Lacoue-Labarthe seems to have become more critical over time.

I would like to conclude with a few comments about "The Origin of the Work of Art," which, as mentioned earlier, was first delivered as a lecture in 1935.

Heidegger's terms, turns of phrase, and trains of thought exist in at least two registers: the more general and explicit philosophical one to which I have devoted most attention thus far, and a more circumscribed, contextually shaped if not determined ideological one. For example, the key idea that the translation of terms and concepts from Greek to Latin creates an inauthentic rootlessness in Western thought (23) takes on a suspicious if not sinister ring at a time when Jews and "gypsies" were persecuted because of their putative rootlessness. The criticism of the translation or transition from Greek to Latin also plays into the suspicion of, and hostility to, "cosmopolitanism" of which Jews were seen as special bearers.[23] Heidegger also has a totally unsituated, excessively vague, extremely questionable allusion to "the essential sacrifice" as one way in which "truth grounds itself" (62). The reader is never told what this essential sacrifice may entail. And references to destiny, the nation, and "the simple and essential decisions in the destiny of an historical people" (48) echo many comparable comments in Heidegger's pro-Nazi writings of 1933–34. The entire orientation to Greek art and the idea that the temple is a paradigmatic work of art are at least suspect in terms of Nazi monumentalization and appropriation of the reference to Greece in particular and to a pre-Christian, "Aryan" and "pagan" world in general, where the sacred or the charismatic was immanent in experience and available for regeneration by the Nazi movement itself. I have indicated how, in a seemingly naive fashion that contradicts his understanding of art as an ontologically performative historical leap that opens or creates a world, he tells us that the Greek temple "simply stands there in the middle of the rock-cleft valley" (41). This view of the temple is reminiscent of the deceptive way he earlier refers to Van Gogh's painting of "a pair of peasant shoes" as simply facilitating "the visual realization of them" in what he puts forward as "a matter . . . of direct description" (32–33). Yet the situatedness of the temple becomes a crucial consideration, including the way in which the nonrepresentational (like the representation of what is taken to be a pair of peasant shoes) is not utterly decontextualized and thus cannot be construed, without further ado, as available for any philosophical investment. If the temple is indeed where the nation "first returns to itself for the fulfillment of its vocation" (42), one would like to know more about that vocation and the

23. I thank Ethan Kleinberg for bringing this point to my attention.

function of the temple in the society and culture in question, including the issue of what kinds of ritual or sacrifice are going on in the temple itself. The appeal to a lost past that did not escape "world-withdrawal and world-decay," but that nonetheless was more authentic and sacral than the present, is also a motif that fits well with conservative-revolutionary rhetoric in general and Nazi ideology of the time in particular. Heidegger does not investigate the possibility that this idealized, phantasmatic past is not lost but absent or nonexistent and that nostalgic appeals to it, along with the experience of it as a lost "presence," are ideologically coded and open to political abuse.

Perhaps the epitome of seemingly decontextualized but contextually and ideologically suspect discourse in "The Origin of the Work of Art" takes place when Heidegger in a sense sees through Van Gogh's painting to its supposed truth, rendered in terms of his own lyrical, mythologized, and somewhat kitsch evocation of the little old peasant lady who lived in her shoe. I quote a pathos-charged passage:

> There is nothing surrounding this pair of peasant shoes in or to which they might belong—only an undefined space. There are not even clods of soil from the field or the field-path sticking to them, which would at least hint at their use. A pair of peasant shoes and nothing more. And yet—
>
> From the dark opening of the worn insides of the shoes the toilsome tread of the worker stares forth. In the stiffly rugged heaviness of the shoes there is the accumulated tenacity of her slow trudge through the far-spreading and ever-uniform furrows of the field swept by a raw wind. On the leather lie the dampness and richness of the soil. Under the soles slides the loneliness of the field-path as evening falls. In the shoes vibrates the silent call of the earth, its quiet gift of the ripening grain and its unexplained self-refusal in the fallow desolation of the wintry field. This equipment is pervaded by uncomplaining anxiety as to the certainty of bread, the wordless joy of having once withstood want, the trembling before the impending childbed and shivering at the surrounding menace of death. This equipment belongs to the *earth,* and it is protected in the *world* of the peasant woman. From out of this protected belonging the equipment itself rises to its resting-within-itself. (33–34)

After about forty years of life in Ithaca, New York, I am quite sensitive to the call of this somewhat maudlin rhetoric. (I even have a pair of peasantlike clogs with which I trudge through the mud and snow, shivering both at the wintry cold and "the surrounding menace of death.") Heidegger does not hesitate to surround the peasant shoes and fill in their presumably undefined space with a discourse that ventriloquates the shoes and their bearer not only in terms of an occupation—the peasantry—and a gender and age—an old woman—which nothing in the painting suggests. Indeed he speaks not only for the subaltern but for her footwear. In so doing he evokes peasant life and the shoes in the tones and terms of volkish "blood and soil" ideology that was common on the far right in Germany and was capitalized on and adapted to very particular uses by the Nazis. This space is rather well defined and much surrounds it. And Heidegger's discourse at this point resonates with aspects of his pro-Nazi speeches and writings in 1933–34, for example, his reference, in his 1933 rectoral address, "The Self-Assertion of the German University," to "the spiritual world of the Volk" as "the power that comes from preserving at the most profound level the forces that are rooted in the soil and blood of a Volk."[24] Yet the process of initial decontextualization, followed by projective recontextualization and *Erfüllung* (or filling in) via an evocative use of free indirect style, functions to eliminate the need for critical self-contextualization that would take the discourse from an abstractly philosophical, indeed mythological and purely allusive, poeticizing level and subject it to norms of critical argumentation, a process one might deem altogether necessary when crucial political and ethical concerns are at issue.

Here, at least for comparative purposes and in the interest of setting up a counterforce to Heidegger's reading, one might mention the article of Meyer Schapiro, "The Still Life as Personal Object."[25] Schapiro argues that the shoes were actually Van Gogh's, and the significance of this fact is that they should be seen and interpreted not in terms of the presumably rooted peasant but with reference to the rootless artist and urban dweller—someone Lyotard, however problematically, would include among the (lowercase) "jews."[26] One important piece of evidence Schapiro adduces is the testimony of Paul Gauguin who lived with Van Gogh in 1888. Gauguin asked Van Gogh why he kept the run-down pair of hob-nailed shoes. Van Gogh answered:

> My father . . . was a pastor and at his urging I pursued theological studies in order to prepare for my future vocation. As a young pastor I left

24. *The Heidegger Controversy*, 33–34.

25. Included in Marianne L. Simmel, ed., *The Reach of Mind: Essays in Memory of Kurt Goldstein* (New York: Springer, 1968), 203–9.

26. Jean-François Lyotard, *Heidegger and "the jews,"* trans. Andreas Michel and Mark S. Roberts, foreword David Carroll (1988; Minneapolis: University of Minnesota Press, 1990), as well as my discussion of the book in *Representing the Holocaust*, 96–99.

> for Belgium one fine morning, without telling my family, to preach the gospel in the factories, not as I had been taught but as I understood it myself. These shoes, as you see, have bravely endured the fatigue of that trip. (208)

In *La vérité en peinture* (*The Truth in Painting*) Derrida discusses Heidegger's "Origin of the Work of Art" and comments extensively on Schapiro's essay. He is critical of the appropriative way Schapiro introduces seemingly conclusive evidence or juridical exhibits (*pièces à conviction*) (259, 296).[27] He argues that Schapiro's reading is reductively referential yet also as projective as Heidegger's ascription of the shoes to a peasant woman. He also notes that the argument in Heidegger's essay counters this type of reading and that Heidegger contradicts himself in his own referential ascription of the shoes (338, 386). In his typically intricate reading, Derrida seems to see the debate as an attempt of two professors, Heidegger and Schapiro, to appropriate the shoes for themselves and to have them fit the feet of their interpretations.

Derrida takes the shoes along labyrinthine *Holzwege* (wood paths) that destabilize any definitive reading and place any attribution of ownership of the shoes in radical doubt. He even questions whether the shoes may be seen as a pair. And he asserts: "Let's posit as an axiom that the desire for attribution is a desire for appropriation," and appropriation is bound up with identification, propriety, the proper, and property (260, 297). Derrida's reading is itself radically decontextualizing, expropriating, and self-questioning yet nonetheless insists on the interested, ideologically freighted, perhaps overdetermined, nature of any "reading" of Van Gogh's painting. And he insists on the mimetic rivalry between the two "professors" in their attempts to provide the right reading of the painting and the shoes. Does Derrida himself enter this rivalry in which, as he notes, the shoes are a fetish standing in for some larger, unnamed object of contention? Derrida admits at points that he may be coming to Heidegger's defense at least for delimited purposes: "We must begin and we must read Schapiro's *Note* against which I have the intention of defending systematically, at least for this designated exercise [*l'exercice en commission*—the translation has "committee exercise"], Heidegger's cause" (294, 335 translation modified). It is of some psychoanalytic interest that Derrida, while he does not simply decide in favor of one reading or the other but suspends or places them both in doubt, curiously begins with a misspelling of Schapiro's

27. *La vérité en peinture* (Paris: Flammarion, 1978). Translated as *The Truth in Painting* by Geoff Bennington and Ian McLeod (Chicago: University of Chicago Press, 1987). Page references will be given in the text with the French pagination following the English.

name in an initial note (as Shapiro) before turning to "Schapiro" in the body of his text. What would Derrida himself have made of this (Freudian? editorial? proof-reading?) slip in a *parergon* to an essay in which the *parergon* or frame will be a crucial concern? Is it alien to all processes of identification or appropriation?

It is indeed noteworthy that Derrida insists on the significance of a fact that for him is "far from being indifferent or extrinsic... or at least the extrinsic always intervenes, like the *parergon,* within the scene" (271, 310). Schapiro dedicated his essay to the memory of his friend Kurt Goldstein. Schapiro, Derrida observes, indicates that Goldstein brought Heidegger's essay to his attention. Derrida also observes that Goldstein fled Nazi Germany in 1933, after having been imprisoned there, and taught with Schapiro at Columbia University from 1936 to 1940: "These were the very years when Heidegger gives his lectures on *The Origin of the Work of Art* and his course *Introduction to Metaphysics* (the two texts where he refers to Van Gogh)" (271, 310). Derrida observes that, in the *Introduction to Metaphysics,* Heidegger quoted, from his 1933 rectoral address at the University of Freiburg, the sentence: "For 'spirit' is neither empty acumen nor the noncommittal play of wit nor the busy practice of never-ending rational analysis nor even world reason; rather, spirit is the determined resolve to the essence of Being, a resolve that is attuned to origins and knowing [*wissende Entschlossenheit zum Wesen des Seins*]."[28] This sentence is not simply directed against Hegel; it might also be read (like the discussion of *Gerede* in *Being and Time,* which it recalls) as having antisemitic connotations, since Jews (along with shallow intellectuals and French civilization) were at the time typically seen in the terms Heidegger contrasts with true spirit. *An Introduction to Metaphysics* also contains the well-known, much-discussed, at best equivocal statement: "The works that are being peddled about nowadays as the philosophy of National Socialism but have nothing whatever to do with the inner truth and greatness of this movement (namely the encounter between global technology and modern man)—have all been written by men fishing in the troubled waters of 'values' and 'totalities'" (199). Controversy surrounds the issue of whether the words included in parenthesis, which seem to bring a modicum of calm to Heidegger's own troubled waters concerning the Nazis, were in the original version or were later added for publication in 1953.

28. Heidegger, *An Introduction to Metaphysics,* trans. Ralph Manheim (New Haven: Yale University Press, 1959), 49. The text, delivered as a lecture in 1935, was reworked for publication in 1953.

In his discussion, Derrida makes at most an oblique, allusive reference to the Holocaust as a charged "event" that may have informed Schapiro's heated, at times accusatory, "note" to Heidegger. ("There is persecution in this narrative, in this story of shoes that are to be identified, appropriated, and you know about how many bodies, names and anonymities [*noms et anonymats*], namable and unnamable, make up this story" (274, 312.) Derrida does not mention Heidegger's Nazi affiliation, which was most pronounced in 1933–34, or the series of highly compromised speeches and writings he put forth at that time. As I have intimated, when Derrida's *La vérité en peinture* was first published (1978), the basic facts concerning Heidegger's Nazi turn were known, at least in certain circles, but were not as widely disseminated or discussed as they would be after the publication of Farias's book. Whatever one makes of these silences in Derrida's text, the mention of Goldstein and aspects of his context would not seem enough as a critical analysis of the dubious dimensions of Heidegger's text, and they may even tend to get lost in the labyrinthine commentary that follows them, focusing on exegetical problems in the readings of Heidegger and Schapiro. Here a certain kind of prolonged, experimental, self-questioning, intricate close reading may function to obscure considerations that should be given a degree of salience, even if they are not made to settle all questions or reduce the text to its more dubious contextual implications. Such a seemingly close reading may even at times threaten to miss the forest for the trees or at least to obscure some very prominent growths by lavishing attention on byways, possibilities, allusions, analogies, virtualities, and problematic or undecidable aspects of reading and interpretation.

I would further point out that the story Schapiro recounts has a possibly beneficial deflationary effect with respect to Heidegger's rhetoric, even if one may question (as Derrida does) Schapiro's desire to pin down the shoes and tie art to some undoubted, deceptively pedestrian empirical reality. At least it complicates the picture in that it would seem to indicate that the significance of the shoes for Van Gogh was not simply that they somehow designated the condition of the rootless urban artist rather that the rooted imaginary peasant. Rather, their significance for Van Gogh alluded to the artist's memory of his father as pastor and to his own early role as preacher. This early self in one sense followed in the footsteps of the father and, in another, departed from them in his preaching the gospel to factory workers according to his own (not his father's) understanding of the gospel. The shoes would thus seem to act as an ambivalent memorial to the father and to his own early self that took a different path from the father's. Indeed, they might in this way be seen as displacing the Greek temple in a different sense from the one Heidegger invokes. And the shoes have both a complex religious significance and a pronounced sociopolitical meaning that differ from Heidegger's emphasis on the auratic nature of peasant life—a significance and a meaning that are not univocal and that may even resonate with Derrida's own concern for ghostly hauntings and overdetermined significations.[29]

One may supplement and counter what I have asserted concerning Derrida's approach in *Truth in Painting* with a reference to his remarkable essay, "Faith and Knowledge: The Two Sources of 'Religion' at the Limits of Reason Alone," in which he quite pertinently questions whether we know what is meant by religion and whether this term, so easily invoked (like the term "postsecular" itself), has ever had or can have a singular meaning or reference, however much it may come under the hegemonic control of a given religion or political formation.[30] Derrida nonetheless feels the need to respond to the

29. It would be of interest to provide an extensive contextualization of Heidegger's ontological approach to art with respect to aesthetics in both the Weimar and the Nazi periods. This undertaking is beyond the scope of my inquiry. Worth more extensive investigation is Heidegger's feeling of rapport with the Norwegian Knud Hamsun to whom he refers in *An Introduction to Metaphysics.* (The widely popular Hamsun, awarded the Nobel Prize for Literature in 1920, later supported the pro-Nazi Vidkun Quisling, was charged with but not convicted of treason, and was fined for alleged membership in Quisling's political party.) The relation to Hamsun is evident in "The Origin of the Work of Art," especially in the passage about the putative peasant woman and her shoes, which echoes a passage in Hamsun's 1917 *Growth of the Soil.* The relation between Heidegger and Hamsun is noted critically by Schapiro and in turn commented on by Derrida. See the discussion in Laurie Schneider Adams, *The Methodologies of Art: An Introduction* (New York: IconEditions, 1996), 175–57. On the relation between Heidegger and Ernst Jünger, see Michael E. Zimmerman, "Ontological Aestheticism: Heidegger, Jünger, and National Socialism," in *The Heidegger Case: On Philosophy and Politics,* ed. Tom Rockmore and Joseph Margolis (Philadelphia: Temple University Press, 1992), 52–89. Especially significant in work emerging from Heidegger's orientation is Hans-Georg Gadamer's approach in *Truth and Method* (1960; New York: Seabury Press, 1975) that takes Heidegger in capaciously hermeneutic, humanistic, and harmonizing directions and does not address the problem of his Nazi turn.

30. In *Religion,* ed. Jacques Derrida and Gianni Vattimo (1996; Stanford: Stanford University Press, 1998), 1–78. Still, in this complex essay, Derrida's own opening to what he might resist calling the "postsecular" is both engaging and at times contestable, for example, when he affirms "another 'tolerance'" [beyond that of the Christian tradition] that "would be in accord with the experience of the 'desert in the desert'" [a hyperbolic moment of "kenosis" or abstraction and emptying of experience]. This "tolerance" would "respect the distance of infinite alterity as singularity" and "would still be religio as scruple or reticence, distance, dissociation, disjunction, coming from the threshold of all religion in the link of repetition to itself, the threshold of every social or communitarian link" (17). Derrida recognizes that his approach "resembles to a fault, but without reducing itself to" a "via negativa," and he seems to address in extreme, even absolute, terms an "originary" level of possibility that presumably both undercuts and gives rise to history but does not seem to interact with it in a mutually interrogative way. He also asserts that the presumably "axiomatic (quasi-transcendental) performative" in witnessing or testimony "amounts to saying: 'Believe what I say as one believes in a miracle'" (63–64). One might instead argue that testimony bears witness to experience

pressing political as well as "religious" question of the role of religion and its putative return today. After alluding to the treatment of radical evil by Kant in his *Religion within the Limits of Reason Alone* (1793), he disquietingly observes:

> Question, demand: in view of the Enlightenment of today and of tomorrow, in the light of other Enlightenments (*Aufklärung, Lumières, illuminismo*) how to think religion in the daylight of today without breaking with the philosophical tradition? In our "modernity," the said tradition demarcates itself in an exemplary manner—it will have to be shown why—in basically Latin titles that name religion. First of all in a book by Kant, in the epoch and in the spirit of the *Aufklärung,* if not of the *Lumières: Religion within the Limits of Reason Alone* (1793), [which] was also a book on radical evil. (What of reason and of radical evil today? And if the "return of the religious" was not without relation to the return—modern or postmodern, for once—of certain phenomena, at least, of radical evil? Does radical evil destroy or institute the possibility of religion?) Then, the book of Bergson, that great Judaeo-Christian, *The Two Sources of Morality and Religion* (1932), between the two world wars and on the eve of events of which one knows that one does not yet know how to think them, and to which no religion, no religious institution in the world remained foreign or survived *unscathed, immune, safe, and sound.* [Derrida has traced the relations of these terms to religion and its dual or multiple meanings.] In both cases, was the issue not, as today, that of thinking religion, the possibility of religion, and hence of its interminable and ineluctable return? (41)

To Derrida's disturbing question and demand, I would simply add the contention that the problem of interpreting Van Gogh's painting points to a basic problem in reading Heidegger—how best to negotiate (or, in Heidegger's terms, to circle in the circle of) the relations between a mode of thought that provocatively wants (at times in a seemingly religious, even mythological, perhaps postsecular register) to rethink traditions and traditional concepts in basic, disorienting ways, insistent contextual issues to which that thought may not be reduced but which may at times constrain and raise questions for it, and the broader problem of the nature of historical and critical analysis.

---

and indeed has a performative force not reducible to a statement of empirical fact about events but still not posit such performativity as quasi-transcendental or equate it with a demand for belief as in a miracle, even though the experience to which the testimony refers may at times seem to be "beyond belief."

# Chapter 6

# Reopening the Question of the Human and the Animal

> For sin shall not have dominion over you: for ye are not under the law, but under grace.
>
> —Paul, Romans 6:14

> The creature itself also shall be delivered from the bondage of corruption into the glorious liberty of the children of God. For we know that the whole creation groaneth and travaileth in pain together until now. And not only *they,* but ourselves also, which have the first fruits of the Spirit, even we ourselves groan within ourselves, waiting for the adoption, *to wit,* the redemption of our body.
>
> —Paul, Romans 8:21–23

> For one believeth that he may eat all things: another, who is weak, eateth herbs. . . . For the kingdom of God is not meat and drink; but righteousness, and peace, and joy in the Holy Ghost.
>
> —Paul, Romans 14:2, 17

> Whether therefore ye eat, or drink, or whatsoever ye do, do all to the glory of God.
>
> —Paul, I Corinthians 10:31

> Only truths (thought) allow man to be distinguished from the human animal that underlies him. . . . In contrast to the fact, the event is measurable only in accordance with the universal multiplicity whose possibility it prescribes. It is in this sense that it is grace, and not history. . . . For Paul, the Christ-event is heterogeneous to the law, pure excess over every prescription, grace without concept or appropriate rite.
>
> —Alain Badiou, *Saint Paul: The Foundation of Universalism*

Striking in its insistence and durability is the quest or desire for a decisive criterion with which to differentiate humans from other animals as well as the human from the animal in human beings. At issue in this quest is both the nature of a judgment that distinguishes between the human and the animal, along with humans and other animals, and the consequences or implications it may have for interactions both among humans and between humans and other species. I would like to reinforce and contribute to the argument (which, despite indications to the contrary, I hope is becoming increasingly prevalent) in favor of judgment that is differential in complex, qualified ways; does not assume a decisive binary opposition or caesura between human and animal; is attentive to complex differences within what is classified as human or animal; and does not have self-serving, anthropocentric, oppressive, or exploitative functions or consequences.

The point of my inquiry is not to deny all differences or distinctions between humans and other animals. But it is to question both the adequacy of the concept of exclusively human rights and the motivation as well as the functions of the misguided quest for a kind of holy grail—a decisive criterion or conceptual Grand Canyon that divides into two the deceptively massive categories of human and animal. I would also ask whether differences that may be adduced are sufficient to serve as a criterion or divider that justifies the human practices and attitudes in the treatment of animals that presumably follow from such a criterion. In the absence of such a decisive, differentiating criterion, any attempted justification of a given treatment of animals (for example, killing and eating or experimenting on them) has to be based on considerations that are typically controversial and debatable, involving problematic normative judgments, that do not have the logical, ethical, or religious force—and conscience-calming function—of a decisive criterion or clear-cut divide in which much of importance is obviously invested.[1]

1. For a statement of opposed positions on the question of animal rights, see Carl Cohen and Tom Regan, *The Animal Rights Debate* (Oxford: Rowman and Littlefield, 2001). Cohen assertively argues that humans are fundamentally different from animals. This fundamental difference has far-reaching consequences, including the denial of rights to animals and the justification of their use by humans for food and experimentation, with very limited restrictions on human practices (for example, the prohibition of ill-defined unnecessary cruelty). Regan defends the inherent, noninstrumental, independent moral value of not only moral agents, such as adult humans, but also of moral patients, including animals as well as certain categories of humans (such as small children and the seriously deranged or enfeebled). He draws from this view extensive restrictions on human practices with respect to eating and experimenting on animals. He is also concerned with factory farming and the way animals are treated in captivity. Despite his pertinent concerns and important disagreements with Cohen, Regan tends to argue in rather delimited ethical terms and does not situate problems in a broader political and ecological perspective. He also has an excessively limited conception of the capacities of all other animals. For a discussion of empathy and morality, including a sense of fairness, in primates, see Frans de Waal, *Primates and Philosophers: How Morality Evolved* (Princeton: Princeton University Press, 2006). Moreover, as Richard Sorabji notes in *Animal Minds and Human Morals: The Origins of the Western Debate* (Ithaca: Cornell University Press, 1993), 216, with reference

Humanism itself has often been defended or attacked for dubious reasons: defended as the most enlightened philosophy in the history of "mankind" or attacked as a departure either from true religion or from what is taken to be an even more enlightened or perhaps suitably disabused, nihilistically accomplished theoretical perspective. Without entering into the complexities and functions of various defenses and attacks, one may recognize the basic inadequacies of humanistic idealism and argue that the most valid and ethico-politically pertinent dimension of the critique of humanism is that which points to humanism's possible role in an anthropocentric perspective that, at least surreptitiously or unintentionally, validates whatever serves human interests and, as a consequence, projectively situates other animals, or animality in general (including the animal in the human being), in the position of bare life, raw material, or scapegoated victim. In fact the human-animal divide is often premised on a dubious comparison between an idealized rights-bearing "normal" human—usually a healthy adult in full possession of his or her faculties—and an excessively homogeneous category of the animal.[2] The obvious question is whether these mutually reinforcing frames of reference provide a sufficient basis for the understanding of problems or the elaboration of viable alternatives.[3] A related issue is whether the concept of human

---

to Regan's book, *The Case for Animal Rights* (Berkeley: University of California Press, 1983), Regan believes that inherent value is equal and admits of no degrees, and he relies on a unifying principle (or theory) in terms of inherent value. See also Peter Singer's groundbreaking *Animal Liberation: A New Ethics for Our Treatment of Animals* (New York: Avon Books, 1975), as well as the book he edits, *In Defense of Animals* (Oxford: Blackwell, 1985). My argument has implications for the question of animal rights but does not directly engage that complex debate.

2. As a result, any proximity between human and animal may well be seen as paradoxical and derive from a questionable comparison between an excessively generalized notion of human extremity if not pathology and of abused animals deranged by extreme stress or trauma. Such a notion of proximity is found in the work of Slavoj Žižek and Eric L. Santner, and it accords with the approach of Giorgio Agamben, discussed below. See Eric L. Santner, *On Creaturely Life: Rilke, Benjamin, Sebald* (Chicago: University of Chicago Press, 2006), and Slavoj Žižek, Eric L. Santner, and Kenneth Reinhard, *The Neighbor: Three Inquiries in Political Theology* (Chicago: University of Chicago Press, 2005).

3. The widespread but not universal public outcry in the summer of 2007 against the role of the star football player Michael Vick in a dog-fighting enterprise involving the brutal killing (electrocution and drowning) of dogs that did not perform with the desired brutality is a welcome indication that the issues I discuss are entering the "public sphere" in more than marginal ways. For a historical and philosophically critical survey of at least ancient Western literature that in certain ways parallels my argument, see Richard Sorabji, *Animal Minds and Human Morals.* On a moral level, Sorabji believes that a crucial problem is that of relevant differences between humans and animals but denies that one needs a unifying principle or theory to decide what differences are morally relevant. He asserts that "depression induced by caging or lighting conditions, fear induced by slaughterhouse procedures, would be agreed by many to be morally relevant. Where we do not agree on the moral relevance of an alleged analogy, we may still agree that the onus is on us to find a morally relevant disanalogy" (217). He

rights should be replaced, or at least supplemented, by that of claims that are so basic or fundamental that they are situated beyond sovereignty and should not be infringed by supposedly sovereign states (or other entities). Indeed, legitimate claims that limit human assertiveness would place the concept of sovereignty in doubt and apply in important respects to other animals or even ecological systems. Whatever the strategic necessity of an appeal to rights in the current context of law and ethical debate, the limitations of "rights discourse" suggest that one rethink the entire issue and displace the notion of rights in the direction of competing claims, in good part to take distance from predictable, conventional expectations, such as the requirement of a mutual implication or even a strict reciprocity of right and duty or obligation that prompts the question—often the rhetorical question—of whether a dog or a cat can have obligations to counterbalance putative "rights."[4]

A question concerning humanism is whether it has always required a radical other, perhaps even a quasi-sacrificial victim and scapegoat, in the form of some excluded or denigrated category of beings, often other animals or animality itself. As categories of humans (such as women or nonwhite "races") have been critically disclosed as the encrypted other of humanism, however universalistic in its pretensions, the other-than-human animal in its animality has been left as the residual repository of projective alienation or radical otherness. Forms of posthumanism may still divorce the human from the animal and anthropocentrically seek the differential criterion (or essence) identifying the human, even when that criterion paradoxically points to an enigma or indistinction: a traumatic split, signifying stress, or anxiety-ridden form of self-questioning that serves to set apart the human or its "post" avatars, such as *Dasein* or creaturely life.[5]

---

concludes with the "hope that what will be drawn from Aristotle is the need for a multiplicity of considerations, not the possibility of applying a single criterion" (219). I think that this multiplicity of considerations must be attentive to differences within the overly homogenizing categories of humans and other animals. And I agree with Sorabji's plea for self-critical caution and at times tentativeness in making arguments with important consequences for human and animal life. For a discussion of the way early modern thought and culture displaced or continued anthropocentric assumptions prevalent both in Christianity and in Greek thinking, see Nathaniel Wolloch, *Subjugated Animals: Animals and Anthropocentrism in Early Modern European Culture* (Amherst, N.Y.: Humanities Books/Prometheus Books, 2006).

4. There is a range of activities to which the mutuality, if not the strict reciprocity, of rights and duties or obligations applies, and perhaps should apply more fully, for example, with respect to the salary levels of CEOs or sports stars. There is also a range of cases to which it does not apply, such as the care of infants, the sick, and the disabled. It also does not apply to the care of companion animals even when they reach an age where they cannot offer the companionship and type of interaction for which they are "prized." The question is whether and to what extent the latter range of cases should be extended and the claims of other beings recognized.

5. See, for example, Santner's *On Creaturely Life* and Žižek, Santner, and Reinhard's *The Neighbor.* If, however, one grants limited validity to the notion, enunciated by Žižek, that "what

One especially dubious function or consequence of a decisive divide between humans and other animals is to situate the latter in a separate sphere that makes them available for narrowly anthropocentric uses and even exposes them to victimization as if they were simply beyond the pale of ethical and political concerns. At best, actions, including violent actions, against other animals are subject to much lesser legal sanctions than comparable actions performed against humans.[6] Paradoxically, the projection of other animals into a separate sphere may take two seemingly contradictory but at times conjoined forms: the reduction of the other to infra-ethical status, for example, as raw material, purely instrumental being, or mere life, and the

---

makes an individual *human* and thus something for which we are responsible, toward whom we have a duty to help, is his/her very finitude and vulnerability" (138), then we would in certain respects be more acutely responsible toward nonhuman animals as well as certain categories of humans such as infants. The argument I am making might also conceivably be supported by Heidegger's view that *Zusage* (trust, confidence, accord, acquiescence) is more "originary" in "thought" than is questioning. I would suggest that one might at least see them as equally significant or (in Heideggerian terms) "equiprimordial." See Derrida's discussion of *Zusage* in "Faith and Knowledge: The Two Sources of 'Religion' at the Limits of Reason Alone," in *Religion,* ed. Jacques Derrida and Gianni Vattimo (1996; Stanford: Stanford University Press, 1998), 59–63.

6. In the State of New York, for example, it is not mandatory for veterinarians to report cruelty to animals. New York State Agriculture and Markets Law section 353A stipulates that cruelty to any animal is a class A misdemeanor making a person subject to up to one year in prison, having the animal removed, and up to three years probation and a court order barring animal ownership for up to three years. "Lawful" hunting, fishing, trapping, and animal testing are not defined as acts of cruelty. A second offense is a felony but applies only to companion animals and only if the animal shows signs of aggravated cruelty. As a felony, the second crime is punishable by up to two years in prison, loss of the animal, fines up to $5,000, and up to five-years probation and a court order preventing animal ownership for up to five years. Agriculture and Markets Law section 351 section B makes it a misdemeanor to own, possess, or keep any animal for fighting. These regulations obviously leave much room for interpretation in both judging that an infraction has taken place and in determining a penalty. And it is debatable whether penalties could be termed prohibitive. It would be important to have accurate statistics concerning enforcement and application of penalties. A recent case in Ithaca, New York (City Court case 10952), indicates what is probably a strict level of enforcement if one has a motivated district attorney, an active SPCA, and significant community outrage. A twenty-three-year-old student, taking care of another person's dog for a night, became angry with it for chewing a speaker wire. He severely beat the dog and poured bleach and laundry detergent on it, causing severe burns and impaired eyesight for life. The dog had a significant laceration one inch by two inches wide, and some of its skull was showing through. The officer in charge of the investigation said the accused acted "cocky and arrogant" and "made numerous comments that this incident meant nothing to him, that he would do it again, and that he knows how the criminal justice system works, and guaranteed that the prosecution of the case would result in an ACD [adjournment in contemplation of dismissal] in City Court." During the trial the accused indicated remorse for his actions, which he even claimed (in contradiction to the police report) that he felt immediately after the acts themselves. On a plea bargain he was convicted of felony animal abuse and sentenced to six months in jail. See *News 10 Now,* October 11, 2007, and the *Ithaca Journal,* May 11, July 6, and September 17, 2007. Information is also available online at http://www.pet-abuse.com/cases/10952/NY/US.

elevation of the other to a supra-ethical status as sacrificial or quasi-sacrificial victim as well as utterly opaque or enigmatic other (whether within or outside the self). One may also foreclose the issue of denigration or victimization of other animals as an ethical and political problem by restricting one's concern to humans and leaving other animals out of the equation or at best referring to them only, or predominantly, in anthropocentric ways, including their reduction to a form of radical alterity. Here anthropocentrism may serve invidious functions insofar as it ascribes certain abilities or considerations only to humans and induces an excessive generalization of the category of anthropomorphism, typically on the unexamined assumption that one has an unproblematic, clear-cut idea of what is distinctively human and that there is indeed a decisive criterion that divides the human from other animals or perhaps the human from animality in the human being. (The charge of anthropomorphism may even serve as a screen for anthropocentrism.)[7]

A decisive difference between humans and other animals may, in certain contexts, also be linked to the postulation of decisive differences between categories of humans based on gender, sexual orientation, race, and class. Traditionally, women were seen as closer to nature and to other animals, for example, with respect to menstrual cycles. They have also been seen as dominated by sensation, passion, and emotion, indeed hysteria and suggestibility, and, by that token, less open to reason and self-control. Their putative affinity for suffering, compassion, melancholy, and endless mourning has functioned to make them seem peculiarly suited for abjection. At times same-sex acts have been classified as animalistic. People of color and entire societies have been presented as *Naturvölker,* in the tell-tale German term, ahistorically caught or captivated in more or less compulsive cycles of repetition; mired

7. For a critique of anthropomorphism, which is self-confidently anthropocentric and follows the prevalent "us and them" format, see Clive D. L. Wynne, *Do Animals Think?* (Princeton: Princeton University Press, 2004). See also the excellent, generally nonanthropocentric, exploration of the abilities of various other animals (including language acquisition, inventing, planning, episodic memory, and even deceptiveness) in Virginia Morell, with photographs by Vincent J. Musi, "Minds of Their Own: Animals Are Smarter Than You Think," in *National Geographic* 213, no. 3 (March 2008): 37–61. The article quotes Wynne as making a comment that would place in question a decisive differential criterion separating the human from the animal: "We're glimpsing intelligence throughout the animal kingdom. It's a bush, not a single-trunk tree with a line leading only to us" (quoted, 54). One may note that theories of lyric tend to be anthropocentric and to assume that address to other-than-human others must be explained—indeed explained away—perhaps as a defense against meaninglessness, trauma, and the Lacanian "real," or as either narcissistic or projective of human relations, rather than being situated in a wide-ranging relational network that may even have ritual or ceremonial dimensions. Here there may be a place for a certain kind of "postsecular" theory of lyric, especially if the secular is correlated with the anthropocentric.

in a magical, mythical, or ritualistic "mentality"; and marked by subhuman animalistic practices such as sexual license and cannibalism.

Forms of prejudice that have been recognized and condemned with respect to humans may find a refuge in conceptions and treatment of other animals. For example, the notion of purity of breed with respect to dogs has racist overtones, including the quasi-ritual horror at mixing breeds, the prejudice against "mutts," the complementary fashioning of expensive "designer" crossbreeds, the breeding for traits that may be detrimental to the animal, and the profiling of certain breeds (including at times discriminatory legislation) when the way dogs have been handled and bred by sometimes vicious humans may be the primary source of a problem. Indeed kennel clubs, along with similar breed registries for other species, may be among the last bastions of unexamined racism, reproducing, vis-à-vis other animals, barriers and attitudes that have been challenged with respect to humans.[8]

There have, I think, been signs of a growing awareness that a decisive, differentiating criterion radically dividing the human from the animal or humans from other animals is nonexistent or at best phantasmatic. The putatively decisive criterion often if not typically rests on a scapegoat mechanism whereby traits causing anxiety in humans are gathered up, expelled, and projected exclusively onto other animals. Human culture nonetheless often seems to depend on the viability and strength of the opposition between humans and other animals (often along with the rest of nature) or even on the belief that humans, in some basic and not simply contingent sense, are not animals. When that decisive opposition is threatened or weakened, whether because other animals share too much of the presumed distinguishing characteristic or because humans seem to have too little of it, anxiety or even panic may set in. The very notion of human being seems typically to rely on an essentializing figuration or conception of humanity whereby the essence or very being of the human "as such" is its humanness in contrast to the animality of the animal. When the human and the animal are seen as combined, the human in the human being is often decisively distinguished from the animal, typically by postulating some fundamental quality or essence that radically separates the truly or authentically human from the animal, at the

8. Drawing on the work of Jean-Pierre Digard, Harriet Ritvo, and Mary Elizabeth Thurston, Boria Sax asserts: "The breeding of animals first produced the concepts of 'race' and 'pure blood,' later adopted by the Nazis. In the latter nineteenth century dog shows... featured a eugenic pursuit of moral and aesthetic perfection that mirrored the enormous emphasis on pure family lines, on 'pedigree,' in aristocratic houses." *Animals in the Third Reich: Pets, Scapegoats and the Holocaust,* foreword Klaus P. Fischer (New York: Continuum, 2000), 83.

limit, through the idea that the human is made in the image of God. The animal side is typically the inferior or lower bodily stratum that is the seat of desire, affect, dependence, and compulsion or captivation. Captivity (with cages, performing monkeys, zoos, and so forth) seems less questionable, even redundant, insofar as the animal is already captivated by its instincts or its self-enclosure. And the human may be understood not as an embodied being but as a human spirit temporarily inhabiting or even visiting a more or less inferior if not despicable animal body—a view certain Gnostics drove to an uncomfortable extreme.

It is significant to note that in Kant, there is an appeal to a presumably universalistic but discriminatory conception of ethics in the argument that morality itself is what separates "man," as a being with access to the sublime, from the rest of nature. Here the Kantian sublime, which may perhaps be seen as a displacement of the sacred, serves in its linkage with morality as a decisive criterion separating humans from, and elevating them above, the rest of nature. Hence Kant can assert: "Sublimity is contained not in any thing of nature, but only in our mind, insofar as we can become conscious of our superiority to nature within us, and thereby also to nature outside us (as far as it influences us)."[9] Moreover, the prevalent critiques, as well as the "strategic" defenses, of essentialism have typically been restricted to human groups without questioning the human–other animal divide. And when humans behave in ways that appear to be distinctively human—indeed in ways that may suggest certain differences between them and other animals of a less self-serving kind, for example, with respect to all-too-human practices of victimization, torture, or genocide—humans, in a self-serving paradox, are said to be bestial or to regress to mere animality. This would seem to be a prototypical scapegoating gesture that blames the victim. Through a form of self-fulfilling performativity, the animal must be "brutalized" to become the image of brutality that in actuality characterizes particularly vicious and humiliating human practices in the treatment of others, perhaps more than it characterizes other animals.[10]

9. Immanuel, Kant, *Critique of Judgment,* trans. and intro. Werner S. Pluhar, foreword Mary J. Gregor (1790; Indianapolis: Hackett, 1987), 123.

10. A recent article on elephants is noteworthy. See Charles Siebert, "Are We Driving Elephants Crazy?" *New York Times Magazine* (October 8, 2006): 42ff. Siebert discusses the way complex elephant societies have been drastically destabilized and traumatized by extensive human poaching, captures, killings, and massacres, including the disruption of generations-long family structures and even mourning rituals. The result has been aberrant behavior of improperly socialized elephants, including aggressions against people and even rapes of rhinoceroses.

Over time in Western culture, and often at one and the same time, there have been various candidates for the distinguishing characteristic or criterion, for example, soul, reason, spirit, thought, dignity, nobility, sublimity, emotion, ethical status, culture (cooking food, for example), language, expectation of (or being-towards) death, sexuality (especially perversion), or (perhaps the most laughable) laughter itself, which has also been seen as something absent in the Christ figure or "lamb of God."[11] The bewildering heterogeneity of seemingly endless criteria used to arrive at the same conclusive divide attests to the force of the desire for that divide or radical separation. And the extent to which other animals share in a characteristic—but typically not enough to question its decisive role in differentiation—is estimated by an appeal to an "us and them" comparison or analogy, with the human being as the center of reference. (For example, animal symbolism is examined to determine the extent it is like a human language; an animal, say the lion, is analogically attributed dignity by comparison with a human role such as kingship; or an animal's avid attachment to an object, especially when separated from its "master," is compared or contrasted with shoe fetishism.)[12] The very idea of a constitutive lack or defect in the human, which Lacan both affirmed and related to the notion of original sin, as well as the idea that animals, unlike

11. See the especially interesting perspective on laughter in man and its absence in Christ in Charles Baudelaire, "De l'essence du rire," in *Oeuvres complètes* (Paris: Editions du Seuil, 1968), esp. 373–75. What Baudelaire termed "le comique absolu" may be argued to unsettle the boundary between human and animal. In making a humanistic appeal to an ethic of dignity, even such an exemplary witness and thinker as Primo Levi frequently invoked the dubious opposition between human and animal, with dignity situated on the side of the human and indignity (or "inhumanity") on the side of the animal: "The transformation from human beings into animals... was a logical consequence of the [concentration camp] system: an inhuman regime spreads and extends its inhumanity in all directions, also and especially downward; unless it meets with resistance and exceptionally strong characters, it corrupts its victims and its opponents as well." *The Drowned and the Saved* (1986; New York: Vintage Books, 1989), 112. Why is the corrupting transformation designated as one from human to animal, with the animal, by implication and by association with the degraded victim, situated "downward"? What Nazis did to Jews and other victims would seem to have little or nothing to do with the behavior of other animals except through their treatment at the hands of humans. See also Levi's references to animals on pp. 36, 54, 89, 99, 114, and 169, as well as the references to dignity on pp. 41, 46, 49, 128, and 132.

12. In *On Creaturely Life,* Eric Santner quotes Jonathan Lear as asserting: "It is only a slight exaggeration to say that there is nothing about human life we hold less in common with animals than our sexuality. We can imagine a bird happening to make a nest out of a lady's shoe; we cannot imagine her getting excited about it" (quoted, 98n). This comment, which may say more about possible limitations of human imagination than about birds, is analogous in structure to Heidegger's assertion, quoted by Agamben, that "not even the lark sees the open." Giorgio Agamben, *The Open: Man and Animal,* trans. Kevin Attell (2002; Stanford: Stanford University Press, 2004), 57. Is not a shoe the fetishist's womblike nesting place? In Heidegger does *Dasein* ever see the open?

humans, are unable to lie or to pretend to pretend, itself serves as another drastic divide between human and animal (as Derrida noted and radically placed in question).[13] If one were to play the game of seeking the elusive, decisive differentiating criterion, one might propose that the human is an animal that generates endless invidious distinctions, especially in the anxiety-ridden, self-serving quest to distinguish itself from other animals. (Or, to put the point somewhat differently, if there is a specific difference between human and animal, we cannot specify it since we "are"—or overly identify with—it in its lability and excess.)[14] The major problem here is not so much

13. An obvious question here is whether humans are simply able to deceive or to pretend to pretend without doing something, however unconscious, that gives them away. A supplementary consideration is put forth by Lacan himself: "What constitutes pretence is that, in the end, you don't know whether it's a pretence or not" (quoted by Slavoj Žižek, "Neighbors and Other Monsters: A Plea for Ethical Violence," in *The Neighbor,* 143). Žižek himself is inclined (in a manner similar to Agamben) to identify "the *differentia specifica* which defines a human being" as "the difference between human and the inhuman excess that is inherent to being-human" (175). With respect to Lacan's view and related issues, see Derrida's "And Say the Animal Responded?" in *Zoontologies: The Question of the Animal in Contemporary Theory and Culture,* ed. Cary Wolfe, trans. David Wills (Minneapolis: University of Minnesota Press, 2002), 121–46. Lacan's version of the *felix culpa* is one more reason why one should not construe lack or loss as constitutive (or as *manque à être*) and thereby conflate it with a transhistorical, anxiety-producing absence or void (*béance*)—a nonlocatable trauma of sorts or a propensity to undergo traumatization that Lacan names the "real"—that humans at a certain level share with other animals, who may also be traumatized and suffer, sometimes at the hands of humans. On this issue, see my "Trauma, Absence, Loss," *Critical Inquiry* 25 (1999): 696–727, a version of which is chap. 2 of *Writing History, Writing Trauma* (Baltimore: Johns Hopkins University Press, 2001).

14. As an epigraph to his thought-provoking *Things Hidden since the Foundation of the World,* trans. Stephen Bann and Michael Metteer (1978; Stanford: Stanford University Press, 1987) René Girard quotes Aristotle's *Poetics* 4: "Man differs from the other animals in his greater aptitude for imitation." In his Socratic-style "dialogue" with his interlocutors (Jean-Michel Oughourlian and Guy Lefort), Girard proceeds to trace in fascinating intricacy the significant role in human culture of mimetic desire, including the ambivalence between model and rival, the conflict between undifferentiated doubles, and the resort to a sacrificial scapegoating mechanism. But he overgeneralizes the undoubted importance of mimetic desire in the attempt to have it reductively "explain" virtually all significant aspects of culture and society, even subordinating the repetition compulsion to it and finding literary works and social (or what he terms "interdividual") relations to "basically say the same thing... bring[ing] all of them back to the same mimetic process" (339). He presents the autonomization of intensified mimetic desire as the very origin of "hominization," culture, and the nexus among violence, eroticism, and the sacred, including scapegoating and sacrificialism, at times in ways that render the latter mere derivatives or appendages of mimetic desire. He also paradoxically combines an extreme variant of secular enlightenment, which presumably demystifies all other religions (and theories) as more or less blindly indentured to the mimetic mechanism, with his own prophetic-apocalyptic "revelation" that declares Christianity to be the only true religion of love that presumably transcends sacrifice, violence, and mimetic rivalry. Indeed for him there are basically in culture only the extreme options of violence and love—the total transcendence of violence in Christian love, on the one hand, and, on the other, the violence of generalized mimetic crisis with its violent (but no longer available) "resolution" in sacrificial scapegoating.

the distinctions (although many if not all of them, in their radically decisive form, might be argued to be specious) but the very desire to postulate them with their invidious functions and consequences, particularly in the attempt to reduce or eliminate the problematic or contestable dimensions of certain human practices.

The paradoxical, complex relations between figuration of the other as raw material (or bare life) and as scapegoated, quasi-sacrificial victim demand sustained attention, for they are often objects of neglect, disavowal, or confusion. They share the crucial function of placing the other-than-human animal, or animality itself, in a separate sphere or category of otherness to which ethical and political considerations do not apply, or at best apply in very reduced form, because the other is either sub- or supra-ethical in status. But they perform this operation in significantly different and seemingly contradictory ways. Without recognizing the tensions generated by this movement, one may unself-consciously oscillate or equivocate between the potentially charged and eventful language of sacrifice and the neutralized and analytically reduced, at times euphemized, language of raw material and mere life—or the comparably subdued or sanitized language of the pest and pest control. Conversely, one may foreclose one of the two discursive practices in favor of the other, at present perhaps with an emphatic, seemingly secular tendency to dismiss the sacrificial as irrelevant and to assert that the animal is (or in modernity has been made into) raw material or mere life adapted to purely human purposes. Still, within the very same sentence, the animal may be presented as sacrificed, utilized, or eliminated as a pest for the good of humans. Similarly, a discriminated-against or persecuted group of humans may be figured as other-than-human animals of an infra- or supra-ethical sort, and responses may oscillate between different linguistic, representational, evaluative, and affective registers. (*Pace* Giorgio Agamben, Nazi discourse about Jews pushes prevalent equivocal tendencies to contradictory extremes, with the Jew figured as a powerful, world-historical, subversive force, a phobic, ritual contaminant, a pest or vermin, and even a rag, piece of refuse, excrement, or, in Agamben's sense, mere life.) It is, of course, on the basis of negative figurations of the animal that one may invoke it in a derogatory fashion in characterizing groups of humans. Typically, in a disavowal of characteristics that internally mark those who scapegoat, along with a simultaneous attempt to reduce internal

---

This variant of an all-or-nothing frame of reference obscures the role of institutions, norms, and practices that mitigate or sublimate violence without utterly transcending it.

anxiety to focalized or determinate fear of a phantasmatic other, groups of humans may even come to be projected beyond humanity and share the fate of other-than-human animals (treated "like" rats, dogs, cattle, pigs, or even wild or savage beasts).[15]

The reduction of the other, including the animal, to the status of raw material involves not attributing qualities to, or recognizing claims of, the other that place normative constraints on its manipulation for human purposes or interests, whether as use or exchange value.[16] At best any limitations are seen as unilateral gifts or (perhaps character-building) normative impositions that humans undertake on their own virtuous, creative, or performative initiative, functioning as more or less gratuitous signs of human good will, uniqueness,

15. In *Coloniser. Exterminer: Sur la guerre et l'État colonial* (Paris: Fayard, 2005) Olivier Le Cour Grandmaison observes that French colonizers in Africa saw sub-Saharan blacks (like American slaves) as comparable to the beast of burden [*bête de somme*] that is "obedient and able to endure hardship... to be domesticated... a 'good negro' capable of being employed inside the house," hence part of a dependable work force (82; my translation). By contrast Arabs (like American Indians) were taken to be more intractable, like wild or savage beasts *(bêtes fauves)*. (The division between black and Arab, however, was not absolute, for the "bad negro" could at times take on the traits of the wild beast, as was the putative case with the rebellious Herero [89]). The jackal, as an animal that could never be tamed, was a favorite reference point, but other beasts and the practices applied to them could also be invoked: "At times 'smoked out like foxes,' in the famous words of Bugeaud, 'Arabs' are always treated as savage animals [*animaux sauvages*] that, once killed, are abandoned after their head has been taken [as a trophy] to certify the success of a victorious tracking" (157; my translation). In metropolitan France, lower classes were also racialized and bestialized, seen as *"'indigènes' de l'intérieur"* (284) in terms similar to those used for Arabs, and military leaders from Algeria (such as Thomas Robert Bugeaud) were instrumental in putting down workers in 1848, resorting at times to means that had been used in the colonies. (Although Le Cour Grandmaison does not dwell on this point, I would note that assimilated elites in the colonies were termed "*les évolués*"—those who had "evolved" under French "civilizing" influences.)

16. It is noteworthy that the U.S. Food and Drug Administration (FDA) requires animal testing of new drugs (as well as testing on human volunteers) before drugs can be marketed. This requirement lessens the significance as well as the market value of alternative modes of testing drugs. For the argument that animal testing does not produce results sufficiently applicable to humans and that alternative methods of testing are both available and more effective, see Jean Swingle Greek and C. Ray Greek, *What Will We Do If We Don't Experiment on Animals? Medical Research for the Twenty-first Century* (Victoria, B.C.: Trafford, 2004). The authors conclude that "very small [genetic] differences between two species will be multiplied exponentially until the two systems are very different in the property being examined, for example drug toxicity" and that society should not continue "to waste resources on misleading experiments on animals" (214). Interestingly, this argument based on genetic difference converges with those stressing similarities, for example, with respect to suffering, to reach comparable conclusions about the undesirability of experimentation on animals. Deborah Blum reports that an analysis by Betsy Todd, citing a 1990 General Accounting Office study, indicates that "51 percent of the 198 drugs approved by the Food and Drug Administration, from 1976 to 1985, caused serious postapproval adverse reactions, including permanent disabilities and deaths." *The Monkey Wars* (New York: Oxford University Press, 1994), 211.

or superiority.[17] Hence other animals are not recognized as limiting human assertiveness but instead taken as passive objects of its dominion, unilateral norms, or program of ethical self-development. What is done to animals is often seen as justified insofar as it brings actual or even hoped-for benefits to humans.[18] At the limit, reduction to raw material, which takes an extreme form in processed meat wherein the animal is converted into the analog of particle board, also entails the nonrecognition of any claims inhering in the other, and not simply projected, granted, or attributed by humans—claims that compete with, and may serve as countervailing forces to, human rights or claims. (I would parenthetically note that social constructivism, not in general but in the radical or extreme form of secular [or postsecular] creationism

17. For one of the more sensitive anthropocentric arguments that construes animals in terms of dependency and uses this view to argue that "the animal side of human nature" itself involves often denied or undervalued dependencies, vulnerabilities, and disabilities, see Alasdair MacIntyre, *Dependent Rational Animals: Why Human Beings Need the Virtues* (Chicago: Open Court, 1999). MacIntyre's argument assists in the questioning of the rashly generalized, dehistoricized assumption that there is simply a zero-sum relation, in terms of either resources or compassion, between a concern for oppressed or dependent humans and for other animals.

18. Hoped-for future applications or benefits are often prominent in the comments of animal researchers discussed in Deborah Blum's *The Monkey Wars.* (Uncritically replicating a common sacrificial frame of reference that in effect begs or suspends ethical questions, Blum conveys, in free indirect reportage, the views of many of her interlocutors: "The animal is being experimented on for ethical reasons, as an acceptable substitute for the human being" [205].) Blum observes that Seymour Levine of Stanford University "discovered... that if he takes adolescent squirrel monkeys—comparable to teenagers [*sic*]—and isolates them for several weeks, he gets a persistent chemical depression [apparently not common in other kinds of monkey], remarkably like the imbalances found in severely depressed humans. The possibilities for testing drugs and other treatments, he thinks, are limitless" (103). The obvious, recurrent issue in such experimentation is whether what will "cure" or work for certain other species or varieties will do the same for all, or even delimited categories of, humans. Moreover, there is the problem that animal research and experimentation, while seeming to have certain successes in the treatment of humans, may also have negative consequences, at times in the very same cases. According to Blum, animal research helped in finding a vaccine for polio as well as for measles and mumps (204), and heart transplants were developed in dogs (205). (Later in the book, she informs the reader that polio research cost the lives of hundreds of thousands of monkeys but also that monkeys not taken for research are often hunted and killed in their native habitats [250ff].) She points out that monkeys carry many viruses that may infect humans. Polio vaccine, grown in monkey kidneys, contained viruses that were suspected to have been a factor in causing AIDS but seemingly proved to be what she terms a "lucky miss" (233), although the progeny of polio-vaccinated mothers may face problems: "In the late 1980s, scientists tracking the life histories of 59,000 pregnant women, all vaccinated with the Salk polio vaccine, found that their offspring had a 13 times higher rate of brain tumors than those who did not receive the vaccine" (228–29). Moreover, serious doubts remain concerning viral transmissions to humans receiving primate organ transplants, including, among many others, Epstein-Barr and SA8 (the baboon version of the deadly B virus, a strain of herpes) (236). Thus far certain major diseases are still very much with us despite years of research and experimentation on animals (cancer, AIDS, Parkinson's, Alzheimer's, and so forth).

that makes the specifically human the quasi-divine "endowing" source of all meaning and value in the world, may unintentionally be an ultimate outcome as well as dubious facilitator of this reduction. And an unqualified emphasis on the excessive asymmetrical gift, pure act, or supererogatory event of grace may also induce the nonrecognition of limits to human or superhuman assertiveness or even passive-aggressive "being" with respect to other animals.)

Keeping in mind these general considerations, I would like now to focus on some figures and texts that may help to bring greater specificity to my account. Those I discuss seem to be becoming part and parcel of an emerging canon in the humanities that provides reference points for discussion and debate on the relation of the human and the animal. Heidegger provided an extensive critique of the "world picture" in which the other is enframed within a *Gestell* that makes of it an instrumentality or stock for exclusively human purposes or interests, although his valuable critique is itself jeopardized by his appeal to a sometimes exclusionary notion of a hierarchy of beings linked to language as a differential, decisive criterion whereby one may assert that the animal is constitutively lacking or at least "poor" in world (*weltarm*).[19] Giorgio Agamben has extended the Heideggerian critique (and overlaid it with Benjaminian motifs) in the direction of concepts of the state of exception and of naked, mere, or bare life, which he sees as crucial in understanding extreme or limit events and experiences in the modern world. In my judgment, his thought-provoking approach harbors problematic elements on which I shall exert pressure, especially since his views have had such pronounced resonance in important critical circles.[20] Indeed, in view of Agamben's status as a widely recognized major modern thinker, critical scrutiny of his approach to the vital question of the human and the animal, which connects with many other dimensions of his thought, has a more general interest, especially for

19. See "The Origin of the Work of Art" in *Poetry, Language, Thought* (New York: Harper and Row, 1971), 15–87. See also my discussion in chapter 5.

20. See, for example, the approach to Agamben and his views on the animal in Santner's *On Creaturely Life* and Žižek, Santner, and Reinhard's *The Neighbor.* Santner's approach to Agamben, both problematic and thought provoking, should be read as a valuable counterpart and "countervoice" to my argument. A crucial question bears on the ethical and political possibilities and limits in Santner's triangulation of Agamben, Badiou, and Žižek, involving what Santner terms the "deanimation of the undead" as a messianic but purportedly nonredemptive act related to loving openness to the neighbor as uncanny and possibly "monstrous" other, the valorization of attentive "melancholic immersion" in "creaturely life," and an affirmation of "miraculous" epiphanies. In brief: What is the potential of a politics of "neighborly" love and miracles? In "Miracles Happen: Benjamin, Rosenzweig, Freud, and the Matter of the Neighbor," Santer's contribution to *The Neighbor* (76–133), one of his most contestable moves is to place Freud and psychoanalysis in a German-Jewish tradition of thought, involving "psychotheological" tendencies and including such figures as Rosenzweig and Benjamin as well as Agamben.

the intellectual or cultural historian with a concern for the present state and possibilities of cultural criticism and critical theory.

In *Remnants of Auschwitz,* Agamben applies the concept of bare life to the *Muselmann,* the most abject concentration camp victim during the Holocaust, who he contends was the instantiation of naked or mere life and thus the transhistorical abject image of everyone, at least in his postapocalyptic image of the contemporary scene wherein the exception becomes the rule.[21] Here one might suggest a somewhat "Žižekian" reading of Fritz Lang's film *M* (1931) that would partially support Agamben's argument. In it a child molester and serial killer, played by Peter Lorre, is hunted and prosecuted by fellow criminals who are impervious to the killer's appeals to monstrous inner forces beyond his control. They condemn him and, in so doing, affirm that, even in the criminal milieu, the exception has not become the rule and that the child molester has gone too far in transgressing limits. In a sense the "ordinary" criminals affirm a normativity, even a normality, that they refuse to see as abolished or unsettled by the acts of the Lorre character who, at the film's end, becomes a cringingly abject and seemingly persecuted figure. One may argue that in important respects the criminal underworld disavows the other within—in a late-Weimar context where the exception was indeed often becoming the rule in terms of street violence, judicial irregularity, routine scandals, and political disorder. For Agamben, the contemporary situation appears to be altogether comparable, and M's world morphs into the modern world writ large. In accordance with this perspective, it does not seem necessary to provide a more qualified understanding of the extent to which different historical situations more or less approximate the state of exception. Late-Weimar Germany and even the Third Reich seem to become not only extreme instances, possible developments, or even clear-and-present dangers of modern sociopolitical and cultural life but the very prototype of modernity in general.

In the context of contemporary American culture and politics, one may well argue that there have indeed been dubious attempts to invoke a state of exception to justify recent practices and policies, including those at Guantánamo and Abu Ghraib, along with the so-called unitary executive that enables the U.S. president to override "checks and balances" and the separation of powers.[22] One may also point to the tendency to collapse the

21. See Giorgio Agamben, *Remnants of Auschwitz: The Witness and the Archive,* trans. Daniel Heller-Roazen (New York: Zone Books, 1999).

22. For a pointed analysis and critique of the "unitary executive," see Elizabeth Drew, "Bush's Power Grab," *New York Review of Books* 53, no. 11 (June 22, 2006): 10–15. The unitary

distinctions between combatant and civilian and between the front line and the "homeland"—a tendency exacerbated by the belief that terrorism is everywhere and warrants every manner of combating it.[23] But Agamben goes well beyond such historical and critical points and engages in sweeping generalizations about modernity as a gray zone of indistinction or shock-infested epoch of accomplished nihilism. Hence he can write:

> Today, at a distance of nearly seventy years [from Heidegger's 1934–35 course on Hölderlin, a temporal marker indicating the obvious importance of Heidegger for Agamben], it is clear for anyone who is not in absolutely bad faith that there are no longer historical tasks that can be taken on by, or even simply assigned to, men. . . . The only task that still seems to retain some seriousness is the assumption of the burden—and the "total management"—of biological life, that is, of the very animality of man. Genome, global economy, and humanitarian ideology are the three united faces of this process in which posthistorical humanity seems to take on its own physiology as its last, impolitical mandate.[24]

---

executive, as well as the idea of the president as "the decider," recall Carl Schmitt's notions of the indivisible sovereign and decisionism. See, for example, *Political Theology: Four Chapters on the Concept of Sovereignty,* trans. George Schwab (1922; Cambridge: MIT Press, 1985).

23. One may well argue that there are signs of a clear-and-present danger in contemporary America not restricted to the cases of Guantánamo and Abu Ghraib or even the more general use (and evasiveness about the use) of torture on terrorists or suspected terrorists. See, for example, Matthew Rothschild, *You Have No Rights: Stories of America in an Age of Repression* (New York: The New Press, 2007). In an article in *The Progressive* 72, no. 3 (March 2008) available online at http://www.progressive.org/mag_rothschild0308), Rothschild discusses InfraGard, an association linking private industry to the FBI and the Department of Homeland Security. At present some 23,000 representatives of private industry (including, according to its website, 350 of the *Fortune* 500) participate in this rapidly growing group whose mission is to provide information to the government and to take action in the event of martial law, allegedly including permission to employ deadly force. In effect, an elect group of private citizens from the corporate sector have been deputized as informants in an association whose clandestine activities are beyond the Freedom of Information Act under the "trade secrets" exemption. One has here an instance of paranoid anxiety about terror leading to the creation of an entity that itself poses a threat to what it is presumably supposed to protect.

24. Agamben, *The Open: Man and Animal,* 76–77. See as well his comparable assertions in *State of Exception,* trans. Kevin Attell (2003; Chicago: University of Chicago Press, 2005) in which the unqualified elaboration of the prevalence of the state of exception ignores counterforces and culminates in a vague apocalyptic call to ill-defined "purity" of word and action: "The only truly political action . . . is that which severs the nexus between violence and law. . . . We will then have before us a 'pure' law, in the sense in which Benjamin speaks of a 'pure' language and a 'pure' violence. To a word that does not bind, that neither commands nor prohibits anything, but says only itself, would correspond an action as pure means, which shows only itself, without any relation to an end. And, between the two, not a lost original state, but only the use and human praxis that the powers of law and myth had sought to capture in the state of exception" (88). In his strong endorsement of Agamben's approach that nonetheless

According to Agamben's "posthistorical," indeed postapocalyptic view, the attempt to overcome the heritage of slavery or apartheid, for example, would apparently not count as a historical task. And critiques or movements contesting forms of genetic manipulation and globalization would be insignificant. I think his rather blurred and hyperbolic approach both alerts one to dangerous developments (there is indeed something to what he asserts) and threatens to repeat or misconstrue them more than it provides critical perspective in carefully understanding and questioning them.

In *The Open: Man and Animal,* Agamben extends his earlier reflections on the more or less unmediated conjunction of mere life, sovereignty, and open possibility. There is of course an initial and perhaps insuperable problem in attempting to formulate Agamben's "argument" since he typically proceeds, in a series of fragmented sections, by way of exegesis, indirection, allusion, and paradox. Indeed, he seems to relish aporia, enigmatic anecdotes, dehistoricized erudition, and unexplicated associations.[25] And he goes

---

seems to resolve its ambiguous or opaquely enigmatic turns, Žižek affirms "those magic moments in which effective universality makes its violent appearance in the guise of a shattering ethico-political *act.*" *Welcome to the Desert of the Real* (London: Verso, 2002), 66. However, Žižek's notion of the "violent" act is not altogether clear. Along with the unwillingness of the "refuseniks" in Israel to serve in the occupied territories, he mentions the rather different case of De Gaulle's initiative in 1940 (see pp. 113 and 153). These examples certainly involved risk and challenged their respective contexts but were not "pure," magical, self-referential, or absolute "acts" approximating apocalyptic-messianic leaps into the "open" or "performative" creations ex nihilo.

25. Hence we learn, for example, that in 1924 Walter Benjamin stayed in Jakob von Uexküll's villa on Capri (39) or that the latter wrote a preface to Houston Chamberlain's *Foundations of the Nineteenth Century,* which somehow marks a proximity between Friedrich Ratzel's theses on *Lebensraum* and Nazi geopolitics (42–43). There is in general an accentuated problem of "voice" in Agamben, who often writes in a generalized free indirect style. In *The Open,* a book of less than one-hundred pages, what Agamben is arguing becomes clear, more or less, only about page seventy-five, after which his style at times modulates into an apodictic assertiveness. For a brilliant defense and enactment of an allusive, paratactic style, see Agamben's *Stanzas: Word and Phantasm in Western Culture,* trans. Ronald L. Martinez (Minneapolis: University of Minnesota Press, 1993). In a turn to postromantic irony, Agamben asserts: "Criticism is in fact nothing other than the process of its own ironic self-negation: precisely a 'self-annihilating nothing,' or a 'god that self-destructs,' according to Hegel's prophetic, if ill-willed, definition" (xvi). Indeed, for Agamben, "there is strictly speaking perhaps only a single book that deserves to be called critical: the *Ursprüng des deutschen Trauerspiel* (The origin of German tragic drama) of Walter Benjamin" (xv). Agamben proceeds to provide, among other things, a philosophical, erudite genealogy of melancholy in its relation to the phantasm, love, and loss that might also be read as a self-genealogy with respect to his other work. Without postulating a simple binary, I think that Agamben's insistent, postromantic mode of sublime utopianism, daring the impossible and in quest of the unobtainable, has different valences in art or in certain forms of poetically inflected philosophy than it has, however differentially, in historical understanding, politics, and ethics. In ethicopolitical endeavors, it postulates an impossible horizon (or *à-venir* in Derrida's sense) that both motivates action and indicates the necessary yet significantly

simultaneously in at least two directions. On the one hand, he repeatedly discusses and seems to affirm the absence or lack of an essence, nature, or vocation in the human. Here he problematizes the distinction between human and animal. It is, it appears, the questionable "anthropological machine" that seeks a radical divide between human and animal only to generate aporias and produce a state of exception or zone of indistinction between human and animal. The machine falters when it attempts to explain the origin of the human from the animal, for then it moves in circles whereby it has to assume what it attempts to derive, for example, language (36–37). On the other hand, Agamben himself seems to assume or require a radical divide between human and animal and to envision the alternative to this divide, or perhaps the nature of the abyssal, alluring divide itself, as a zone of indistinction between human and animal.

There is a sense in which, in Agamben's own discourse, animals in their diversity are not figured as complex, differentiated living beings but instead function as an abstracted philosophical topos similar in certain respects to (perhaps even functioning as a displacement of) the *Musulmann.* (To paraphrase Freud, "Where the *Musulmann* was in *Remnants of Auschwitz,* the animal in *The Open* now seems to be.") Both "the" animal and "the" *Muselmann* function as avatars of the radically "other" (albeit, expectably, an other that is also within the self). And both are discussed in extremely decontextualized, at times homogenized, terms. They also serve as vehicles for a conception of modernity as a posthistorical age of accomplished or completed nihilism marked by the reduction of being to mere or naked life, a kind of ground zero or *Stunde null* of existence. What might possibly be seen as a form of postsecular negative theology in extremis enables Agamben to put forward an empty utopianism of pure, unlimited possibility that transvalues utter

---

different limits of any realized form of justice. But it should not serve as the only standard of critical thought and practice, which must also engage in sustained, historically informed, if contestable, inquiry into the actual, the plausible, and the realistically possible. In relation to certain problems (such as the relation between the human and the animal), it may at times be misleading. With reference to politics, one may note the necessary tension between two statements that follow within a sentence of one another in Max Weber's "Politics as a Vocation": "Politics is a strong and slow boring of hard boards... man would not have attained the possible unless time and again he had reached out for the impossible." *From Max Weber: Essays in Sociology,* ed. H. H. Gerth and C. Wright Mills (New York: Oxford University Press, 1958), 128. Agamben typically reaches for the impossible, if not the utterly opaque, without the "strong and slow boring of hard boards." See also Ernesto Laclau's pointed critique of Agamben's political philosophy, "Bare Life or Social Indeterminacy?" in *Giorgio Agamben: Sovereignty and Life,* ed. Matthew Colarco and Steven De Caroli (Stanford: Stanford University Press, 2007), 11–22, as well as the exchange in Judith Butler, Ernesto Laclau, and Slavoj Žižek, *Contingency, Hegemony, Universality: Contemporary Dialogues on the Left* (London: Verso, 2000).

disempowerment into a valorized *désoeuvrement* or posthistorical, seemingly anomic, worklessness as well as a form of learned ignorance. What is of general interest and concern here is the linkage among an extremely negative if not nihilistic conception of existing social, political, and cultural reality, blank utopian longing, and desire for re-enchantment of the world.[26]

Agamben's all-or-nothing paradoxicalism relishes the conjunction of extreme, unmediated opposites—an orientation that attains its apogee in the ecstatic, "extimate" vision of the indistinct human-animal relation as marked by both a radical divide and (although in a somewhat indefinite key—one both suggested and negated by Heidegger) an imperceptible intimacy. A pole of one striking opposition is an image of blissful immanence in "the hieroglyph of a new in-humanity" to be found in both Benjamin and certain Gnostic postapocalyptic beliefs in which "something for which we perhaps have no name and which is neither animal nor man settles in between nature and humanity and holds itself in the mastered relation, in the saved night" (83). The other pole, seemingly different from immanence and any process of settling or intimacy, is the "central emptiness," gap, or radical divide in which "man" is to risk himself, in what might seem to be an utterly nihilated or evacuated transcendence—a virtual space created by a god that has died without leaving a trace, except for a longing for transcendence itself, however null and void. For Agamben, one should not seek new or more authentic articulations between Being and beings or, for that matter, between humans and other animals. Rather, moving beyond Heidegger's ontological difference, one seeks "to show the central emptiness, the hiatus that—within man—separates man and animal, and to risk ourselves in this emptiness: the suspension of the suspension, Shabbat of both animal and man." What this "central emptiness," functioning as a great divide, might be, itself remains a void that is nonetheless an object of limitless desire. The presumably risky leap into it, or "suspension of the suspension," somehow opens onto an "otherwise than being" that is asserted to be "an existing, real thing that

26. An important collection on Agamben came to my attention after the completion of this book. See *Politics, Metaphysics, and Death: Essays on Giorgio Agamben's Homo Sacer*, ed. Andrew Norris (Durham: Duke University Press, 2005). Included in this collection is Agamben's "State of Exception" (284–97), a concise and lucid exposition of the key notion of the state of exception, including a thought-provoking analysis of the exchange between Carl Schmitt and Walter Benjamin. See also *Giorgio Agamben: Sovereignty and Life* in which Matthew Colarco's approach to the human-animal relation, in his "Jamming the Anthropological Machine" (163–79), may be compared and contrasted with my own. This collection reprints a version of my "Approaching Limit Events: Siting Agamben," 126–62, which may also be found in *History in Transit: Experience, Identity, Critical Theory* (Ithaca: Cornell University Press, 2004), chap. 4.

has gone beyond the difference between being and beings" (92). The vanishing point at which the obscure opposites meet would seem to be the longing for *désoeuvrement* or radical disempowerment—a *Gelassenheit* beyond *Gelassenheit*—that stops action, history, projects, and the "anthropological machine" and purportedly holds out the promise of pure possibility as the most open of the open.

A further enigmatic conjunction in Agamben is between pure possibility and the reduction of being to mere or naked life, for it is the emergence of mere naked life in accomplished nihilism that simultaneously generates, as a kind of miraculous antibody or creation ex nihilo, pure possibility or utterly blank utopianism not limited by the constraints of the past or by normative structures of any sort. Mere or naked life (under the control of a sovereign power) seems equivocally to be both the object of Agamben's critique and, paradoxically enough, the necessary if not welcome condition for his own sense of pure possibility and unlimited, empty utopian aspiration. One thus has the *mysterium coniunctionis* of an all-time low and an unimaginable high. Indeed for Agamben the historical condition of accomplished or completed nihilism in which the post-Auschwitz world presumably finds itself is an utterly decontextualizing or traumatizing situation—a state of exception or anomic, dehistoricized aporia-ridden interregnum—that is marked by the extremes of absolute sovereign power, mere life, and pure possibility.

I have intimated that, in a manner perhaps typical of Agamben's vision of philosophy as poetically allusive yet conceptually rarefied theory, *The Open* has virtually nothing specific to say about other-than-human animals or their lives. His interacting insights and blindnesses track those of Heidegger, and Agamben even seems at points to accept the division between *Dasein* that worlds or, especially through language, opens a world—more precisely, enters "the essential domain of the conflict between disconcealment and concealment" (60)—and the animal's exclusion from this "domain" because of its enclosure or captivity in an environment.[27] The allusion to Heidegger's politics is in terms of his interest in the polis and his notion of strife in "The Origin of the Work of Art" (72). (The difficult, fraught issue of Heidegger's relation and that of his thought to Nazism remains *hors texte.*) Agamben

27. One may note that Agamben's prose, like Heidegger's which it emulates, is itself quite "animal-like" when it addresses the supposed difference of the animal, that is, it is not accessible (*offenbar*) or is at most "open in an inaccessibility and an opacity" (55). I would further note that humans might be seen in terms approximating Heidegger's view of the animal (which lacks world-disclosure or even confrontation with existential conditions) when they are presented as living fully within a *habitus,* functioning on the basis of an unquestioned environmental set of practices, and, even more so, when they are locked within a repetition compulsion.

further complicates Heidegger's view of the animal in a tangled discussion in which he to some extent approximates man and animal by having man be uncannily open to the closed or concealed. Hence he quotes approvingly Heidegger's gnomic assertion that "this announcing pointing toward that which makes Dasein authentically possible in its possibilities is a *necessary compulsion [Hinzwingen] toward the singular extremity of this originary making possible*" (67). (Here somewhat less mesmerizing but still difficult references might be to Freud's notion of the unconscious as an uncanny openness to the closed, concealed, or enigmatic and to Sartre's supplementary idea that "man" is *disponible* and condemned to be free.)

Agamben manifestly wants to outdo or go beyond Heidegger by intensifying or perhaps leaving behind *Gelassenheit* (or letting Being be) and instead affirming a letting of what is beyond or outside of Being be. The paradoxical kernel as well as the thought-provoking appeal of his thought is perhaps best formulated in a comment he makes about Heidegger's 1929–30 course on "The Fundamental Concepts of Metaphysics"—a reference that might pari passu be applied to Agamben:

> For in the abyss—and, at the same time, in the peculiar proximity—that the sober prose of the course opens up between the animal and man, not only does *animalitas* become utterly unfamiliar and appear as "that which is most difficult to think," but *humanitas* also appears as something ungraspable and absent, suspended as it is between a "not-being-able-to-remain" and a"not-being-able-to-leave-its-place." (50–51)

Although Agamben's insistence on the caesura, gap, or "open" between man and animal, especially within man, resonates with Heidegger's insistence on the passage from the animal's poverty in world to *Dasein*'s worlding, Agamben's own most powerful, if extreme, countervailing formulations reinscribe movements in Heidegger's thought: "*Dasein* is simply an animal that has learned to become bored; it has awakened *from* its own captivation *to* its own captivation. The awakening of the living being to its own being-captivated, the anxious and resolute opening to a not-open, is the human" (70).

Agamben's evident interest is in "awakened" human vacuity or paradoxically abyssal possibility rather than in the lives of other animals, their treatment at the hands of humans, or the way their behavior and relation to humans may itself have enigmatic dimensions that place in question any radical divide. The only other-than-human creature Agamben discusses at length in a fascinating and fascinated manner is the tick. It is noteworthy that Agamben's extended discussion of Heidegger immediately follows and perhaps echoes that of the tick, and he is both intimately close to Heidegger's thought and at times struggles to free himself from its captivating embrace (at the end of the book even seeming to invoke Benjamin as a deus ex machina or distancing lever with respect to Heidegger). He indicates that the work of Jakob von Uexküll, from which he draws for the analysis of the tick, was itself significant for Heidegger's notion of the captivation or captivity of the animal in its environment in contrast to *Dasein*'s disclosive worlding and relation to the open. The tick out-vampires the vampire as a blood-sucking creature with minimal sensory attachment to its prey whose vital fluid it continues to ingest until it falls to the ground and deposits its eggs, hence existing and perishing in a kind of all-consuming, compulsively choreographed *Liebestod*. For Agamben, the tick is "immediately united" to its minimalist environment "in an intense and passionate relationship the likes of which we might never find in the relations that bind man to his apparently much richer world" (47). The tick in a sense is as close as one gets to a purely absorbed and immanent relation to the world.[28] Yet Agamben's reading of Benjamin seems to convert the latter into a kind of sublime, diaphanous, ticklike being whose vision of a beatific union with nature, in a noncoincident "immediate constellation," is epitomized in "sexual fulfillment" (83). While never negating this unmediated vision of reconciliation with animal nature, Agamben moves, as I have indicated, to the notion of a "central emptiness," a radical divide or caesura between the human and the animal within "man" that, I think, misleadingly pinpoints or fixates less locatable sources of unsettlement and uncanniness in existence. One could redescribe Agamben's "central emptiness" as an insufficiently situated version of transhistorical, structural, or existential trauma that, in Agamben's account, may well induce an evasion or misconstruction of specific historical, social, and political problems, including the status and use of the animal in society (as well as differing regimes and conceptions of political authority, not all of which can be reduced to the problematic of absolute sovereignty).[29] Or, to put it metaphorically, in Agamben there is still

28. In a quizzical manner, Agamben refers to the puzzling, unexplained reference by Uexküll to a seemingly "undead" tick in a sleep-like state, artificially isolated from its environment and kept "alive" for eighteen years under laboratory conditions (47).

29. Agamben asserts: "The juridical system of the West [*sic*] appears as a double structure, formed by two heterogeneous yet coordinated elements: one that is normative and juridical in the strict sense (which we can for convenience inscribe under the rubric *potestas*) and one that is anomic and metajuridical (which we can call by the name *auctoritas*)" (*State of Exception*, 85–86). This formulation goes in the direction of the aporia between normativity and anomie and, in early Benjaminian fashion, sees legal order and normativity as "always already in the process of ruin and decay" (86). The "machine, with its empty center," which is based on this aporia, has, for Agamben, "continued to function almost without interruption from World War One, through fascism and National Socialism, and up to our own time" (86–87). This

at least at times a Grand Canyon between the human and the animal, but now it is shrouded in mist and inhabited by an invitingly spectral creature, a coming communal being beyond Being whose postapocalyptic "tock" may, for all we know, return us to the world of the tick.

One may note here what Agamben does not thematize: the relation of his thought to trauma. For he assumes a totally posttraumatic as well as postapocalyptic condition of the world that is, at the same time, anomically open and closed—open to all radically contingent possibilities and closed in upon itself as mere life.[30] The misleading description of the animal as captivated by its environment might also seem to describe, in displaced and somewhat disguised or modified form, the condition of disarmingly traumatized, disoriented humans, stunned or reduced to a benumbed (yet also manic) passivity and fatalistically caught up in compulsive repetition. Indeed, the Heideggerian notion, reinscribed by Agamben, that boredom is the "human" phenomenon closest to what Heidegger discusses as the captivity (*Benommenheit*) of the animal might more readily be applied to the symptom and to boredom when it is symptomatic of depression and restlessness (in both human and other animals, for other-than-human animals seem most prone to anxious, restlessly agitated boredom—and thus on Heideggerian grounds most like *Dasein*—when held in captivity by humans).[31] The blind hope for a contentless utopia might also be read as the desperate phantasm of an empathically traumatized, or at least rhetorically attuned (*bestimmt*), postromantic visionary with an often unchecked penchant for hyperbole and an aesthetic of the sublime.

It is, moreover, unclear how Agamben's view bears on a nonsentimentalizing concern for other animals or a critique of humanism as itself concealing a scapegoat mechanism that misleadingly condenses anxiety, projects it outward, reductively names or focalizes its source, and excludes or even

---

view, reminiscent of the notion of "totalitarian democracy" prevalent in the 1960s, creates a sense of inevitability, along with extreme disempowerment, and downplays attempts to qualify, divide, and problematize sovereignty in forms of constitutional democracy.

30. This is figured in *Remnants of Auschwitz* as a post-Auschwitz condition in which one paradoxically lives on after the end awaiting another apocalypse that may herald or perhaps coincide with the "open."

31. See especially Agamben's discussion in *The Open: Man and Animal* (57–62). Agamben does not indicate that Heidegger himself recognizes flexibility in the "captivity" of the animal in its environment. But this point might not modify Agamben's approach in that this flexibility in Heidegger operates in a rather narrow range and does not lead to a basic rethinking of the relation of animals to their habitats and to other animals. It distinguishes Heidegger's understanding of the animal from the Cartesian machine but is not made to question the radical divide between human and animal.

victimizes animals (including the animal in the human). Despite his insistent desire to avoid anthropomorphism and even to outdo Heidegger in undoing the "anthropological machine," there is a crucial sense in which Agamben's perspective remains insistently anthropocentric in its fixation on an apocalyptic or postapocalyptic idea of "man's" existence as both radically disempowered and blankly open to all possibilities. The all-too-open possibility in Agamben's argument is that the animal or, more precisely, animality (or perhaps postanimality) may once more be situated as radically other, this time in the service of a posthuman, postsecular, quasi-transcendental notion of an abyssal leap into a radical divide, caesura, or "open." The approach taken in *The Open* does not itself open onto a possibly critical and politically pertinent inquiry into what Agamben's thought might be taken to invite: the question of the extent to which certain animals, employed in factory farming or experimentation, may be seen in terms of the concept of bare or naked, unprotected life.[32]

The relation of *The Open* to a sociopolitically and ethically pertinent critique of the use and abuse of other-than-human animals—and even of the animal in the human—remains at best an open question. It is also unclear to what extent Agamben is questioning the radical divide between human and animal or reinforcing it, in however paradoxical a manner. For what is obscured in at least one prominent if not dominant dimension of Agamben's approach, culminating in a turn to a "central emptiness" dividing humanity and animality, is the way the human being is always already a compromise formation or hybrid traversed by multiple fault lines, anxieties, and possibilities that must be negotiated and cannot be unified by a division or border, however indistinct or "open," between human and animal (or speaking being and living being). The danger in Agamben is the reduction of multiple, not readily localizable openings (or "opens") in humans in order to arrive at a pathos-charged putative massive divide or abyss between human and animal

32. It is also significant that Marx and the critical historical analysis of capitalism do not constitute significant reference points for Agamben. Hence in *The Open* he does not discuss the commodification of relations between humans and animals along with the effects of the insertion of animals and nature more generally within the commodity system. (The phenomenon of canned hunting [or fenced-in reserves where hunters in effect shoot animals as if they were fish in a barrel and may even be given their money back if they do not get a kill], along with internet hunting [where one sights an animal, pushes a button, witnesses a kill, and is sent a trophy], intensifies the question of how animals are treated and the role of commodification in that sometimes callous treatment.) If there are dimensions of marxism with which Agamben's thought might seem to resonate, it is not so much the analysis of the historical constraints and situational possibilities of capitalism but instead Marx's own more hyperbolic indictments, messianic inclinations, and blankly utopian aspirations.

in "man." (A related danger is slippage from the recognition of displaced religious and theological motifs in "modernity," which should be subject to careful and critical scrutiny, to a relatively uninhibited, insufficiently discriminating, even politicized, desire for "postsecular" re-enchantment or at least [post]apocalyptic re-visioning of the world.) Moreover, the differences between and among animals—as well as the proximities and distances between humans and other animals—are more diverse and significant than any megadivide between (or foundational trauma separating) human and animal, whether within man or between humans and other animals. (To put the point in somewhat misleading graphic terms, one should not envision the human and the animal as two circles that are either separated by a gap/divide or intersecting with a shared portion forming a zone of indistinction. Rather the two are superimposed like tectonic plates with multiple, variable, unpredictable, even seismic movements between—and within—them. Or to formulate the point in terms Agamben's thought might itself be read to invite: the human and the animal are always on an undecidable threshold with respect to one another—a threshold that is being continually contested and negotiated.) And the differences within and among humans, ranging from genocidal violence or victimization to trust and mutual aid, might also seem to be more significant than any human-animal divide, even if the latter is paradoxically and at times confusingly conjoined (as in Agamben) with an incommensurable notion of intimacy or "peculiar proximity."[33]

33. For Santner the crucial divide between human and animal is what he terms signifying stress, bound up with the (cringing or abject) subjection to the "inhuman" yet all-too-human excess and drive-destiny of transhistorical structural trauma (the Lacanian real or death drive). Indeed it is significant that the very notion of "creaturely life" serves as a "postsecular" way of radically distinguishing the human from the animal. However, like Agamben and with particular reference to the work of W. G. Sebald, Santner also paradoxically sees an uncanny proximity of the human and the animal when animals are subjected by humans to conditions of exceptional stress—indeed he even finds creaturely life "at the intersection of human and animal dementia" in a zone where human and animal are "abandoned to a state of exception" (*On Creaturely Life,* 145–46). He refers to the Sebald-narrator's statement in *Austerlitz* that "the only animal which has remained lingering in my memory is the raccoon"—a captured raccoon in a cage caught up in a compulsively repetitive gesture of "washing the same piece of apple over and over again, as if it hoped that all this washing, which went far beyond any reasonable thoroughness, would help to escape the unreal world in which it had arrived, so to speak, through no fault of its own" (quoted, 144). One overall difficulty in Santner's approach flows in good part from his attempted triangulation of Agamben, Badiou, and Žižek, especially via Saint Paul as the Benjaminian, messianic, militant, hunchbacked dwarf of inner-light psychotheology, who secretly pulls the strings of historical materialism (*The Neighbor,* 125–33). Santer himself criticized this difficulty in his earlier book, *Stranded Objects: Mourning, Memory, and Film in Postwar Germany* (Ithaca, Cornell University Press, 1990, esp. 19): what I have referred to in terms of the tendency to subsume specific social or historical problems in a structural, transhistorical level of analysis rather than to relate the two in a critical manner. For example, the *Musulmann*

The posthumanism or nonhumanism that Agamben seeks might be better served by a more differential, complex understanding of a field of distinctions, differences, proximities, voids, enigmas, wonderments, uncanny twists, and possibilities that cannot be condensed into a human-animal divide or "central emptiness," whether within "man" or between humans and other animals. Indeed it may be basically misleading to conceive the relationship between human and animal on the model of a foundational trauma, however weakly reminiscent of the Fall and the *felix culpa* of original sin that requires some redemptive act of grace or, as in Agamben, some postredemptive, nonetheless ecstatic leap that may even be confused with a political initiative.[34]

---

becomes an example or perhaps exemplar of Agamben's *homo sacer* and is analogized to Kafka's Gregor Samsa as an instantiation of cringing signifying excess (*The Neighbor,* 100–103). This decontextualized reading both occludes the historical situation of *Musulmänner,* including the role of Nazis in reducing them to an extreme condition, and simultaneously construes victims in one-sided, analytically reduced fashion. (For Nazis, Jewish victims were not simply *homo sacer* in Agamben's sense but both something close to that "banned" figure of mere life and, in a confused, paradoxical manner, the polluting, world-historically conspiratorial objects of quasi-sacrificial processes of purification and redemption. Moreover, in his own distinctive way, Gregor Samsa is both pest and a being whose death is experienced in a quasi-sacrificial manner as liberating or even redemptive by his family, as is evident in the closing scenes of the novella.) The world Santner presents is by and large one of extreme abjection, traumatization, and nonsensical "humor" or peculiarity (*On Creaturely Life,* 146–48) from which the only release is "miraculous."

34. It is noteworthy that, in H. G. Wells's 1896 novel *The Island of Doctor Moreau* (New York: Dover, 1996), the uncanny attempt is indeed made to traumatize animals into becoming hybrid humans by experimentally combining "signifying stress" with torture, but should this extreme effort be taken *tout court* as emblematic of *la condition humaine*? Wells's remarkable novel combines elements of the Gothic tale, the horror story, the detective story, and of course science fiction (or its semblance), along with the themes of repeated traumatization, scapegoating, colonization, misogyny, and experimentation on "lower" forms of life. And the arguments in it, especially those of Doctor Moreau, are repeated, at times uncannily, in justifications for later research. Moreau's "Beast People," the products of his experiments, are a composite of "vivisected" animals and the colonized. They also incorporate aspects of people of color and Jews (or perhaps Semites in general) whose mode of prayer is imitated by Moreau's creatures. While Prendick, the narrator, is himself an amalgam of conventional prejudice and horrified reaction once certain limits are crossed, Moreau is the transgressive experimenter situated, in his own mind, beyond ethical concerns. In his striking, indeed sublime apologia, Moreau appeals to the scientific research imperative, aesthetics, and "religious" or "spiritual" considerations, all related to the desire to transcend the body and its limits. He presumably chooses "by chance" the human form as his combinatory center of reference in experiments, yet also because "there is something in the human form that appeals to the artistic turn of mind more powerfully than any animal shape can" (54). He spells out the experimental method of question and answer leading endlessly to new questions and experimental answers, and he sings the praises of "intellectual passion" and "intellectual desire." He expostulates: "The thing before you is no longer an animal, a fellow-creature, but a problem.... I wanted—it was the only thing I wanted—to find out the extreme limit of plasticity in a living shape" (56). Recognizing no limits to experimentation, Moreau denigrates sympathetic concern with the body in pain because pain is only of the body and hence a "materialist" affair (54)—"the mark of the beast from which

Agamben himself takes leave of his reader with a paradox-laden, posthistorical, (post)apocalyptic, "beyond-beyond" gesture ("beyond both knowing and not knowing, beyond both disconcealing and concealing, beyond both being and the nothing" [91]), a gesture that points to an indistinct "figure of the 'great ignorance'" in which "living beings can sit at the messianic banquet of the righteous" without historical tasks yet undertaking a supposedly "unprecedented inquiry into the practico-political mystery of separation" (92).[35]

J. M. Coetzee seems not to know Agamben's work, but there are at least certain affinities between Coetzee and Derrida that invite a reading of the former with the latter's work serving as a significant subtext to the novels.[36] In any event, like some of Derrida's own later texts, Coetzee's *Lives of Animals* has become another significant reference point in the discussion of the

---

they [the Beast People] came" (55). He needs the "bath of pain" to conduct his transfigurative experiments and "burn out all the animal" (59). From his radically transcendental (yet also remorselessly naturalistic) perspective, "pain and pleasure—they are only for us, only so long as we wriggle in the dust" (55). Moreau's method of experimentation in converting other animals into variegated "Beast People" involves their systematic traumatization as objects of repeated violence, but it also inculcates into them categorical laws which they chant while swaying: "Not to go on all-Fours; *that* is the Law. Are we not Men?" (43). The "Laws" include: "Not to suck up Drink," "Not to eat Flesh or Fish," "Not to claw Bark of Trees," and "Not to chase after other Men," whose rhythmic recitation is followed by the inevitable question: "Are we not Men?"—a question whose referent is destabilized in the narrative. The "positive" side of the Law makes a dreaded divinity of Moreau, the "maker," "wounder," and "healer" who lives in "the House of Pain" (43). With the apocalyptic end of Moreau and his hellish island paradise, as well as the "regressive," "generalized animalism" and "dwindling shreds" of humanity of its inhabitants (first appearing in females who "began to disregard the injunction of decency" [96–97]), the narrator, marked by Moreau and showing genocidal inclinations toward what he now refers to (yet also resembles) as the "Beast Monsters," manages to get back to England. He is disoriented, even feeling at times that he too "was not a reasonable creature, but only an animal tormented with some strange disorder in its brain," yet seeking peace and quiet with "wise books" and "experiments in chemistry"! He concludes his narrative, "in hope and solitude," invoking the equivocal, seemingly illusory, even eerily Moreau-like, desire to find in "the vast and eternal laws of matter... that whatever is more than animal within us must find its solace and its hope [*sic*]" (104).

35. For a recent inquiry into a large body of literature bearing on the relations among secularization, rationality, disenchantment, and enchantment, see Michael Saler, "Modernity and Enchantment: A Historiographic Review," *The American Historical Review* 111 (2006): 692–716. In his attempt to elaborate a complex concept of "disenchanted enchantment," Saler criticizes binary and dialectical notions of the relation between enchantment and disenchantment, but he may not sufficiently explore their contexts, effects, and rationales. Still, Saler's article has the virtue of indicating and discussing a large body of material on a difficult topic. Unfortunately, he does not treat Agamben or the uses made of his work, especially in terms of "postsecular" and (re)enchanting orientations.

36. For an insistently Derridean reading of Coetzee, see Derek Attridge, *J. M. Coetzee and the Ethics of Reading* (Chicago: University of Chicago Press, 2004).

human-animal relationship, especially in its bearing on the issue of "animal rights."[37] Beginning as the 1997–98 Tanner Lectures at Princeton University as fictionalized lectures within lectures, and subsequently integrated or inserted as chapters into a more recognizable novel, *Elizabeth Costello,* the text is itself a curious, hybridized mutant that has a disturbing afterlife in the mind of the reader. Perhaps its most problematic element is the comparison between the Holocaust and the treatment of animals in the rather unqualified form it takes in the views of Elizabeth Costello, the text's central protagonist, who herself is intent on questioning any radical human-animal divide. In Agamben there is arguably an implicit analogy, or a relation of discursive displacement, between the most abject Holocaust victims (the *Muselmänner*) and the animal (or animality), but his argument invokes the animal as an abstract topos for an anthropocentric analysis of aporetic human complexity. In Costello the comparison between the treatment of animals and the Holocaust is altogether explicit, and it is directed at the plight of animals as actual living beings, although a hermeneutic of suspicion may be all-too-readily deployed to see her motivation as self-centered.[38] Coetzee carefully stages Costello's commitment to animals that leads to both powerful assertions and questionably leveling comparisons. Her intemperance is itself a sign of her beleaguered conviction concerning the justice of her beliefs. Yet Holocaust comparisons, whose rhetorical force is at times overwhelming and whose

37. Coetzee, *The Lives of Animals,* ed. and intro. Amy Gutman (Princeton, N.J.: Princeton University Press, 1999) with essays by Marjorie Garber, Peter Singer, Wendy Doniger, and Barbara Smuts. Without the accompanying essays, this is integrated as chapters or "lessons" 3 and 4 in *Elizabeth Costello* (New York: Penguin Books, 2003).

38. Such suspicion is prompted when Costello, in response to the question of whether her vegetarianism comes from moral conviction, answers: "No, I don't think so. . . . It comes out of a desire to save my soul" (89). However, Costello's Holocaust analogy finds support in Charles Patterson, *Eternal Treblinka: Our Treatment of Animals and the Holocaust* (New York: Lantern Books, 2002), which came to my attention only after this present book was almost completed. Patterson provides a rich compendium of empirical material pertinent to the problem of the treatment of animals. One might suggest that, for Patterson, the Holocaust analogy becomes more pertinent to the extent one takes seriously, and sees as dubious, important dimensions of that treatment. In chapter 5 he discusses actual cases of people drawn to animal advocacy at least in part because of Holocaust-related experience, notably their own or that of intimates, and in chapter 6 he treats the work of Isaac Bashevis Singer. Patterson's title is taken from Singer's "The Letter Writer," where one finds the arresting statement: "In relation to them, all people are Nazis; for the animals it is an eternal Treblinka." Patterson observes that, in the United States, 9.4 billion animals (over 8 billion of which are chickens) are slaughtered annually, amounting to more than 25 million a day (71). It should be noted, however, that, in Patterson's often manifesto-like account, the putative way "American eugenics and assembly-line slaughter crossed the Atlantic and found fertile soil in Nazi Germany" (53) is, with respect to the causation and dynamic of the Holocaust, seen in overly unmediated or one-dimensional terms and expressed in labile metaphors (see also 49–50, 72, and 109).

function is at best problematic, may not be necessary to make certain points or explore certain issues. One issue, suggested at times in Coetzee's text, is the structure of the "open secret," which is prevalent with respect to potentially unsettling recognitions, such as certain conditions of factory farming, slaughterhouses, and experimentation on animals.[39] In the open secret, one knows enough to know that one does not want to know more. This is somewhat like knowing when to turn off, or change channels on, the TV in anticipation of a scene one does not want to see. And one resists trying to see or find out more because the resulting knowledge might threaten defenses. The open secret implies not mere indifference but an active or performative process whereby compassion or empathy with the other is blocked or

39. See *Elizabeth Costello,* 64, 65, and 80. The case of Harry Harlow raised ongoing questions about the protection of animals used in experimentation and whether certain experimental practices invited forms of abuse. Before his death in 1981, Harlow tried to prove experimentally the need for interaction and love. His "proof" *a contrario,* which makes Bentham's Panopticon seem benign, included an experiment that subjected baby rhesus monkeys to what he termed the "Pit of Despair"—a stainless-steel isolation chamber to which the monkeys were confined for long periods of time without contact with other monkeys or humans. Harlow "discovered" what might, outside of a delimited disciplinary habitus, seem obvious: the deprived monkeys became disoriented and lacked animation. They were not recognized by others of their species who, among other responses, tried to gauge out their eyes. The inventive Harlow added to the "Pit of Despair" a "Rape Rack" where adult females raised in conditions of isolation were tied and raped. The offspring of these unions received no maternal care from their alienated mothers who instead abused them, for example, by eating their fingers or crushing their heads. See Deborah Blum's *The Monkey Wars* (79–83, 87–97) as well her *Love at Goon Park: Harry Harlow and the Science of Affection* (New York: Berkley Books, 2002). Blum argues that Harlow's approach was "mainstream" or even progressive for his time, and she often strives for ameliorative, upbeat messages, even ascribing later improvements to the impact of, or reaction to, Harlow's experiments. Especially in the earlier book, Blum provides much important information and attempts, in however strained a manner, to be balanced in showing both sides of every issue. See her discussion of the passage of a revised Federal Animal Welfare Act in 1985, which was largely due to the pressure of animal protection groups and achieved despite the often staunch resistance of major pro–research-and-experimentation institutions such as the National Institutes of Health, the American Psychological Association, and the National Association for Biomedical Research, as well as many individual scientists experimenting on animals, including primates. She notes that the National Center for Research Resources, through which federal primate centers were being run, was dedicated to "one theme": "to supply scientists with the tools that they need. In this case [AIDS research], the tools happen to be monkeys" (252). A special provision for monkeys included in the 1985 law was the need for attention to their "psychological well-being," although the determination of that condition was left to individual institutions undertaking experimentation, subject to review of federal inspectors of which there were very few provided. Before the passage of the law in 1985, animal experimenters could treat animals largely as they saw fit. See Blum, *The Monkey Wars,* esp. 24ff, 113ff, 121ff, and 184ff. Often with a decided preference for "human interest" stories, Blum focuses on individual researchers, professional organizations, government agencies, and animal rights activists but says very little about agribusiness and corporations invested in animal research and experimentation.

rendered ineffective, and one does not seek, or turns away from, available information.[40]

A further issue, which I have already raised, is the equivocal status of the other-than-human animal as raw material or mere life and as quasi-sacrificial victim and scapegoat. Even in the slaughterhouse, the perception of the animal as mere life is a consolatory, conscience-saving move that may not hold up both because of quasi-sacrificial motifs, explicit in kosher killing but perhaps not limited to it, and because of the more or less disavowed feeling that an animal is not mere life. A corollary of the argument I am trying to make is that, whether or not one believes humans have the right to kill other animals for food, or even whether human rights or claims should be weighed more heavily than those of other animals, the question of how other animals live before they die, and the manner in which they are killed, insofar as this question comes under human control, is an important ethicopolitical issue. To the extent that it is under human control or supervision (and this extent is broadened to the degree that human behavior affects ecological processes), the question of how animals live before they die or are killed, and the very manner in which they die or are killed, might be proposed as the "ethical minimum" that should be recognized and confronted by anyone with respect to the issue of "animal rights." Such a recognition would involve the obligation to find out how animals are treated both before and when they are killed, especially when the destination of the animal may be one's dinner plate.[41]

40. See the analysis and critique of the notion of indifference, whose structure is not limited to German attitudes toward Jews during the Holocaust, in Carolyn Dean, *The Fragility of Empathy after the Holocaust* (Ithaca: Cornell University Press, 2005), chap. 3.

41. For an account of the meatpacking and slaughtering system in North America, see Donald D. Stull and Michael J. Broadway, *Slaughterhouse Blues: The Meat and Poultry Industry in North America,* foreword Eric Schlosser (Belmont, Calif.: Wadsworth/Thompson Learning, 2004). In his foreword, Schlosser summarizes the book's argument about North America, where four companies control 85% of the market and the majority of underpaid workers are impoverished immigrants (many of them Latino): "The North American meatpacking industry has been transformed since the early 1970s—without most people realizing it. Slaughterhouses are now located in rural areas that rarely get much attention from the national media. . . . As Stull and Broadway demonstrate, the current system needlessly harms workers, consumers, and the environment. It mistreats animals. It brings poverty, drug abuse, and crime to rural communities. When all the social costs are tallied, our cheap meat is much more expensive than we can afford" (xiii–xiv). It is significant that Schlosser's own key text, *Fast Food Nation: The Dark Side of the All-American Meal* (2001; New York: Harper Perennial, 2005), remains anthropocentric and says little about the often devastating effects of the fast-food industry on animals processed to meet its needs, although the implications of its practices and policies should be apparent to the reader. Stull (an anthropologist) and Broadway (a geographer) focus on social and ecological dimensions but also provide information about the treatment of animals. A recent innovation they discuss is the chicken catcher, a machine that scoops up factory-farmed chickens. They report the views of a chicken grower: "According to Shawn, the machine, which looks

Coetzee's *Lives of Animals* is itself introduced and followed by a series of interesting commentaries. In her valuable contribution, Barbara Smuts, for example, observes that the protagonist and animal-rights activist in the story, Elizabeth Costello, makes no reference in her impassioned defense to "real-life relations with animals," although she lives with cats—"the individuals with whom she interacts most often and, perhaps, most intimately" (108). This observation should be qualified in important ways, and the qualification is significant since similar observations appear rather frequently in a manner that Smuts manifestly seems not to intend, that is, in the critique of animal-rights activism as itself abstract if not narcissistic and projective. "Real-life" relations to animals do inform Costello's comments, and the fact that they are not made to bear the brunt of the argument may be credited to her attempt to enter into a critical exchange with philosophers that the latter would not dismiss out of hand as overly personal, contingent, sentimental, and autobiographical. The first section of the novella, featuring a lecture followed by a few questions from the audience, is after all entitled "The Philosophers and the Animals," and the perspective of the philosopher (or at least of a certain type of philosopher) is epitomized in Costello's own daughter-in-law. In the second section, "The Poets and the Animals," experiential concerns are not altogether excluded. In her final response to her debating partner in the seminar setting, Costello observes: "Anyone who says that life matters less to animals than it does to us has not held in his hands an animal fighting for its life" (65). She adds with undue self-disparagement and debatable deference to both poetry and experience: "If I do not convince you, that is because my words, here, lack the power to bring home to you the wholeness,

---

somewhat like a combine, 'sucks the birds up' and onto a conveyor by means of rotary blades, and then 'shoots' them out of a 'gun' directly into the coops on the truck. It still takes seven operators to run the machine and handle the coops, and the machine stresses the birds and causes wing damage and other injuries. The machine cannot empty a house any quicker than the human catchers, it requires the same number of personnel, and there is more injury, so what is the benefit? The only one Shawn could see was that it eliminates the catchers, who he says are illegal immigrants. Machine operators will be employees, not contractors as the catchers had been, but, according to Shawn, it takes a long time to train them [the human catchers], and they don't stay long" (50–51n). From Stull and Broadway's analysis, it seems difficult not to conclude that the most (perhaps the only) "humane" conditions for animals before slaughter are provided by "free range" life, which is typically incompatible with factory farming and mechanization under intensified, even rampant, commodification. In *Eternal Treblinka,* Charles Patterson notes that many states have passed laws that exempt "food animals" from state anticruelty statutes, thus not protecting farm animals from abuse and neglect. He concludes that, counter to what is happening in Europe, "the American meat and dairy industries have successfully convinced their friends in state legislatures and Congress that what agribusiness does to animals should be 'beyond the law' " (71).

the unabstracted, unintellectual nature, of that animal being. That is why I urge you to read the poets who return the living, electric being to language; and if the poets do not move you, I urge you to walk, flank to flank, beside the beast that is prodded down the chute to his executioner" (65). (One may observe that the last-named procedure is followed by Temple Grandin in her attempt to design better—should one say more humane?—devices for slaughtering animals.)[42]

Elizabeth Costello's own varied if not heterogeneous "lectures" on humans and animals do not have an easily summarized line of argument, and they may even go in different if not contradictory directions. One opposition or contrast that helps to structure her approach is that between the philosopher as the vehicle of human reason that seems, beyond a certain point, closed to other animals and the poet as the bearer of living feeling and the "sympathetic imagination" that is open to all others. Reason is described as anthropocentric, especially when it takes a decidedly analytic form as "the specialism of a rather narrow self-regenerating intellectual tradition whose forte is reasoning" (69). This reason seems to conform to a massive "us and them" dichotomy that may be chipped away at certain points only to be reconstituted at others. In Pascal's formulation, the poet—or perhaps the poetic—is the bearer of "heart" that has reasons that reason may not know. One of those heart-felt reasons for Costello is sympathy. She is bold enough to postulate of the death camps that "the horror is that the killers refused to think themselves into the place of their victims, as did everyone else.... In other words, they closed their hearts. The heart is the seat of a faculty, *sympathy,* that allows us to share at times the being of another" (79). Of course this would seem to ignore the role of sadomasochistic killers and the more complex issue of violence that was directed at others experienced or figured as bearers of anxiety-producing, supposedly impure, contaminating, or perhaps subversive and conspiratorial forces one refused to recognize in oneself. Costello goes on to discuss sympathy, seemingly accepting the questionable ideas that sympathy is identification with the other and that

42. See Temple Grandin, *Thinking in Pictures and Other Reports from My Life with Autism* (New York: Knopf, 1996). Grandin, who entertained the possibility that some form of sacrificial ritual was necessary to control slaughter and its possible excesses, asserted: "I do not believe that my profession is morally wrong. Slaughtering is not wrong, but I do feel very strongly about treating animals humanely and with respect" (201). One may note that, for Saint Paul, ritual sacrifice, including its prescriptions and constraints, was unneeded since "we are sanctified through the offering of the body of Jesus Christ once *for all*" (Hebrews 10:10). Christian ritual contains little that regulates the relations between humans and other animals and is focused on the relations between humans and other humans or God.

such identification is itself a preservative against cruelty and genocidal behavior. Thus a crucial issue for Costello is whether one can be, think, or feel like another—say, a bat, in the famous example she adopts from Thomas Nagel. Here one might object that sympathy in a fully identificatory form is very problematic as a moral or ethical sentiment in that it induces projective or incorporative identification and that the type of empathy or compassion Costello seems to be seeking would be better construed as an affective response that may involve elements of identification but nonetheless is also informed both by acknowledgement of the other as other and by the realization that sympathy or empathy alone, however desirable on an ethical level, is not sufficient as a response to social and political problems. At the very least, it requires supplementation by norms and processes linked to forms of sociopolitical practice. But such considerations take one beyond the world envisaged by Costello, although they may not contradict it.[43]

43. This world was envisaged by Hannah Arendt for whom norms and forms of political practice were crucial. But one may note that, in *Eichmann in Jerusalem: A Report on the Banality of Evil* (1963; rev. and enlarged ed., New York: Viking Press, 1965), Arendt can attempt to explain Eichmann (for example, in terms of the banality of evil and the inability to "think"), but she cannot understand him because of an absence of empathic rapport. She is unable to imagine herself as even possibly someone who cannot "think" in the philosophical sense of exercising critical judgment. The paradoxical result is that Eichmann becomes her opaque, radical other, arguably in a position structurally analogous to that of the fully objectified entity. With reference to the Hegelian-Heideggerian frame of reference that Arendt elaborates in *The Origins of Totalitarianism* (1966, 1968; new ed., New York: Harcourt, 1985, for example, 192 and 454–59), Eichmann is also in the position of the other-than-human or even sub-human animal (as well as the African *Natürvolk*) that does not have a world or share a world with civilized humans. One might of course argue that Eichmann did exercise judgment, however misguidedly, in concluding that Jews were "life unworthy of life," even a distorted form of sacrificial victim, fit for slaughter in keeping with the will of the "god-like" *Führer.* In "Lesson 6" ("The Problem of Evil") of *Elizabeth Costello,* Costello offers a perspective that provides at least qualified support for Arendt's orientation. She puts forth a strict ethical limit to aesthetic representation and experimentation, even a limit to the "sympathetic imagination" that she earlier seemed to affirm in unqualified terms. She finds herself at a conference with a fellow author, Paul West, with whose book *The Very Rich Hours of Count von Stauffenberg* (New York: Harper & Row, 1980) she disagrees in a fundamental way, and her criticism can be mitigated but not blunted by her consideration for the author (who in any event meets her overtures with a wall of silence). She finds that West's (for her, successful) attempts at "conjuring up" (172) scenes of torture and execution of Hitler's would-be assassins do basic harm to both writer and reader of West's words. As she puts it: "Certain things are not good to read *or to write.* To put the point in another way: I take seriously the claim that the artist risks a great deal by venturing into forbidden places: risks, specifically, himself; risks, perhaps, all. I take this claim seriously because I take seriously the forbiddenness of forbidden places. The cellar in which the July 1944 plotters were hanged is one such forbidden place. I do not believe we should go into that cellar, any of us. I do not believe Mr. West should go there; and, if he chooses to go nevertheless, I believe we should not follow" (173).

It may come as no surprise that the story of Abraham and Isaac is not a reference in Coetzee's celebrated text where the critique remains largely immanent and the framework relational and this-worldly. In the various discussions of the Biblical account in Genesis 22, the focus has traditionally been on the dilemma of Abraham and his relation to God. This focus may seem unexceptionable from a certain religious perspective, even when it takes the radically self-questioning form it does in Kierkegaard. But it is significant that even Derrida, in his *Gift of Death,* occludes some seemingly obvious problems.[44] First, there is the status and plight of Isaac as sacrificial victim who is the "gift of death" that Abraham is willing to offer his God. The fact that the question of the victim does not become a key problem for Derrida may seem surprising since in sacrifice the typical gift is the victim. The actual sacrifice of the ram as a substitute for Isaac is a seeming nonissue, as it tends to be in other accounts of the Abraham story. The ram (caught in a thicket by his horns—as if already trapped and bound) seems at best to be an "extra" that remains offstage. And Isaac as potential sacrificial victim plays at most a cameo part. At least in the *Gift of Death,* the dialogue is almost exclusively one that involves Abraham, God, and Derrida. Neither the human nor the other-than-human animal as sacrificial victim is given a "voice" or a significant role in the excessive focus on the excessive gift. And there is not a sustained consideration of a crucial issue: whether aspects of sacrifice, such as oblation or gift-giving, may be validated only insofar as they may be extricated from the very process of victimization that has been essential to sacrifice.

Derrida recognizes that God (or his angelic messenger) stops the human sacrifice and that Abraham displaces it onto the animal. But Derrida understands the Akeda "as if Abraham had already killed Isaac" in the instant of Abraham's decision. And he sees Abraham as a religious figure who confronts an impossible paradox or aporia between "absolute" duty (dictated by the command of a radically transcendent, hidden, secret god) and ethical duty toward his beloved son Isaac. Abraham responds "absolutely to an absolute duty" (72). Derrida seems to accept this frame of reference or to render it in a free indirect style that conveys both his proximity to Abraham and his (at times projective) identification with Kierkegaard. Derrida's powerful reading not only appears to marginalize the problem of victimization in sacrifice and to stress both the gift and the uniqueness or singularity of the object of

44. Derrida, *The Gift of Death,* trans. David Wills (1992; Chicago: University of Chicago Press, 1995).

sacrifice. It also relies on a notion of the absolute in terms of which there is an absolute duty conjoined with radical transcendence and necessary secrecy. One may, I think, take this as a postreligious (or postsecular) as well as aesthetic perspective that construes Abraham as an agonized (but not tragic) figure of the sublime for whom even mourning, much less any other form of mediation or negotiation of aporetic double binds, is unavailable. Derrida is in the closest proximity to Kierkegaard but, aside from the seeming difference in his relation to the "leap of faith," his mode of identifying with Kierkegaard obscures the way Kierkegaard himself did not simply affirm the "madness" of Abraham's decision, which implies, for Derrida, the madness of all decisions. Rather Kierkegaard raised the question of Abraham's possible madness as a consideration that rendered his decision, along with all comparable decisions, radically problematic. Derrida may assume this problematic madness, for he elsewhere asserts that Abraham's intended sacrifice of his son "was always madness."[45] In any event, the further question that perhaps remains more active in Kierkegaard than in Derrida is whether the questionable gesture may well be to think one can place oneself in the (sublime?) position of the chosen one who enters into an impossible vis-à-vis with the radically transcendent other, takes up an "absolute" duty, affirms an aporia or differend between absolute and ethical duty, and "decides" it madly through a suspension of ethical duty in performing sacrifice.

My truncated comments concerning *The Gift of Death* should immediately be countered and contested on the basis of Derrida's own reflections in such important later writings as "The Animal That Therefore I Am (More to Follow)."[46] In them Derrida is intent on radically questioning the massive

45. "Faith and Knowledge: the Two Sources of 'Religion' at the Limits of Reason Alone," in *Religion,* ed. Jacques Derrida and Gianni Vattimo, 43.

46. Trans. David Wills, *Critical Inquiry* 28 (2002): 369–418. See also "And Say the Animal Responded?" "L'animal que donc je suis" and "Et si l'animal répondait?" have appeared in book form in *L'animal que donc je suis,* ed. Marie-Louis Mallet (Paris: Editions Galilée, 2006), and in English as *The Animal That Therefore I Am,* ed. Marie-Louis Mallet, trans. David Wills (New York: Fordham University Press, 2008). For a discussion of rams and (among other things) their role in sacrificial processes, including the biblical account of Abraham and Isaac, see Derrida's essay "Rams: Uninterrupted Dialogues—Between Two Infinities, the Poem," in *Sovereignties in Question: The Poetics of Paul Celan,* ed. Thomas Dutoit and Outi Pasanen (2003; New York: Fordham University Press, 2005), 153–63, whose original publication followed *The Gift of Death* by eleven years. However, Derrida's insistent affirmation of incommensurability, total alterity, and aporia enjoins a contestable, hyperbolic assertion of the necessity of "violent sacrifice": "Always singular and irreplaceable, these laws or injunctions remain untranslatable from one to the other, from some to others, from one language to another, but that makes them no less universal. I *must* translate, transfer, transport (*übertragen*) the untranslatable in another turn even where, translated, it remains untranslatable. This is the violent sacrifice of the passage beyond—*Übertragen: übersetzen*" (162). Instead of positing an originary status for violence and

divide between the putatively homogeneous categories of the human and the animal, a divide he sees as pervasive in the philosophical and theoretical traditions, including such recent figures as Levinas and Lacan. The purpose of this divide is to establish what is proper to "man," or definitive of the human "as such," and thereby, whether intentionally or not, to legitimate human uses and abuses of other animals (one might perhaps add the animal in "man" as well). Derrida questions this divide not to postulate a pure continuity, which he observes would be at odds with his emphasis on difference and alterity. Rather he attempts to deconstruct and criticize the binary opposition between the categories of the animal and the human as well as the accompanying limit or divide between human and animal, which, he avers, "through and beyond all their disagreements, philosophers have always judged and *all* philosophers have judged... to be single and indivisible" (408). (I have indicated ways in which Agamben might be added to the list of philosophers in this respect.) Derrida seeks instead a more explicitly problematic, internally differentiated, self-questioning, but not simply indistinct or blurred, understanding of human and animal, including the animal in the human.

Noting the far-reaching effects of Bentham's seemingly simple question concerning animals, "Can they suffer?," Derrida observes:

> Being able to suffer is no longer a power, it is a possibility without power, a possibility of the impossible. Mortality resides there, as the most radical means of thinking the finitude that we share with animals, the mortality that belongs to the very finitude of life, to the experience of compassion, to the possibility of sharing the possibility of this nonpower, the possibility of this impossibility, the anguish of this vulnerability and the vulnerability of this anguish.[47]

---

conjoining it with sacrifice, I would argue instead that one should moot the question of the originary and situate any transhistorical notion of violence (or trauma) as explicitly and questionably speculative as well as requiring careful, critical analysis of its imbrication with specific traditions and singular historical forms of violence.

47. Derrida adds: "Once its protocol is established, the form of this question changes everything" (text extract and quote, 396). This question concerning suffering, Derrida contends, unsettles other questions, such as that of the *logos* or of language as *le propre* of man, disturbing them "by a certain *passivity*" and a vulnerability (but should one conflate the two?) that are shared by all who are able, indeed cannot not be able, to suffer. And, in unsettling the overly self-confident quest for the distinctive criterion or "*propre*" of "man," Derrida places special emphasis on an openness to compassion, including the compassion that Nietzsche felt as "he was mad enough to cry for an animal, under the gaze of, or cheek to cheek with a horse. Sometimes I think I see him call that horse as a witness, and primarily, in order to call it as a witness to his compassion, I think I see him take its head in his hands" (403). Before he evokes this pathos-charged (is it "sentimentalizing"?), hauntingly phantasmatic, and chimerical scene, which he intends with a seriousness accompanied by Nietzsche's own appeal to laughter,

The end of the passage moves toward now-familiar paradoxical and chiasmic formulations. Yet Derrida is struggling with the limits of language in the attempt to articulate and convey, among other things, the inability of language itself to be erected into the distinguishing property (*le propre*) or essence of man and established as the decisive criterion that separates and acts as the unbreachable limit or divide between the human and the animal. He may, arguably, go too far in acknowledging human disempowerment, but he relates it to the experience of compassion rather than fixating on it or linking it to distinctively human virtues or to a leap into an abyssal divide somehow related to what is presumably other than being (although the latter move might conceivably be associated with Derrida's own latter-day notion, invoked repeatedly in *The Gift of Death,* that *tout autre est tout autre:* every other is radically other or, in a sense, transcendent and opaque or enigmatic, like the Hidden God—one crucial instance of the radically other than Being).[48] Still, one can almost imagine Derrida as a character, an unlikely philosopher in Coetzee's *Lives of Animals* who rises from the audience to raise questions and make "poetic" comments that support the attempts of Elizabeth Costello to respond to the less comprehending or compassionate, cuttingly analytic questions of other philosophers and even some poets who would at all cost keep their firm hold on that unfailing, monumental criterion.[49]

---

Derrida formulates the aporia that unsettles an overly self-confident quest for the "proper" of man.

48. The "*tout autre*" seems to be related to the portmanteau concept of "*divinanimalité*" that somehow approximates the divine and the animal and brings the animal into the range of the divine and the enigmatic other. See *L'animal que donc je suis,* 181. The notion that "tout autre est tout autre" might be better understood as indicating not that every other is utterly or totally other but that, within every other, there is something totally other, concealed or secret (designated in psychoanalysis as the unconscious or [with Jean Laplanche] the enigmatic signifier). For a chronological, contextualizing discussion of the displacement of theology in Levinas's notion of ethics with respect to the totally other, which situates the historical origins of his thought in interwar France rather than in specifically Jewish traditions (even asserting a more direct relation to Protestant theology), see Samuel Moyn, *Origins of the Other: Emmanuel Levinas between Revelation and Ethics* (Ithaca: Cornell University Press, 2005). See also the convergent argument in Ethan Kleinberg, *Generation Existential: Heidegger's Philosophy in France, 1927–1961* (Ithaca: Cornell University Press, 2005). While knowledge of the more immediate contexts of Levinas's thought is informative and important, the theological issue of transcendence and immanence, along with their secular displacements, goes well beyond interwar France. And, as both Moyn and Kleinberg recognize, insistence on transcendence and its relation to the singular individual is crucial in Levinas.

49. Basing his argument largely on Derrida's recent work, Cary Wolfe in *Animal Rites: American Culture, the Discourse of Species, and Posthumanist Theory* (Chicago: University of Chicago Press, 2003), which came to my attention only after the completion of the present book, criticizes the quest for a decisive criterion separating the human from the animal, in terms that partially converge with the argument I offer. Wolfe's book is well worth reading and provides

Before concluding, I would like to add a caveat with respect to the issues I have tried to explore. Certain Nazis reveal how a sentimental concern for other animals may be combined with extreme, even genocidal, mistreatment of groups of humans. Indeed, their practice brings home the point that the legitimate interest in other animals within a larger ecological perspective is not a panacea and must be articulated with an ethicopolitical conception of relations among humans in a viable, noncompensatory, non–zero-sum manner.[50] Whatever doubts one may raise about Hitler's vegetarianism or Nazi affirmations concerning the value of animals and nature, it is still chilling to read Himmler's reported words to his masseur and confidant Felix Kersten, as the Reichsführer waxes poetic about the murderous nature of hunting "innocent, defenseless and unsuspecting" deer or asserts that "nature is so

---

many valuable analyses and insights. There are differences in our approaches aside from the fact that Wolfe does not discuss the influential work of Agamben. Wolfe relies on a notion of posthumanism without investigating its possible anthropocentrism, and his appeal to psychoanalysis in very limited. I would especially take issue with his insistence (of course he is not alone) on absolute nonreciprocity and total alterity in ethical relations, along with an unqualified insistence on a division among spheres or role-specific areas in modern life. (I think ethics is subordinated to theology when it is understood only in terms of absolute nonreciprocity, total otherness of the other, and the pure asymmetrical gift.) The amalgamation of Derrida and Luhmann at the end of his book is ingenious yet problematic, even though one might argue that it is invited by Derrida's own turn at times to formalization along with seemingly fatalistic, mechanistic, and biological "logics" (such as autoimmunization), which he correlates with psychoanalytic notions of the uncanny and the repetition compulsion (for example, in "Faith and Knowledge: The Two Sources of 'Religion' at the Limits of Reason Alone"). I would argue that in social and cultural life specific areas are indeed differentiated and there is a striving in various groups—especially professional groups—for autonomy and normative self-definition. This is part and parcel of the history of professionalization. But Wolfe like Luhmann (and Bourdieu) may take this movement too much at face value. The various spheres or roles are never defined with the desired precision or exclusivity. Hence, *pace* Luhmann, their relations are not simply incommensurable or able to generate formal paradoxes or aporias. There may of course be dilemmas and role conflicts. But this is very different from paradoxes in a formal system like mathematics. Wolfe may be too formalistic here, and his formalism is related to his insistent desire for the paradox or aporia. Finally, unlike Wolfe, I would not associate ethics with passivity but rather with a form of acknowledged or even affirmed vulnerability that does not exclude agency (including agency related to processes of working-through, a concept that finds no place in Wolfe's account).

50. It is self-defeating to assume that there is simply a zero-sum relation, in terms of either resources or compassion, between a concern for oppressed or dependent humans and for other animals. The view of Hitler as a vegetarian, as well as its significance, is still being debated. It seems that he avoided meat, when he did, because of stomach problems and anxieties about cancer or other forms of bodily "impurity." But he did not completely give up favorite dishes such as sausages, liver dumplings, and stuffed and roasted game. He would also viciously beat dogs with a whip despite his fondness for them. He held nonviolent vegetarians, notably Gandhi, in contempt and, when he came to power in 1933, vegetarian societies in Germany were subjected to restrictive controls. See the useful, at times contestable, summary and references in Charles Patterson, *Eternal Treblinka,* 125–28. (I thank Peter Staudenmaier for his comments on this aspect of Patterson's book.)

marvelously beautiful and every animal too has a right to live.... After the war I will issue the strictest regulations for protecting animals." Himmler asks Kersten to stop, after the latter is bold enough to assert: "You are not quite so gentle when it's only a matter of men." Kersten adds, for the eyes of the reader of his memoirs: "How can one reconcile the facts that the same man who pities the fate of hunted animals blandly ignores the fate of men?"[51]

One may perhaps anticipate the time when the issue of the other-than-human animal, understood in nonanthropocentric, broadly relational and

51. Felix Kersten, *The Kersten Memoirs, 1940–1945,* intro. H. R. Trevor-Roper, trans. Constantine Fitzgibbon and James Oliver (London: Hutchinson, 1956), 116–18. Kersten elsewhere indicates how the question is more complicated than he seems to imply, notably with reference to the sources of Himmler's incapacitating stomach cramps that Kersten interprets in psychosomatic terms. See the appendix to the *Memoirs,* 309–12. See also Boria Sax, *Animals in the Third Reich: Pets, Scapegoats, and the Holocaust.* Himmler's view, as reported by Kersten, cannot simply be generalized to apply to all Nazis. While contending that "the Nazis, whatever their motives, were right in much of their humane legislation" concerning animals (165), Sax's book brings out the complex, often contradictory attitudes of the Nazis toward animals and the ways these attitudes resembled other policies and orientations of the regime. For example, attesting to the phantasmatic nature of the image of the Jew, an animal might be declared "Jewish" and shot (22). Nazis themselves might identify with predatory animals, for example, the wolf. Sax speculates that "an unarticulated purpose of the Nazi animal protection laws was to accustom people to think of euthanasia as a positive thing. By desensitizing people, the killing of animals helped open the way for the mass murder of human beings" (169). On an empirical level, he asserts that "some members of the SS were required to rear a German shepherd for twelve weeks, then strangle the dog under the supervision of an officer" (169). The function of this activity as a ritual inverting ordinary norms and fostering the desired trait of Nazi "hardness" would seem obvious. Nobel Prize winner Konrad Lorenz, who had a pronounced Nazi affiliation he never openly discussed (135), speculated that Aryan-like breeds ("lupus dogs"), such as the German shepherd, were descended from the wolf, while Semitic-like breeds ("aureus dogs") were descended from the Mesopotamian jackal (89–90). Sax also observes that, in the immediate postwar period in Germany, "there was widespread hunger, and the few animals that had survived the war were generally sacrificed for food. Hardly any animals were left for the purposes of research" (133–34). And he points to contemporary "confused and contradictory attitudes toward animals, adored as pets and brutalized as meat" (23). He argues that "one result of the taboo against comparisons to the Holocaust is that it gives analogies an excessive rhetorical force" and, without asserting a moral equivalence, he compares factory farms and death camps (18). One of his most pointed arguments is that "what is most disturbing in factory farms is not that animals are killed but that they are not allowed to live. They are not allowed individual stories; they cannot explore the world or choose their mates. Turkeys bred for supermarkets have such enormous breasts that they cannot reach one another to reproduce except by artificial insemination. Our discomfort goes far beyond the issue of the capacity of animals to feel pain. It seems to me entirely likely that many animals in industrial farms may be so brutalized by the combination of genetic manipulation and lack of stimulation that they lose the capacity to suffer very much. If that has not already happened, it soon may" (166–67). Here one does seem to have an image of the living dead, or the undead, bred to feed humans. Yet Sax apparently does not see how the Nazi idea of an Aryan master race, under a supreme Führer, however much it presumably modeled itself on a fantasy of "natural" predators, did not question anthropocentrism but affirmed one extreme particularistic form of it (42).

ecological terms, will be conjoined with such crucial questions as race, class, and gender in critical-theoretical inquiry.[52] Yet, while there are indeed signs of this development, there are also countertendencies. In conclusion I would only mention the much-discussed book *Empire* by Michael Hardt and Antonio Negri.[53] Despite its extremely speculative and utopian dimensions, *Empire* (like its sequel, *Multitude*)[54] has almost nothing to say about other-than-human animals, especially within the context of an argument about global citizenship. Other-than-human animals seem to remain perpetual *sans papiers,* excluded even from the ill-defined "multitude" that Hardt and Negri oppose to the invasive Empire. Their neo- or postmarxist approach remains insistently anthropocentric, even when it turns, at the very end of the book in a surprising gesture, to Saint Francis, the birdman of Assisi. The saint becomes a model of the postmodern "militant." However tempting it might be, one should not dismiss their gesture as a reversion to the "flower power" of the sixties. But, in their final evocation of unrealized possibilities, in which Saint Francis seems to mutate into a premodern Foucault, the allusion to other-than-human animals is obscured by its inclusion in a rather nebulous generality. Here are the concluding words of *Empire:*

> Francis in opposition to nascent capitalism [the structure of the Church at the time might be a more plausible reference here] refused every instrumental discipline, and in opposition to the mortification of the flesh (in poverty and in the constituted order) he posed a joyous life, including all of being and nature, the animals, sister moon, brother sun, the birds of the field, the poor and exploited humans, together against the will of power and corruption. Once again in postmodernity we find ourselves in Francis's situation, posing against the misery of power the joy of being. This is a revolution that no power will control—because biopower and communism, cooperation and revolution remain together, in love, simplicity, and also innocence. This is the irrepressible lightness and joy of being communist. (413)

52. In a landmark decision on January 16, 2008, which had important ecological implications, a French court levied heavy fines on those responsible for the 1999 sinking of the tanker *Erika,* an unseaworthy vessel (*navire poubelle* or garbage ship, in the French expression) whose massive oil spill caused extensive damage, including to the ocean, beaches, and wildlife. The giant corporation Total was fined $556,000 and ordered to pay a share of nearly $300 million (192 million euros) in damages to civil parties and the French state. At this writing, the case is under appeal.

53. Cambridge: Harvard University Press, 2000.

54. Hardt and Negri, *Multitude: War and Democracy in the Age of Empire* (New York: Penguin Books, 2004).

One might say many things about this concluding passage where animals are ushered in on a general wave of sentimental, idealistic humanitarianism. I shall simply conclude by indicating that, in the next mutation of critical theory and cultural criticism, one may look forward to a more sustained interaction between theory and historical understanding in which the utopian dimension itself, without offering misleading blueprints, nonetheless becomes less vacuous and more pointed, bringing with it a renewal of historically informed immanent critique and a concern for an other-than-anthropocentric notion of society. A generous reading of the passage from Hardt and Negri, which could serve critically to indicate the limitations of my own essay, would underscore the importance of situating the question of the human and the animal in a broader but differentiated ecological perspective or wide-ranging network of relations that I have only been able to adumbrate. For the questioning of a decisive criterion separating the human from the animal or even from the rest of nature has widespread ramifications, indicating the need for a major paradigm shift in the relations of the human, the animal, and nature in general. Such a shift would not only mark a turn away from anthropocentrism but also point to the inadequacies of "rights" discourse, both human and animal. Without simply taking one back to traditional ideas of natural law, it would lead to a notion of basic claims of beings in an interactive network of relations that places sovereignty in question, including state (or divine) sovereignty, and requires complex, mutual negotiations among claims as well as limits on various forms of assertiveness. The most signficant difference or distinction between human and animal would seem to lie in the direction of all-too-human yet "inhuman" excess related to structural or transhistorical trauma, the Lacanian real, "existential" anxiety, and a void at the center of the human, especially as such forces or factors relate to fantasy structures (including what I take to be the fantasy of a constitutive lack in the human). To the extent such a difference is pertinent, the question is whether it relates to a universal or even quasi-transcendental dimension (if not "core") of the human or whether it is dependent on cultural assumptions and traditions, including the Christian notion of original (or originary) sin(fulness).

# CHAPTER 7

# Tropisms of Intellectual History

Open seriousness, always ready to submit to death and renewal, true open seriousness fears neither parody, nor irony, nor any other form of reduced laughter, for it is aware of being part of an uncompleted whole.

—Mikhail Bakhtin, *Rabelais and His World*

This concluding chapter serves as a retrospect on the concerns of this book and, to some extent, of my intellectual orientation as a whole. It is also a prospect and (to paraphrase Friedrich Schlegel) conveys my view of the historian as a critical theorist looking backward in an anticipatory manner. As I note in the introduction, a version of it was initially written in response to an invitation by the editors of *Rethinking History* for their "Invitation to Historians" series. Except for a few autobiographical comments, which may help illuminate my concerns, I understood the charge for the most part in terms of relating my own intellectual itinerary to larger movements and possibilities in the subdiscipline of intellectual history, the field of history, and the academy more generally.

Intellectual history, in its close relations with cultural history, has undergone many mutations and variations in the recent past, including states of both near extinction and vigorous self-assertion. Until the last fifteen years or so, my goal was to help put a transformed and reinvigorated intellectual history back on the historiographical agenda—an intellectual history distinguished from an older history of ideas and from a reductive social history for which intellectual history was epiphenomenal or even unnecessary (whether because it treated only "irrelevant" or "unrepresentative" elites or because every historian is already an intellectual historian in treating the problem of meaning or "intellection").[1] There was also (and continues to be) much intellectual history in the form of more or less useful contextualizing, erudite road maps of the past that do not themselves go very far in the direction of critical thought about significant problems. I tried to argue that contextualization, while altogether necessary for historical understanding, is not identical with it. It must be supplemented and in certain ways challenged by one's implicated, dialogic relation to the past related to an attempt at responsive understanding requiring interpretation and close reading of both texts and contexts. To some extent there is a tension and a trade-off, at least in practice, between an attempt at the fullest possible contextualization of an artifact, which treats every conceivably pertinent current contemporary with, or antecedent to, it—an attempt that may go to the extreme of contextual saturation and is typically conjoined with a desire for objectifying, perhaps even encyclopedic knowledge—and a critical analysis or exchange

1. For example, A. J. P. Taylor states: "Literature tells us little when we deal, as we must in the twentieth century, with the people of England. The novels of Virginia Woolf, for example, were greatly esteemed by a small intellectual group, and their destruction of the tight narrative frame has influenced later writers. They are irrelevant for the historian." *English History, 1914–1945* (New York: Oxford University Press), 311. William Bowsma writes with a generosity that obliterates intellectual history in any specific sense along with (one infers) academic positions in that field: "We no longer need intellectual history because we have all become intellectual historians." "Intellectual History in the 1980s: From the History of Ideas to History of Meaning," *Journal of Interdisciplinary History* 12 (1981): 280. Less ominously and in a line of thought influenced by the history of "mentalities," yet showing similarities to Bowsma's perspective, Keith Michael Baker supplements his view that all historians face basically the same problem of contextualization with an injunction to see "intellectual history as a mode of historical discourse rather than as a distinct field of inquiry with a clearly demarcated subject matter. . . . The intellectual historian seeks particularly to attend to the intellective dimensions of social action as historically constituted. . . . Intellectual history . . . is the history of intellection. . . . In a word it is the history of meaning." "Ideological Origins of the French Revolution," in *Modern European Intellectual History: Reappraisals and New Directions,* ed. Dominick LaCapra and Steven L. Kaplan (Ithaca: Cornell University Press, 1982), 197–219. In his analysis of intellectual history and the social history of intellectuals, Daniel Wickberg begins with a commendable critique of the construction of intellectual history as a mere epiphenomenon of social history but then winds back to a totalizing variant of the approach he seemingly rejects. He advocates "the ideational history of the social," which takes "the documents and subject matter of the social historian and subject[s] it to the methods and insights of the historian of thought." "Intellectual History vs. the Social History of Intellectuals," *Rethinking History* 5 (2001): 393. In this light, "all history, after all, must be the history of thought before it is anything else" (394). One might agree that one (not *the*) approach to intellectual history is to read William James "in concert with hack journalism of the 1890s, joke books from that era, estate inventories and accounting records" (392) but still object if the concert is such as to harmonize, level, or drown out all the significant divergences and differences, including differences in critical and performative force, among these texts.

that tries to disclose dimensions of an artifact or of the past that have been underemphasized and that pose questions to our own modes of understanding and self-understanding.[2]

As should be evident from the preceding chapters, I think that the alternative to contextualism or a narrow historicism is not theory understood as the universalist surrogate for classical philosophy in which history becomes merely a source book of illustrations, exempla, or signs. This conception of theory, or what I sometimes term theoreticism, has been given a new lease on life by certain tendencies in poststructuralism, postmarxism, and Lacanian psychoanalysis, notably in the influential work of Giorgio Agamben, Alain Badiou, and Slavoj Žižek.[3] The problem, rather, is how to articulate the relations between history and theoretical self-reflection that poses questions to history. A cardinal aspect of this endeavor is the attempt to address the problem of specificity in analysis by not reducing it to either particularity or universality but instead understanding it in terms of the intricate interaction between the historical (or singular) and the transhistorical (understood with all due caution and allowing self-critically for one's limitations). Contextualization in this light becomes a process of situating the singular (text, individual or group, phenomenon or process) in a field of interacting forces without obliterating the critical and transformative, including the performative, dimensions of its resistances and responsiveness or its problematic relation to transhistorical problems and considerations, including the way it continues to address readers or interpreters over time, even the way it may still provoke controversy.

I have argued that, at least in "Western" culture, there may be something like transhistorical or structural trauma (variously figured as original sin, the passage from nature to culture, separation from the mother, the entry into language, the Lacanian real, and so forth). But the problem both philosophically and historically is how transhistorical dimensions of trauma are articulated with historical traumas in ways that resist reduction in either direction (whether it be figuring the Holocaust as an illustration of the Lacanian real,

2. I should make explicit the point that, while I find it fruitful for there to be critical exchange and argument between exponents of different approaches to intellectual history and other (sub)disciplinary approaches, there should also be an openness to different perspectives not only within the profession but within the same department or unit. Such a state of affairs makes for more thought-provoking interactions and benefits students by exposing them to different orientations.

3. For example, the Holocaust or the Gulag may be construed only, or at least primarily, as an instance of the Lacanian traumatic "real," or the *Muselmann* may be transfigured into the sublime image of everyman. One finds these views, respectively, in Žižek's *The Sublime Object of Ideology* (London: Verso, 1989), esp. 50, and Agamben's *Remnants of Auschwitz* (New York: Zone Books, 1999).

on the one hand, or as an apocalyptic event at the origin of all significant post-Holocaust anxiety and "postmodern" disorientation or decentering, on the other).[4] In other words, the problem for a theoretically informed historiography is to elucidate precisely how "pieces of the [traumatic] real" are imbricated in historical experiences and events such as the atrocities of war and genocide. The related problem is how to recognize one's own vulnerability or constitutive anxiety, related to the structural or transhistorical dimension of trauma, without historicizing, localizing, and containing it in misleading ways or projecting its cause onto others as scapegoats.

In making these and related arguments, I have tensely combined a cross-disciplinary mode of inquiry with a concern for disciplinarity that does not establish unbreachable barriers between fields but does concern itself with distinctions and nuances.[5] In these respects my relation to forms of poststructuralism, postmodernism, and postmodernity has always been both sympathetic and critical, and I have been averse to the blurring of all distinctions, a notion of thought as conceptual meltdown, or the resort to unhelpful, overly general or codified, ultimately dogmatic pronouncements (such as: history, in the sense of historiography, is figurative, aesthetic, or interpretive "all the way down," or history is trauma or "what hurts").

But I have certainly argued for the significance of the traumatic in relation to extreme events or experiences and for the relevance to history and historical understanding of literature and the arts in general, in elite, mass, and popular culture. Moreover, although I have been seen as a proponent of the linguistic turn, I have never understood this turn in terms of a literal pantextualism but instead in terms of the role of signifying practices in all their intricate and problematically interacting forms. Still, while finding all texts and documents worth thinking about, I have defended the critical importance of certain significant texts which, paraphrasing Claude Lévi-Strauss, I find to be especially "good to think with." And the linguistic turn was for me inspired as much by M. M. Bakhtin as by Ferdinand de Saussure or even Jacques Derrida (who, as is evident in *Of Grammatology,* is actually a critical reader of Saussure rather than a disciple). In addition to the insistence on supplementing contextualization with an attempt at responsive understanding, a principle

4. See especially my *Writing History, Writing Trauma* (Baltimore: Johns Hopkins University Press, 2001), chap. 2.

5. I was quite pleased when the German translation of my *History & Criticism, Geschichte und Kritik,* trans. Ludwig Hirt, (1985; Frankfurt am Main: Fischer Taschenbuch, 1987), referred to me in an introductory note as a *Grenzgänger,* which could be translated either as border-crosser or as wetback.

of Bakhtin's approach that I have found especially pertinent for intellectual history is the idea that, in thought and argument, a strong adversary is more valuable than a weak ally.[6] Also to be derived from Bakhtin's work is the realization that texts (in the broad sense) that are "good to think with" are in no sense restricted to written works with individual authors or to artifacts of "high" culture but extend to anonymous, popular, and collective phenomena and processes such as dimensions of the carnivalesque, of testimonies and the *testimonio,* even of rituals such as mourning (understood as a key form of working through, without totally transcending, losses and at times involving humor or laughter). Moreover, even symptoms are not simply pathological deformations but modes of responding to difficult if not impossible situations in which what cannot be spoken may nonetheless be shown, enacted, or acted out in ways related to attempts to work through problems. In their own way symptoms are signifying practices, however opaque or gap ridden, and the most critical texts or artifacts may nonetheless have symptomatic dimensions with respect to prevalent ideologies or unspoken assumptions. Even the most "enlightened" manner of thinking critically about them remains at some level implicated in processes that "think" with them.

I find Jorge Luis Borges's whimsical "Pierre Menard, Author of the *Quixote*" to be a text that is "good to think with"—one of the best ever written on the text-context problem.[7] It is also a text that interweaves narrative with the essay form in a critically provocative, parodic, and self-parodic fashion. One might see it as a form of serious play or jesting in earnest—Thomas Mann's definition of art that he borrowed from Goethe. In this small but imposing text (a mere handful of pages), context is crucial but not all-important for (at least limited) understanding.

Borges recounts that Menard writes fragments (not the totality) of the *Quixote* neither by copying or rivaling it nor by becoming Cervantes through identification but by writing or rewriting the *Quixote* in some sense empathically while remaining Menard. Writing becomes a kind of spiritual exercise involving self-discipline and even askesis in the constitutively limited, respectful, yet critical and self-critical, attempt to engage and understand the other (person, text, problem). Crucial in this attempt is the recognition of

6. This is the sense in which I find it fruitful to engage the work of Slavoj Žižek and Giorgio Agamben as well as the consistently insightful, thought-provoking work of Eric L. Santner, for example. For my discussion of Bakhtin, see *Rethinking Intellectual History: Texts, Contexts, Language* (Ithaca: Cornell University Press, 1983), chap. 9.

7. The text is included in Jorge L. Borges, *Labyrinths: Selected Stories and Other Writings,* ed. Donald A. Yates and James E. Erby (New York: New Directions, 1962), 36–50.

untimely, even uncanny, resistances in the other that counteract our attempt to make meaning through projective constructions or identification—indeed resistances that may lead us to change our questions and even to question our assumptions. As Borges puts it: "Needless to say, he [Menard] never contemplated a mechanical transcription of the original; he did not propose to copy it. His admirable intention was to produce a few pages which would coincide, word for word and line for line—with those of Miguel de Cervantes" (39).

Borges intensifies the sphinxlike mystery of Menard by asking on the reader's behalf: "But why precisely the *Quixote*? our reader will ask. Such a preference, in a Spaniard, would not have been inexplicable; but it is, no doubt, in a Symbolist from Nîmes, essentially a devoté of Poe who engendered Baudelaire, who engendered Mallarmé, who engendered Valéry, who engendered Edmond Teste" (40–41). After this parodic series of quasi-biblical "begats," which mingles historical personages and a fictional creature, Borges quotes Menard to respond to (while deepening) the question as well as to situate the intentionality of the author:

> My general recollection of the *Quixote,* simplified by forgetfulness and indifference, can well equal the imprecise and prior image of a book not yet written. Once that image (which no one can legitimately deny me) is postulated, it is certain that my problem is a good bit more difficult than Cervantes' was. My obliging predecessor did not refuse the collaboration of chance: he composed his immortal work somewhat *à la diable,* carried along by the inertias of language and invention. I have taken on the mysterious duty of reconstructing literally his spontaneous work. My solitary game is governed by two polar laws. The first permits me to essay variations of a formal or psychological type; the second obliges me to sacrifice these variations to the "original" text and reason out this annihilation in an irrefutable manner. . . . To these artificial hindrances, another—of a congenital kind—must be added. To compose the *Quixote* at the beginning of the seventeenth century was a reasonable undertaking, necessary and perhaps even unavoidable; at the beginning of the twentieth, it is almost impossible. (41)

Borges here intimates that Menard's "essay" was more daring and difficult, albeit in certain inevitable ways less successful, than Cervantes's undertaking. And he sets up a four-sided relation between himself, Menard, Cervantes, and the reader from whom is demanded responsive understanding and not simply an attempt to contextualize Borges himself as writer of this text, although the latter consideration is not irrelevant to understanding. How it is relevant is intimated in the Menard text itself. Borges takes

Menard's indication of the untimeliness of writing the *Quixote* at the beginning of the twentieth century several steps further through an ingenious, seriocomic comparison of Cervantes's and Menard's endeavors in order to bring out the mind-boggling differences between literally identical words. And Borges is able to further accentuate the differences through belated recognitions related to the passage of time. Hence, for example, he writes:

> Menard's fragmentary *Quixote* is more subtle than Cervantes'. The latter, in a clumsy fashion, opposes to the fictions of chivalry the tawdry provincial reality of his country. Menard selects as his "reality" the land of Carmen during the century of Lepanto and Lope de Vega. What a series of *espagnolades* that selection would have suggested to Maurice Barrès or Dr. Rodriguez Larreta! Menard eludes them with complete naturalness. In his work there are no gypsy flourishes or conquistadors or mystics or Philip the Seconds or *autos da fé*. He neglects or eliminates local color. This disdain points to a new conception of the historical novel. This disdain condemns *Salammbô*, with no possibility of appeal. (42)

Leaving us in doubt concerning the conception of the historical novel he imputes to Flaubert (for whom anything like local color or even historical or pseudohistorical circumstance served primarily to disorient the reader), Borges tacks in another direction in comparing the styles of Menard and Cervantes: "The contrast in style is also vivid. The archaic style of Menard—quite foreign, after all—suffers from a certain affectation. Not so that of his forerunner, who handles with ease the current Spanish of his time" (43).

Rather than give way to the temptation to quote even more of the text, especially the wonderful passage quoting Cervantes's and Menard's identical yet seemingly incommensurable words on "truth, whose mother is history," I shall confine myself to a few more comments. Through not only changes in context but also via the belated recognitions of a responsive reading in a later time, the *Quixote* is drastically transformed. Formally identical words have become radically different in meaning because of differences in subject position, sociocultural and political context, and—last but not least—the resistances, temptations, challenges, and openings faced and engaged by both writer and reader. For the reader this realization can itself be part of a critically transformative experience as well as of an insight into the complexities of the interplay between text and context.[8]

8. I should, however, note that in his ironic, even preposterous, last paragraph, comparable in its quixotism to Menard's own project, Borges sees Menard as enriching the art of reading with

Recently I have been increasingly concerned with relating intellectual history both to cultural history and to historiography and critical theory more generally, especially via certain crucial problems such as trauma, the sublime, and the extreme or limit event (for example, with respect to the Nazi genocide of the Jews and other victimized groups). And I have, throughout my work and despite a partial reorientation since about 1990, affirmed a self-reflexive intellectual history insisting on the importance of a close reading and critical analysis of interacting texts (or signifying practices) and specific contexts that I judge to be particularly pertinent, thereby linking the text-context problem to critical theory and a concern for the mutually implicated dialogic relations between past and present that bear on the future. In this sense, I have insisted that the concept of working-through should not be understood in terms of closure or totalization but rather as an attempt to generate counterforces to acting-out, melancholia, and the repetition compulsion—counterforces that enable transformations in understanding and practice, including a reengagement in sociopolitical life with openings to possible futures. (Such an approach has a necessary normative dimension that I try to make as explicit as possible and thus open to the judgment of the reader or interlocutor.) Moreover, critical self-reflexivity, which is addressed especially to basic assumptions in research and understanding, leads to the injunction: Historian, contextualize (and question) thyself. In these respects intellectual history is not simply the history of meaning, although it does involve inquiry into both the possibilities and limits of meaning—limits that become insistent and at times incapacitating with respect to extreme, traumatizing events and experiences resulting in disorientation and disempowering symptoms.

In seeing contextualization as altogether necessary but not sufficient for historical understanding, I have made a selective appropriation of psychoanalytic concepts, crucially including transference, in revising the notion of objectivity and elucidating the historian's implication in the object of

---

"the new technique" of "deliberate anachronism and the erroneous attribution." Yet Menard's technique (or is it Borges's?) may be termed deliberate anachronism only in a very special sense: that of being untimely or utterly implausible in the context of its own time. But it would simultaneously be a factor if not a force in that porous context, where a notion of plausibility was being destabilized if not undermined to the anxiety-ridden, some might say exhilarating or sublime, point of making almost anything possible. Similarly, erroneous attribution could be applied to Menard only in a rather wayward manner. He did not claim to have written Cervantes's *Quixote* but his own, to wit, Menard's. But perhaps the underlying consideration here is that, in terms of Borges's story itself, authorship is not an absolute or transparent category. Indeed it may always involve erroneous attribution, and the doubly inscribed *Quixote,* or parts of it, come to have at least two problematic authors (but to Cervantes and Menard should one add not only Borges but an endless series of readers?).

study and the need to work through it in critical ways. In accordance with this conception, objectivity becomes not objectification from a god's eye or transcendental position. Rather it is a never-terminated process of working through necessary "transferential" involvements in the object of study, including the tendency to act out symptomatically, or more or less compulsively repeat, dimensions of the object, notably through (projective and/or incorporative) identification.[9] And, especially in the case of extreme, violent events and processes, objectification, in its limited, defensible dimension, may itself be at least partially understood as the creation of a distancing or even "numbing" protective shield for the observer, which both repeats an aspect of traumatization and homeopathically serves to ward off full identification and the upsetting possibility of undergoing secondary traumatization with its anxiety-ridden symptoms. I have also insisted on the affective dimension of historical understanding including the role of empathic response.

Empathy as a component of historical understanding has not been a prominent concern for about a century both because it is incompatible with a scientistic idea of knowledge exclusively as objectification of the other and because it has been conflated with identification, hence seen as a substitute for, rather than a complement and supplement to, critical procedures of inquiry (or even to social and political action). While I believe there is always a tendency toward positive and /or negative identification, I would distinguish desirable empathy from identification and link it to recognition of the alterity of the other as other, thus combining it with possible critical distance and judgment (whether positive or negative). To put the point metaphorically, in empathic response as a component of the attempt to understand, one puts oneself in the other's position without taking the other's place. Empathy is in this sense an opening to the other that is related to transferential implication.[10] One might even argue that there is no need for a conscious attempt

9. Examples of compulsive repetition include ritualistically dismissive analyses of ritual or discussions of scapegoating that scapegoat one's critics or objects of criticism. A much-discussed, analogous process on the political level is the way the post-9/11 "war on terror" has helped to engender those whom it is supposed to ward off (for example, terrorists in Iraq) and come to embody at times "terroristic" techniques of interrogation and surveillance as presumably protective devices.

10. Empathy is also related to the problem of forgiveness, which is further bound up with considerations of justice and generosity. In terms of justice, the victim may demand reciprocity at least in the minimal form of apology and repentance. (Such reciprocity may of course never be perfect or even adequate with respect to extreme acts.) There may also be a demand for reparations or even institutional change to create the bases of social justice. Generosity (or the gift) is best understood as existing in a tense, supplementary relation to justice. It rests on an asymmetrical relation whereby the victim grants forgiveness with no expectation of reciprocity

to "feel oneself into" the other because transferential implication always occurs on an unconscious level in positive and negative ways. (This is the case, on a sometimes visceral level, with respect to a writer's style.) But there is indeed a need for alertness to transference so that it may be guided insofar as possible by an informed, responsible awareness. In any event, empathy, including the active acknowledgement of otherness, is crucial for responsive historical understanding, and it does not exclude the attempt to take critical distance when warranted, work through past problems, and (as Walter Benjamin advocated) recapture unrealized, desirable possibilities that have arisen in the past. Any process of working-through should also be open to the role of humor and the joke, including the role of gallows humor in those who have been through devastating experiences—the type of humor that is likely to emerge not in isolation, when one is at one's most depressed and melancholic, but in social interaction, whether actual (as in survivor groups) or imagined.[11]

---

or return, in a kind of act of grace or even *acte gratuit.* Demands for justice may at times be linked to resentment and revenge, but they also are differentiated from the latter in that they are not predominantly affective and relate to broader normative and sociopolitical considerations. The desire to detach justice from any trace of resentment or revenge may be at play in the recent poststructural tendency to approximate or even conflate justice and generosity (or the pure gift), a vision that would seem utopian. See, in these respects, Jacques Derrida, *Cosmopolitanism and Forgiveness,* trans. Mark Dooley and Michael Hughes, preface Simon Critchley and Richard Kearney (1997; London: Routledge, 2001) and *Given Time: 1. Counterfeit Money,* trans. Peggy Kamuf (1991; Chicago: University of Chicago Press, 1992). See also Julia Kristeva, "Forgiveness: An Interview [with Alice Rice]," *PMLA* 117, no. 2 (2002): 278–95. Also pertinent is Richard Kearney, *Strangers, Gods and Monsters* (London: Routledge, 2003).

11. Samuel Moyn argues that empathy has become the core concept of my work since my turn to the Holocaust, that the concept is related to human-rights discourse into which my thinking falls, that one needs a critical genealogy of the concept of empathy (along with human rights) in the light of its critique by such figures as Agamben, and that I fail to provide normative grounding for an appeal to empathy. See "Empathy in History, Empathizing with Humanity," *History and Theory* 45 (2006): 397–415. Moyn makes a number of pertinent observations but tends to assimilate my recent work (along with that of Carolyn J. Dean) to his own important project concerning human-rights discourse. A critical genealogy of "empathy" and its relation to such concepts as sympathy and sentimental humanitarianism developed in Europe in the eighteenth century may well be desirable, but it has not been my project. For a recent attempt to provide a history of human-rights discourse, with a strong, arguably Eurocentric emphasis on the eighteenth century, see Lynn Hunt, *Inventing Human Rights* (New York: W. W. Norton, 2007). For reasons I clearly delineate (such as its neglect and its misleading conflation with identification), I am trying to put empathy as a problem on the agenda of current historical thought—not to contextualize its past uses, although, if undertaken in a certain way, such an attempt might well be of critical-theoretical interest. In any case, it is inexact to see empathy as the core of my recent thought. It is related to a constellation of other concepts of equal or greater importance, including trauma, transference, melancholy, mourning, the sublime, the uncanny, and working-through, among others. My approach to these concepts comes with an attempt to resist often "crypto-normative" pathologizing forms

To shift gears somewhat abruptly, I note that the first rather massive existential item that may help contextualize my interests and approach, at least as filtered through my own belated recognitions, is that I was very religious until the onset of adolescence.[12] (No in-depth analysis of the transition, either in this text or in my life, will be provided.) Actually my investment in religion continued into my late teens, and my serious interest in religion has been a constant in my thought, increasingly taking the form of concern with the problem of secularization and, recently, the postsecular. The postsecular is entangled with the problem of secularization, and it is just beginning to demand sustained attention. Crucial questions are whether it is a more or less masked return to religion, what dimensions of religion or the sacred it revises or rehabilitates, and what components of the secular (or what is commonly associated with the secular, such as critical rationality) it questions, relativizes, or places in doubt. I find questionable the turn to the "mystical" or the messianic, especially when the latter are seen as modes of, or surrogates for, social and political action. Yet I am more sympathetic to the idea that "modernity" is in need of certain orientations, such as a nonanthropocentric responsiveness to the other, and even ritual or quasi-ritual forms, notably with respect to (nonsacrificial) ceremonial and carnivalesque activities (including mourning)—forms that may be necessary for an ecological understanding of the implication of humans in broader relational networks that counter excessive assertion and check exploitation of other species and natural resources.[13]

---

of thought and to further an explicit statement of normative as well as empirical and analytic aims. The demand for grounding is, I think, misplaced and usually put forth even though one cannot specify what would satisfy its unrealistic, even diversionary, insistence on criteria. As I noted in the introduction, instead of relying on such an inoperative default position, the point is rather to make normative (as well as other) assumptions explicit and to elaborate arguments or put forth considerations that one tries to make as cogent and convincing as possible, while remaining open to counterargument and to the possibility that one may be blind to one's own limitations. My critical reservations about (but not simple dismissal of) rights (including human-rights) discourse should be evident in chapter 6. See also Talal Asad, *Formations of the Secular* (Stanford: Stanford University Press, 2003), chap. 4.

12. The religion in question was Catholicism, but I grew up on a Jewish block in Brooklyn where I was a Shabbes goy, attended many Jewish rituals and ceremonies, and had close Jewish friends.

13. The belief that mourning is impossible or even irrelevant, along with the insufficiently qualified valorization of melancholia, may be implicated in a "past we have lost" scenario in which one postulates or simply assumes some unspecified "traditional" religious context or time when mourning was not only possible but really worked to bring closure, full renewal, or even regeneration. (I thank Sarah Senk for making a similar point.) One may, however self-questioningly, think there is a deficit of effective ritual in "modernity" yet not rely on such a tendentious frame of reference. Idealized, totally successful mourning is better understood on

If one is to appeal to the concept of secularization at all, I think it best to conceive of it neither as a unilinear process leading from the religious to the secular nor as a radical, total discontinuity (or epistemological break) between the two.[14] Nor would I affirm either the identity between religion and secular formations (asserting that marxism is a Christian heresy or psychoanalysis, an offshoot of Jewish mysticism, for example) or a straightforward, unproblematic divide between them (seeing marxism—or psychoanalysis—as the heir to the Enlightenment that demystifies and transcends religion). And one cannot postulate a simple movement from the religious to the secular. Rather, I see the problem of secularization in terms of complex, mutual displacements between the religious and the secular both at any given time and, with variations, over time. Hence there has been an intricate, at times intensely internal dialogic relation, with contestatory elements, between religion and secularity, and more particularly between theology and philosophy, throughout (Western) history. And this interaction may indeed come with marked variations over time, even "ruptures," notably in the form of traumatic events and experiences that are historically decisive (the differentiation of Christianity from Judaism, the formation of the Church, the Reformation, the "death of God"). Yet the ruptures at issue are, I think, best understood on the Freudian model of trauma itself, that is, in terms of a repetition that is nonetheless an unanticipated break or a shattering experience that is within limits intelligible, at best, only belatedly or after the fact (*nachträglich*). On the level of individual experience, a conversion has this quality whether it be religious or secular (a "conversion" to marxism or some other ideological orientation, for example). But something similar may be said of deconversion or a seeming loss of religion, ideology, or existential orientation. In both conversion and deconversion, one has belated recognitions whereby events or experiences of the past are seen differently because of intervening events and experiences, notably including the conversion or deconversion itself. Here the analogy with falling in and out of love is apt, and it helps to bring out the affective component of basic events and experiences. I think this pattern or process of complex displacement or repetition with (more or less decisive or traumatic) change, involving belated temporality, may well apply to historical "development" in general, a mode of development that is not linear but syncopated and uneven. And aspects of history that themselves

---

the analogy of other golden age mythologies as an absence that is phantasmatically construed or experienced as a loss.

14. For further discussion of this point, see, for example, my *Representing the Holocaust* (Ithaca: Cornell University Press, 1994), chap. 6.

have transhistorical dimensions, such as rituals and related practices (such as mourning), may serve either to ward off or to work through the effects of traumatic experiences and events. Hence the recent turn to the postsecular, which might even be construed as an aspect of the problem of secularization, should not come as a total surprise.[15]

After writing what I thought was the final form of this chapter, including the above paragraph, I discovered related thoughts, associated with Freud's notions of the uncanny, displacement, and the return of the repressed, in a book I had not reread since its initial appearance in 1975: Michel de Certeau's *Writing of History.*[16] Certeau writes:

> Modern Western history essentially begins with differentiation between the *present* and the *past.* In this way it is unlike tradition (religious tradition), though it never succeeds in being entirely dissociated from this archeology, maintaining with it a relation of indebtedness and rejection. (2)

> I wonder if the religious "tradition," the home that has been abandoned by a society that no longer lives in it, the home that is no longer even there, cannot be seen historically from the basis of two propositions that can be drawn from Freudian analysis. The first was already expressed by Agathon, the hero of Wassermann's premonitory novel [*Les Juifs de Zirndorf*]: "Neither am I a Jew nor am I a Christian": *neither one nor the other*—a statement of "dispute," of exodus, of historical break. The second is the contrary: *one and the other;* but in the fashion of the quid pro quo and of the straw man—a statement of "debt," of "return," and of bizarre "deformations" which bring the repressed religious elements back in the form of *fictions.* This "displaced" ghost haunts the new dwelling. It remains the rightful heir in the spot that we occupy in his place: such is a current problematic of religious history. (345)

15. At this writing, Google has a significant (about 11,200) but still relatively modest and predictably heterogeneous number of entries under the heading "postsecular." As should be evident from earlier chapters, I find specially relevant and, in certain ways, exemplary or at least influential Giorgio Agamben's *The Open: Man and Animal,* trans. Kevin Attell (2002; Stanford: Stanford University Press, 2004), Eric L. Santner's *On Creaturely Life: Rilke, Benjamin, Sebald* (Chicago: University of Chicago Press, 2006), and Slavoj Žižek, Eric L. Santner, and Kenneth Reinhard's *The Neighbor: Three Inquiries in Political Theology* (Chicago: University of Chicago Press, 2005). Also significant in a somewhat different key is Jacques Derrida's "Faith and Knowledge: The Two Sources of 'Religion' at the Limits of Reason Alone," in *Religion,* ed. Jacques Derrida and Gianni Vattimo (1996; Stanford: Stanford University Press, 1998), 1–78.

16. Trans. Tom Conley (1975; New York: Columbia University Press, 1988).

Among other observations, Certeau makes the provocative point that one way to see the relation between history and fiction is in terms of complex displacements (neither identity nor total difference) that of course must be further explicated in terms of the intricate interplay of similarities and differences. I would add the seemingly obvious: the haunting displacements or returning-repressed dimensions of religion take the form not only of fictions, important as they are, but of less-controlled and perhaps unconscious symptomatic formations in thought and practice.[17] As Lacan emphasized, these returning dimensions are even more uncontrolled and possibly destructive when they are not simply repressed but disavowed or cut off, for then they come back with a vengeance as posttraumatic symptoms or intrusive, seemingly unintelligible, revenants (for example, the irreligious or presumably fully secular individual or group that feels compellingly "called" to engage in sacrificial self-mutilation or "regenerative" violence against others).

An insufficiently explored problem is what might be called founding or foundational traumas in both collective and individual life. (A comparative history of such traumas would be of pronounced critical interest, especially with respect to claims about what is or is not transhistorical.) The founding trauma is a shattering, often divisive, event that splits self and/or society. It should in principle pose the very problem of identity and lead to the understanding of identity as at best problematic. But, paradoxically, it often functions as the very basis or core of identity, which can be unself-questioning if not self-righteous and dogmatic, whether for an individual or a collectivity. And the founding trauma is often repeated in later history in a manner that poses the problem of working it through rather than compulsively repeating or acting it out—perhaps never fully transcending it but coming to terms with it critically in a way that opens different possibilities in the present and future. Indeed the belief that one may fully transcend or heal a trauma once it has occurred is deceptive, and it induces accounts or narratives that tend to deny the very problems that called them into existence (what Eric Santner has perceptively analyzed as fetishistic narratives).[18] A trauma taken as foundational may itself be subsumed in such narratives, for example, when the Holocaust in a Zionist narrative is "redeemed" by the creation of the state

17. As is well known, Certeau was a Jesuit who had taken his distance from the order but nonetheless planned funeral rites administered by them, hence in a limited way returning to the estranged and somewhat uncanny "home" of religious tradition.

18. Eric Santner, "History beyond the Pleasure Principle: Some Thoughts on the Representation of Trauma," in *Probing the Limits of Representation: Nazism and the "Final Solution,"* ed. Saul Friedländer (Cambridge: Harvard University Press, 1992), 143–54.

of Israel or when a revolution, such as the American Revolution, is understood as giving rise to a consensual, gloriously unparalleled nation-state.

A related problem is how different societies and cultures respond to and situate trauma in both structural (or transhistorical) and historical senses (which in empirical reality are typically intertwined), including the role of practices and processes that serve to avert or work through the traumatic. One issue calling for comparative study is whether all collective life and myths of origin, which try to provide self-understanding for collectivities, present trauma as an origin and even tend to sacralize it, figure it as sublime, or constitute it as a founding event. (I would add that the sacred and the sublime might themselves be seen as displacements of one another, one in a religious and the other in a more or less secular key.) The Fall in the Book of Genesis seems to function as a founding trauma of Judaism and Christianity, perhaps even as the shared trauma of the so-called Judaeo-Christian tradition to which later "falls" are often referred. The Crucifixion might be argued to have the status of a sacred founding trauma in Christianity, and one of the most elevated religious experiences for Christians is the imitation of Christ, including the bearing of stigmata, which may be seen in terms of the intergenerational transmission of trauma and the manifestation of posttraumatic symptoms in one who has not experienced the "original" event (crucifixion) that attends the trauma. (There may be an analogy between Christians imitating Christ and intimates of victims and survivors who, through often unconscious identification or *imitatio,* relive or reexperience what others have lived through.) National histories have a traumatic event or series of events at the "origin" of identities within the nation (or the new, "born again" nation)—an origin that subsequently becomes sacralized or memorialized in positive, negative, or equivocal terms and, in the most traumatic instances, typically gives rise to divided heritages. Obvious instances are the French Revolution, the Russian Revolution, and the American Civil War. The Holocaust has itself functioned as a founding trauma both for Jews and for Germans, with later events (Israeli-Palestinian conflict, the West German government versus Baader-Meinhoff) being construed in terms that tend to repeat the "originary" trauma and simultaneously raise the knotty problem of how to work it through in order to lay ghosts from the past to rest, avoid inappropriately intrusive behavior or misplaced amalgamations, and allow openings to a different future. Moreover, one can refer to many cases in individual life of a trauma becoming a violent basis of identity, being endlessly repeated, and constituting the blockage with which one must viably come to terms and to some extent overcome if life is to be livable. As I noted, one needs research into how general this phenomenon of the founding trauma is and how different groups and individuals come to terms with it. What are often called "traditional" societies have severe tests or trials in their myths and rituals, but they may not have founding traumas in the sense that the Crucifixion "founds" Christianity or the French Revolution (at least until very recently) "founded" modern France and set the endlessly repeated, albeit displaced, terms of ideological identification in it (whereby one's interpretation of the Revolution was an index of one's political and ideological position in the present). In recent American history, 9/11—the suicide bombing of the World Trade Center twin towers—was of course constructed by the administration of George W. Bush, often with the complicity of mainstream media, as a new founding trauma for the nation, which apocalyptically changed the world and presumably justified military action against Iraq and the seemingly endless war against terrorism and terrorists (or even terror).

I had a rather serious deconversion experience and a more parodic foundational trauma in my own life that help frame my academic experience, and they probably have analogs in the lives of many others. I shall defer my trauma and say a few words about my deconversion experience (which was traumatic in its own way). That experience itself took a linguistic turn.[19] But language or signifying practice was in no sense divorced from other dimensions of life. I was about twelve years old and, after one of my periodic confessions, I went up to the altar rail to say penance. It was late morning or early afternoon. I found that I could not get through the first few words of the prayer but kept repeating and repeating them in my mind. I left church at the same initial point in the prayer at which I had begun and arrived home having missed dinner. Time had been suspended as I knelt at the altar for at least six or seven hours. I would now say that religious language, in its intimate relation to religious experience, had broken down or fallen apart into fragments or nonsense syllables that could not be fitted together meaningfully. Here the experience of meaninglessness is itself significant in that it is related to a legitimation crisis that may arise in the life of a collectivity as well as of

19. A still earlier childhood experience also took a somewhat linguistic turn. My household was rather crowded and noisy, with people continually coming and going. I learned to read with my hands over my ears and remember vividly the shock I experienced in first entering a library and realizing that it was possible to read without having one's ears' plugged. Related closely to the way I learned to read was the fact that in the home I did not have silent spaces, which phenomenologists such as Gaston Bachelard believe are necessary for reverie and daydreaming. Be that as it may, I prefer modes of critical analysis (including analysis of fantasy, dream, and phantasm) and get impatient with freely associative, predominantly paratactic, loosely linked, quasi-oneiric forms of thought, at least when they try to pass for critical analysis. Still, I attempt, within limits, to respond with sympathetic understanding to certain of them (notably in Benjamin, Derrida, and Heidegger) that I believe open important avenues of thought.

an individual. In any case, what I have been long convinced of (rightly or wrongly) is that I displaced the intensity and insistence of my early religious experience onto academic and intellectual activity which I have taken with seriousness and conviction—but also with a "sacred" parodic sense—a joking relation to my academic and intellectual commitments and a propensity to "crack" jokes during serious (at times overly serious) discussions. I think this combination of factors frames my own polemical tendencies. I argue for what I think, react strongly to what I take as misunderstanding, but generally do not bear grudges (indeed often forget who is an opponent), and have a certain distance from my involvements, which I may even reconsider and revise.[20]

Now to my parodic founding trauma—a joke of sorts. As I was about to leave for graduate school, my father in a semi-demi-Oedipal scene asked me what I was going to study. Being a neophyte unversed in the fine art of learned repartee and not yet realizing that it is a far, far better thing to deconstruct certain questions than to answer them, I responded naively and said: intellectual history. His sly and cutting rejoinder was: what's the alternative, dumb history? There I was, bereft, a flame without a candle. And, on many a sleepless night, I have obsessively pondered that bad joke of a response, remembering Freud's comment that the best joke is the bad joke because it taps the unconscious. Could the old boy have had a point? And what could that perilous point have been?[21]

20. I would simply mention that I went to high school (Bishop Laughlin, then the diocesan scholarship school for all of Brooklyn and Long Island) with Christian Brothers and resisted pressure for Catholic college by attending Cornell. I majored in philosophy and political theory, having the good fortune to do extensive work with John Rawls, David Sachs, Norman Malcolm, and other bright lights of philosophy at Cornell at that time. But one of my most memorable courses was with David Brion Davis who did American intellectual history with a strong emphasis on its trans-Atlantic connections. (This was before his turn to the problem of slavery and his move to Yale.) I originally intended go to graduate school in political theory but changed my mind during a Fulbright year in France. In graduate school at Harvard I worked with H. Stuart Hughes, Stanley Hoffmann, Crane Brinton, and Donald Fleming, among others, and tutored in both history and the interdisciplinary honors program in social studies. Aside from my Fulbright year I was able to spend two additional years in France during the graduate school period. In France I took the seminar of Claude Lévi-Strauss and courses with Raymond Aron, Georges Gurvitch, Roland Mousnier, Jean-Claude Passeron, and others. I was immersed in the atmosphere of structuralism at its height and of poststructuralism in its incipient stages. I remember carrying Foucault's recently published (1961) *Histoire de la folie* around with me for a few weeks and reading it everywhere from café to subway. After returning as a tutor to Harvard, I was told (by Laurence Wylie) that I was the first person there to teach Foucault in a class.

21. For Freud, the joke, producing uncontrollable laughter, taps the unconscious. And laughter, which has been a prominent criterion used to distinguish the human from the animal

I must confess that at times I have been sorely tempted to conclude that he may have had a point. The point, however, is not that all history is either intellectual history or dumb history. Rather one point among others is that varieties of intellectual history, raising and pursuing different questions (including but not restricted to a history of intellectuals and a critical reading of their texts), have a right to exist, with faculty positions devoted to them, as components of a subdiscipline that is valuable for developing critical and self-critical processes of thought. Another point is that all history should have a self-reflexive and critical-theoretical component—indeed a gadfly element—in which the very questions and concepts employed are themselves interrogated, disciplinary limits are subjected to scrutiny, and room is made for the issue of the relation between inquiry into the past and its implications for the present and future.

I have argued for a close relation between the attempt to reconstruct the past and the role of a dialogic relation to it that is bound up with our implication in the questions and issues we raise. I have also insisted on the tense interaction between more constative dimensions of historical discourse (related to accurate reconstruction) and performative dimensions (related to our implication in or transferential relations to the past). Each of these dimensions is important for historical understanding. In a related manner, I have tried to show how artifacts or signifying practices, including "canonical" texts, combine in variable ways symptomatic, critical, and transformative aspects in coming to terms with their contexts. They pose intertextual and "intercontextual" problems for us as readers and historians who are bringing these artifacts into the present with implications for the future. How we read and do research (which, *pace* the belief of some if not many historians, centrally includes reading) and teach others to read and do research are themselves historical acts and not simply "objective" components of the historical discipline. They make a difference in the present and constitute a historical force, however weak and requiring articulation with other "forces" and activities. Hence one should be attentive to the interaction between documentary aspects of texts, which record contextual elements or mark differences, and worklike or more performative aspects, which rework contexts

---

(for example, in Aristotle), also contradicts another differentiating criterion: conscious control of the self or distance from what Heidegger discusses in terms of the "disinhibitor" (more typically treated in reference to "instinct," at least with respect to nonhuman animals). (See chapter 6.) Laughter might be defined as a human disinhibitor that often induces animal-like squeals and antics. For an interesting history of laughter, which does not question its role in separating the human from the animal and thus severely limits its "subversiveness," see Barry Sanders, *Sudden Glory: Laughter as Subversive History* (Boston: Beacon Press, 1995).

and make a difference. And this interaction includes or is transferred to our own use or appropriation of texts and signifying practices in general in a manner that bears vitally on the issue of the relation between historiography and critical theory. It also bears on the question of how we conceptualize an account and how we attempt to turn erudition into learning. These and related problems are denied or foreclosed in an exclusively "objectifying" history for which contextualization (including a big panoramic picture of the past) is (mis)taken as identical with historical understanding.

Certain forms of intellectual history in the United States had their heyday in the 1950s and 1960s. These included Arthur Oncken Lovejoy's rather abstract, formalistic yet rigorous "history of ideas," a predominantly contextualizing social history of ideas, and a more amorphous intellectual history that, when it was not charting the pinnacles of "genius" or the representativeness of "mainstream" figures, tended to focus on losers and oddballs in history, often with a superior, even a supercilious sense of irony. In the 1970s and early 1980s intellectual history tended to be overshadowed by a more enterprising social history that either marginalized certain elites or saw their products in epiphenomenal terms. The most challenging form of this approach was probably that of the Annales school, which had both direct and indirect influence in the United States. Yet the history of mentalities, through which intellectual history was recuperated, tended to flatten out the latter's contours and contestatory power in the interest of focusing on "representative" figures or movements, making "mentality" fit with preexisting social categories or contexts, notably socioprofessional ones, and approximating a retrospective sociology of knowledge. The turn to Clifford Geertz and later to Pierre Bourdieu, whatever its benefits, often served to provide more subtle formulations of older modes of excessive stylization, "sociologistic" reductionism, or insufficiently differential amalgamation of cultural and social categories. ("Thick description" or "field" could readily serve as new labels for objectifying contextualization as tantamount to historical understanding.) Hence, in the 1980s, along with others, I saw my own task as reformulating intellectual history and reasserting its importance as well as defining better its relations with social and cultural history. The initiative moved on two fronts: against a formalistic, free-floating history of ideas and simultaneously against a reductionist, overly contextualizing social or sociocultural history as well as an indiscriminate methodological populism ("history from the bottom up") at least when objectified, taken as a be-all and end-all and detached from any political motivation. More positively, it was to explain how texts or signifying practices worked and how they interacted with—at times challenging—various pertinent contexts of production, circulation, and reception, including our own context in which certain aspects of texts might raise questions for our assumptions in reading them. Pure contextualism or historicization, which uncritically identifies historical understanding with contextualization, in effect denies the contestatory and transformative dimension of texts (in the broad sense) and the ways they make demands on readers for responsive understanding, demands both shaped by current concerns and possibly enabling us to learn from the past and resist projective "presentist" reprocessing of its artifacts, hence provoking us to question our questions if not our selves. Unqualified contextualism may also rely on a dubious concept of understanding something in its own terms and time, as if the past were not itself implicated in its pasts, rife with controversy and uncertainty, and open to its possible futures—not fixed in amber or an unproblematic, "mappable" object of knowledge that fully accounts for and gives meaning to texts. As I intimated, indiscriminate contextualization, which takes a saturation-bombing approach to heaping context onto thought or practice, may do more to confuse issues than to further understanding. While at times more sensitive to problems of reading and understanding, the history of ideas misconstrued the problem of form or the "internal" work or play of textuality in terms of a narrow formalism adapted to macrological patterns or period concepts (the great chain of being, Renaissance individualism, modernity, postmodernity, and so forth). The problem, as I and others saw it, was to elaborate a more fine-tuned, critical, and self-questioning intellectual history, a history not closed to critical-theoretical self-reflection but not simply subservient to a given theoretical orientation or engaged in merely reprocessing the past in terms of present-day concepts, methods, or stylistic maneuvers.

For a while I was seen as a Derridean or as a somewhat younger analog of Hayden White, however incompatible these two representations were.[22] I certainly saw—and see—value in Derrida's and White's work and tried at times to bring them into greater critical contact with one another. But the nature of my response to each of these significant figures was complex and qualified. I thought—and continue to think—that White raises questions in a provocative way. As I put it in a Kantian turn of phrase in a review essay first appearing in 1978: "No one writing in this country at the present time has done more to wake historians from their dogmatic slumber than has

22. In significant ways, for example, in the emphasis on narrative and the aesthetic, the work of important figures such as Frank Ankersmit and Hans Kellner is closer to White's than is my own.

Hayden White."[23] But Kant himself was not simply agreeing with Hume, and, inappropriate analogies aside, I was not simply agreeing with White in whose thought I found overly formalistic and constructivist inclinations. (Radical constructivism, with its air of creation ex nihilo, has seemed to me to be a form of secular creationism, perhaps more dubious than its theological analog in that it ascribes quasi-divine powers to humans, often—and however unintentionally—to the detriment of other animals.) I also thought that White's *Metahistory* was a magnificent baroque edifice that mistook itself for a system and that some of his most valuable insights were his asides and qualifications rather than his central theses concerning the "poetic" system of tropes that presumably formed the projective infrastructure of historical texts. The latter view lent itself perhaps too readily to codification and emulation, and in these respects its effects have been both positive and less positive. Despite the obvious and profound differences between White and Derrida, a similar point could be made about the latter, at least on the level of a style that could be mimetically appropriated, at times in unintentionally self-parodic ways. My own most Derridean venture was my book on Sartre, which did not imitate or emulate Derrida's mode of writing and was explicitly proposed as an experiment in thought intended to provoke counterreadings (features of the book typically ignored, especially when it led to classifying me as a Derridean or—from the perspective of his emulators—a Derridean *manqué*).[24]

At times I have turned to explicit critiques of certain of Derrida's texts or tendencies without, however, denying or downplaying his importance in the field of critical theory, especially with respect to problems of reading and the limits of meaning. I also have insisted that his famous or notorious statement in *Of Grammatology,* "there is no outside-the-text" (*il n'y a pas de hors-texte*)—typically mistranslated as "there is nothing outside the text"—is a way of posing the text-context problem by challenging the simple divide (or binary opposition) between the two and situating both in what he terms a general trace-structure or network of instituted traces, including signifying

23. Included in *Rethinking Intellectual History,* 72.

24. With respect to dimensions of recent thought, into which I have inquired critically in this book, one might arguably see as pertinent Kierkegaard's caveat from a diary entry in 1854: "A corrective made into the norm, the whole, is *eo ipso* confusing in the next generation (when that which it was meant to correct no longer exists). And as long as this continues things get worse with every generation, until in the end the corrective produces the exact opposite of what was originally intended" (232–33). *The Soul of Kierkegaard: Selections from His Journals,* ed. and intro. Alexander Dru (Mineola, N.Y.: Dover Publications, 2003).

practices. My later disagreements with Derrida bear in good part on what I see as his occasional, unfortunate confusion or conflation of deconstruction with all forms of critique.[25]

I see deconstruction (related to immanent critique) as applying to texts and practices that bear elements that may serve in their own critique or self-contestation and that indicate strong divisions in an argument or narrative leading both to aporias and to open possibilities. (Hence one may use Plato to deconstruct Plato, for example, with respect to the role of metaphor, poetry, or myth in relation to philosophy, or Freud to bring out the countertendencies to Freud's scientism or misogynism.) I see (in one sense nonimmanent) critique as applying to texts or practices that are ideologically saturated or overly codified and have at best only minor internal contestations of a self-questioning sort, although they may be riven with symptomatic contradictions and equivocations. Critique not deconstruction is primarily required for stereotypical thinking, propaganda, and prejudice, including antisemitism and racism in general. And (nonimmanent) critique draws its resources from artifacts and practices other than its object, including from internally self-questioning artifacts "worthy" of deconstruction. If one thinks one can

25. As should be evident from preceding chapters, I also have doubts about motifs especially prominent in Derrida's later work, including the excessive gift (or act of grace seen as justice), pure forgiveness, impossible mourning, and absolute alterity (or the *tout autre* as *tout autre*). I would be tempted to speculate that, in certain ways, Derrida in his later work "encrypted" de Man and that his orientation more resembles de Man's than it did before the latter's death and the discovery of the wartime journalism that generated turmoil in and around deconstruction. Still, one may revisit the question of the relation between two of Derrida's assertions that have functioned as founding texts: "There is no outside-the-text" (in the early Derrida) and "every other is radically (or totally) other" (*tout autre est tout autre* in the later Derrida). These assertions seem contradictory or at least paradoxical, and Derrida, to the best of my knowledge, never tried to relate or "think" them together. They might be referred to the notions of immanence and radical transcendence in theology (evoked by the idea that the center is both inside and outside the system that it regulates). "Il n'y a pas de hors-texte," indicating implication in a relational network or "trace structure," might be understood as a charter for deconstruction as a form of immanent critique that allows for situational (not total) transcendence. As Derrida himself intimates in *The Gift of Death*, trans. David Wills (1992; Chicago: University of Chicago Press, 1995), "tout autre est tout autre" would place every other in the "position" of absolute alterity of the Hidden God, hence somehow outside the text. In this sense the assertion might be seen as sacrilegious. I have tried to indicate that its paradoxical status would be mitigated but not eliminated if it were replaced (perhaps glossed) with the assertion that in every other (as well as in oneself) there is a radically other (or enigmatic) dimension possibly construed in terms of the unconscious and pointing, for Lacanians, to a void in the symbolic. Moreover, implication in a relational network would not obviate the possibility of traumatic breaks that might well be experienced as a searing exposure or "openness" to the totally other.

deconstruct an artifact or practice requiring criticism, one makes something analogous to a category mistake and may end up rewriting history, employing deconstruction as a Cuisinart and going in apologetic directions (for example, turning collaboration into resistance). I think this occurs in Derrida's reading of Paul de Man's World War II journalism, especially in the case of a markedly antisemitic article. But of course the distinction between deconstruction (or immanent critique) and (nonimmanent) critique is itself not a clear-cut binary opposition, and certain artifacts or practices call for both. I would also note that I have become increasingly insistent in pointing out that the deconstruction of binary opposites (male/female, private/public, inside/outside, good/bad, and so on) does not lead to the obliteration or blurring of all distinctions but to the need to articulate distinctions and differences more carefully and more subtly, including the elaboration of arguments concerning how strong or weak one believes certain distinctions are or ought to be. This point applies to the distinction between perpetrator and victim, which, in some cases, may be very strong, in others more equivocal, and ideally would be overcome insofar as one got beyond the entire grid of victimization to enable different kinds of relation not dependent on victimization or scapegoating. The point also applies to the distinction between areas of expression (for example, fiction and history) and disciplines (for example, historiography and literary criticism or philosophy).

The problem of disciplinarity has been of special concern to me, as, I think, it must be to anyone who works responsibly with graduate students who at some point enter the professional job market. One has to elaborate problematic distinctions between and work through disciplines rather than simply collapse them, believe one can readily transcend or leap beyond them, or become fixated on disciplinarity and border maintenance. For example, it is evident that there is a realistic dimension to (at least some) fiction and a performative dimension to history, even when performativity is reduced to a minimum through naturalized procedures of objectification and research. But, while I see value in Michel de Certeau's view that history and fiction are displacements of one another, this view must be further explicated in a manner that does not obliterate the distinctions or differences between the two. Otherwise there is no basis for a mutually interrogative relation between them. One may agree that a fact is an event (or a representation of an event) under a description. But it is significant that historians as historians may not simply invent facts (the figure of Pierre Menard and his texts, for example) while writers of fiction may. When they do, these "facts" must be postulated as counterfactuals or framed as parts of a hybridized account in which the historian is playing multiple roles. Moreover, history makes truth claims not only on the level of facts but on that of interpretive and explanatory structures, however difficult it may be to validate such claims. Fiction may also be implicated in, or even make, such claims, for example, in the way it construes a problem or series of events (the Holocaust, slavery and its aftermath)—indeed the way it provides a reading of problems, events, or "the times," but it does so more indirectly and figuratively. The notion that both history and fiction are in some sense figurative or poetic on a "foundational" level is both problematic and not directly applicable on other levels of discourse, although of course historians make use of figurative language in accounting for the past. Yet figurative language in history is itself related to truth claims in ways it need not (but of course may) be in fiction or poetry. When one finds a statement like "war is hell" in a history, it must be substantiated by, or come as the epitome of a series of, propositions or assertions that are subject to modes of substantiation, including empirical inquiry.

In any event, I think that the challenge at this point is not to repeat hyperbolic claims about the fictionality or aesthetic nature of history. (The *bourgeois* has already been thoroughly *épaté.*) The challenge is rather to elaborate more qualified and subtle conceptions of differences within disciplines as well as interactions—including similarities, differences, and zones of indistinction or undecidability—between them and areas of cultural practice or fields in general, without resorting to conflation or binary opposition. For example, historiography and fiction are closer on more structural levels of narration than they may be on the level of fact related to event. But there may also be differences on structural levels. I have argued, for example, that historians are under special constraints with respect to the use of a free indirect style that in certain respects I take to be the modern discursive analog of a middle voice. A free indirect style performatively intermingles the voice of the historian (or other inquirer) with his or her objects or subjects of analysis. When and how the use of such a free indirect style is legitimate should be questions for critical reflection and debate. I have suggested that, in historiography, a careful use may be most warranted and perhaps even necessary in treating empathically the most equivocal and internally divided dimensions of history. An example drawn from one of my areas of interest is the plight of Jewish councils or certain capos in camps who were themselves in double binds and subjected to impossible conditions and (non)choices. In cases of more clear-cut perpetrators or victims, the use of such a free indirect style (giving "voice" to Hitler or "speaking for" the *Muselmann,* for example) may be questionable for different reasons, perhaps even in areas other than history.[26] (Identification with and speaking in the voice of the perpetrator and the victim are dubious in different ways, and what empathy may or may not require with respect to each is not obvious.) I would note that the generalization of a free indirect style has been common in certain forms of literary criticism (for example, in Shoshana Felman's at times moving contributions to *Testimony*), and it seems to be validated for historiography by Hayden White, at least with respect to what White terms the "modernist" event such as the Holocaust (figured by White, in insufficiently differentiated terms, for example, with respect to perpetrators, victims, ambiguous perpetrator-victims, bystanders, and so forth).[27] Whether one ideally wants to overcome or transcend all distinctions between history and fiction toward some meta- or postmythological (fully postsecular?) signifying practice, which, for example, generalizes a free indirect style or some analog of a middle voice, is a difficult problem, and its consequences are far from clear although its possible dangers may at times be more evident.

I think that on balance both the New Historicism and cultural studies, which in the United States arose largely within departments of literature, have been positive developments with many possibilities for fruitful interaction with intellectual and cultural history.[28] And they manifest a concern for both history and critical theory in relation to the study of literature and culture in general. The New Historicism (for example, in the work of

26. For a critical discussion of George Steiner's free indirect voicing of Hitler in the novel *The Portage to San Cristóbal of A. H.*, see my *Writing History, Writing Trauma*, 199–201. I discuss Giorgio Agamben's attempt to speak for the *Muselmann* via Primo Levi in *History in Transit*, chap. 4.

27. See Shoshana Felman and Dori Laub, *Testimony: Crises of Witnessing in Literature, Psychoanalysis, and History* (New York: Routledge, 1992), and Hayden White, "Historical Emplotment and the Problem of Truth," in *Probing the Limits of Representation*, 37–53. See also White's *Figural Realism: Studies in the Mimesis Effect* (Baltimore: Johns Hopkins University Press, 1992), chaps. 2 and 4. To put the point with extreme brevity and without any pretense to conclusiveness, I think that "empathy" with the perpetrator involves the recognition that, under certain conditions, extreme (even "thoughtless") acts might be possible for oneself, while empathy with the victim involves respect and compassion that are not tantamount to identification or speaking for the other.

28. On the New Historicism, see H. Aram Veeser, ed., *The New Historicism* (New York: Routledge, 1989), and Brook Thomas *The New Historicism and Other Old-Fashioned Topics* (Princeton: Princeton University Press, 1991). For a thought-provoking book, in general inspired by a New Historicist perspective and written by a scholar in a department of English, see Joan Dayan, *Haiti, History, and the Gods* (Berkeley: University of California Press, 1995). For a sampling of approaches in cultural studies, see Lawrence Grossberg, Cary Nelson, and Paula Treichler, eds., *Cultural Studies* (New York: Routledge, 1992). See also my discussion in *History and Reading: Tocqueville, Foucault, French Studies* (Toronto: University of Toronto Press, 2000), chap. 4.

Catherine Gallagher, Stephen Greenblatt, Marjorie Levinson, Alan Liu, and Louis Montrose) has been strongly marked by its response to poststructualism in general and deconstruction in particular, and those doing cultural studies have come to recognize the disadvantages of more atheoretical and monolingual orientations. Comparative literature may include theory as one of its vital components (if not as one or more of its "languages") and be much broader than literary studies in its self-definition, even taking critical distance on the earlier understanding of it as a comparison of national traditions of literature. And German studies and French studies are particularly open to sustained interaction with critical theory in its different guises. For example, the journal *New German Critique,* which has been a primary conduit for German cultural studies, early had an inclination toward Frankfurt school "critical theory" that was broadened to include constructive, though at times critical, engagement with predominantly French poststructuralism. And attempts to "queer" the canon, which may make use of creative anachronism, decontextualization, and recontextualization, often run parallel to certain "decentering" ventures in deconstruction. Still, there is a problem in finding suitable academic employment for graduate students who come out of interdisciplinary programs, and in the United States there are few such programs (say, in cultural studies) that have the ability to hire faculty on tenure-track lines. And few departments of literature have made the wholesale move to cultural studies, and at present there may even be a reaction against such a move, with a call for a return to the "literary." Moreover, a history department will rarely employ someone without a degree in history, and a German studies department will hesitate to hire someone with a degree from a department such as history, even if the candidate has an informed interest in literature and cultural studies as well as fluency in the German language. These rules are in general suspended only for senior scholars who may be added to enhance a department's offerings or profile, but such a gesture does relatively little to transform the structure of a discipline as it affects hiring within departments. At best there may be preference shown for someone with a solid, even relatively traditional, departmental training who also has a degree of competence in a related area, such as a literary critic who has read broadly in historiography or a historian who knows something about critical theories beyond the point of not appearing uninformed in warding them off.[29]

29. Here I would simply note that my own interest in critical theory and in literature is extensive and long standing both intellectually and institutionally. At Cornell I have long been

Two conferences, leading to collective volumes, were significant in my intellectual life, inducing not "conversion" experiences but shifts in orientation or at least invitations to elaborate preexisting concerns and interests. (One might take them as attesting to the importance of dialogic relations in the thought of scholars.) The first was the 1980 conference at Cornell, which Steven L. Kaplan and I organized and resulting in the book that we co-edited, *Modern European Intellectual History: Reappraisals and New Perspectives.* Before this conference I had published *Emile Durkheim: Sociologist and Philosopher* (1972) and *A Preface to Sartre* (1978). At about the same time or subsequent to the conference, I published *Madame Bovary on Trial* (1982), *Rethinking Intellectual History: Texts, Contexts, Language* (1983), *History & Criticism* (1985), *History, Politics, and the Novel* (1987), and *Soundings in Critical Theory* (1989). The second conference was organized by Saul Friedländer at UCLA in 1990 and led to the publication that he edited, *Probing the Limits of Representation: Nazism and the "Final Solution."* Friedländer's idea was to bring together scholars who had done substantial work on the Nazi genocide (as he himself has of course done) and those whose work he found interesting but who had not devoted sustained attention to it. From the interaction he hoped some new questions or perspectives might be generated. I found the conference and the ensuing volume to be quite productive, and they helped to reorient my work. Afterward I published *Representing the Holocaust* (1994), *History and Memory after Auschwitz* (1998), *History and Reading: Tocqueville, Foucault, French Studies* (2000), and *Writing History, Writing Trauma* (2001). In 2004 I published a book that, like this present one, spans

a member of graduate fields in Comparative Literature and in Romance Studies, and I have recently accepted a joint appointment in Comparative Literature to go along with my appointment in the Department of History (where I was initially hired in 1969). Also significant for my pronounced cross-disciplinary interests is the fact that for a little over a decade (until 2003) I directed Cornell's Society for the Humanities, which brings together an outstanding group of scholars to address an annually changing focal theme (such as my parting legacy, the theme for 2003–04, "Exploring the Secular and the Sacred.") The book I edited, *The Bounds of Race: Perspectives on Hegemony and Resistance* (Ithaca: Cornell University Press, 1983), stemmed from a conference related to an earlier focal theme, in which fellows at the Society participated. Moreover, I have been associated with the School for Criticism and Theory (SCT), where I taught for two sessions while it was at Dartmouth and, on its move to Cornell, was associate director (1996–2000) and, from 2000 to 2008, director of the program. SCT brings together an extraordinary teaching faculty and a comparably remarkable group of advanced graduate students and generally younger to midcareer faculty from over twenty countries for an intensive six-week session (mid-June to the end of July) of seminars, colloquia, lectures, study groups, and related events. These responsibilities have given me the rare opportunity to combine intellectual activity with administrative work to which one is genuinely committed. I should add that at Cornell I have been fortunate to work with an outstanding series of graduate students.

what might loosely be seen as these two periods: *History in Transit: Experience, Identity, Critical Theory.*

I do not think that the initiatives undertaken in my work since 1990 have been sufficiently seen in relation to my earlier work. John Toews, who made an important and influential contribution to the discussion of the linguistic turn to which I shall recur, wrote a thoughtful review of *Representing the Holocaust* for the *American Historical Review* in which he did see the book as an attempt both to expand and to focus more sharply my earlier concerns by selecting an important historical problem and treating it in terms that had broad implications for understanding the interaction between texts and contexts.[30] Indeed, all my books have at least one theoretical or methodological chapter that tries to connect present with past concerns and future prospects. Hence, for example, "Canons, Texts, and Contexts," which is the first chapter of *Representing the Holocaust,* is a rejoinder to and partial critique of "Rethinking Intellectual History," which is the beginning chapter of my book bearing the same title. The former moves from a defense of noncanonical readings of canonical texts (prominent in *Rethinking Intellectual History*) to expanding and contesting the canon with implications for the study of problems or even fields of study such as the Holocaust that, while having their own canons (with Raul Hilberg's *Destruction of the European Jews* coming close to being the field's bible), have not had significant effects on the rethinking or reading of canons in intellectual history. The two issues of noncanonical readings of canonical texts and revising as well as contesting canons come to a head in my chapters on Heidegger and on de Man in *Representing the Holocaust.* This concern to connect initiatives in my work over time is not related to system building but to a (post-postmodern?) desire for critical self-understanding and cognitive responsibility in relating arguments and forms of analysis to one another. Still, in the way I try to formulate problems or compose an account, I am often most concerned with both the lucid exposition of complex issues and the development of points or perspectives that do not lend themselves to easy summary or rote application. (I may of course deceive myself here as elsewhere.) All my works, including essays not included in my books, have been conceived not as overviews, syntheses, or treatises but rather as interventions in an ongoing dialogue or debate.

30. John Toews, "Review of LaCapra, *Representing the Holocaust,*" *The American Historical Review* 100 (1995): 129–30. See also Sander Gilman, "Review of LaCapra, *Representing the Holocaust,*" *Modern Philology* (November 1996): 276–79.

This approach leads to a stress on what one thinks has been underemphasized at a given juncture, especially in historiography but at times in other fields or disciplines. The corollary is criticism of that which one finds to be dubious or overemphasized. In this undertaking there is a prominent place for modulations of rhetoric depending on context and audience—a place, for example, for both hyperbole and understatement or irony. (One difficulty with the work of certain proponents of deconstruction is the lack of a modulated rhetoric, which induces the same baroque complexity if not mannerism in deconstructing a text by Plato or Freud and in discussing a speech by Ronald Reagan or in writing a letter to a newspaper.) Over time I have taken different approaches to various critical theories depending in part on their status in the academy. Hence I defended deconstruction despite reservations when it was in a marginal position, and I more openly criticized certain tendencies in those affiliating themselves with it (or other modalities of poststructuralism) when their position was more secure if not at times assimilated into a homogenizing or compulsively repetitive discourse that somewhat predictably made all the right moves whatever the topic or object of analysis.

The Cornell conference of 1980 has been seen by a number of commentators as marking a turning point in the history of intellectual history, especially with respect to a "linguistic turn." Gérard Noiriel manifests dismay at this turn and the interest of recent members of the Annales school in it.[31] For him it signals the American menace and the dismal decline of social history whose glory days he associates with the illustrious lineage of Marc Bloch. By contrast, François Dosse heralds the linguistic turn as a most fruitful *évènement,* indeed something warranting the transposition of the very term "intellectual history" into the French language, a linguistic move that signals the attribution to intellectual history of a key role in historiography.[32] Dosse accurately sees the importance of the linguistic turn not in a spurious pantextual imperialism but in a rethinking and rearticulation of questions and methods and in an attempt to link intellectual and social history in a cogent, nonreductive manner. He writes:

> The true mutation is elsewhere than in the expansion of the field of intellectual history; it is in what is termed the *linguistic turn,* which has profoundly overturned this area of study, displacing the questions, modifying the methods of approach and giving greater rigor to the studies

31. Noiriel, *Sur la "crise" de l'histoire* (Paris: Belin, 1996).

32. François Dosse, *La marche des idées: Histoire des intellectuels—histoire intellectuelle* (Paris: Editions La Découverte, 2003).

undertaken.... The great event in this attempt at articulating social history with contributions from the *linguistic turn* is due to two American historians at Cornell university, Steven Kaplan and Dominick LaCapra who took the initiative in organizing a conference on the theme in April 1980 at Cornell University in New York State, giving rise to a publication of the presentations centered on the manner of conceiving intellectual history.... As for Dominick LaCapra he comes forward as an advocate of the linguistic turn, which he considers as very positive for the intellectual historian. He places himself in an initiative that tries to overcome the classical dichotomy between the internalist point of view and an externalist approach, and he does so through a rearticulation of these two dimensions. On the model of Austin's distinction between the constative and performative registers, LaCapra establishes two levels in the study of a work. On the one hand one may seek out the documentary level, which refers to the literality, the factuality which the observer accounts for when he speaks of the empirical reality of the past that he reconstructs. Then another level may be approached, which LaCapra qualifies as "worklike"; it refers to the interpretative dimension, the role of imagination and engagement of an intellectual history that enters into dialogue with the past starting from questions of the present. Evidently, these two levels are in constant interaction and must be studied in the perspective of critical historiography. Documentary reading of texts has largely predominated to that point, and LaCapra insists on the pertinence for intellectual history of the new interest in diverse uses and interpretations of discursive formations studied in their temporal dynamic. The domination without balance [*partage*] of the documentary conception has engendered the exclusion of fiction from the domain of study of the historian, even if LaCapra recognizes in Hayden White the merit of having reintroduced this literary dimension as a resource for meaning. (207 and 212–14; my translation)

I might want to introduce further qualifications in Dosse's account, which he expands and nuances himself, but I find his summary to be useful. It remains to be seen whether his point of view is shared to a significant extent by younger French historians who may bring about further modifications or even mutations in the now largely diverse if not splintered Annales school.[33]

33. For an excellent analysis of tendencies in the Annales school until about a decade ago, see Philippe Carrard, *Poetics of the New History: French Historical Discourse from Braudel to Chartier* (Baltimore: Johns Hopkins University Press, 1992).

I would note that the linguistic turn with respect to the gamut of signifying practices should not be conflated with the narrative turn. Narrative is indeed an important signifying practice, and transformations of narrative in the modern period as well as before it (for example, in the picaresque novel) are complex and deserving of careful inquiry. In this sense Borges's Menard piece, while exceptional in certain respects, is also a prototype of tendencies in modern (and postmodern) literature. Narrative represents an obvious area for informed comparisons of historiography and literature, including the novel and, more broadly, heteroglossic and carnivalized discourses or practices such as the Menippean satire. And the turn to narrative in historiography, philosophy, and literary criticism is a remarkable development, indicating dissatisfaction with overly "scientistic" and analytic approaches. But one overstates the case if one collapses the linguistic turn into the turn to narrative or construes narrative as the primary instance of the human mind, as theorists such as Fredric Jameson, Jean-François Lyotard, Paul Ricoeur, or Hayden White are at times prone to do. And it is less insightful to try to reduce seemingly nonnarrative elements (the lyric, the statistical analysis, the polemic, the parody, the satire, the dialogue, and so forth) to narrative as a putative urtext than it is to trace the intricate relations between narrative and other-than-narrative forms or modes. Among the nonnarrative forms that interact with narrative and are at times incorporated into unconventional narrative (Robert Musil's *Man without Qualities* or Thomas Mann's *Doctor Faustus,* say) is the essay itself, and it is significant that theorists who privilege narrative themselves tend to write in an essay form that often remains untheorized in their work.

All of my own writings, like those of many others, take the form of more or less extended essays in the etymological sense of the word. (The present book is no exception even if it has narrative interludes.) They are attempts (*essais*) at revising understanding and critically inquiring into problems. Montaigne was an early proponent of the essay form, and the essay has found numerous practitioners and theorists since his time, including Georg Lukács, Theodor Adorno, and Jacques Derrida. Marking the move to the "meta" level of commentary that inquires into assumptions, Derrida uses as an epigraph to his seminal essay, "Structure, Sign, and Play in the Discourse of the Human Sciences," Montaigne's assertion that "we need to [*il y a plus affaire à*] interpret interpretations more than to interpret things."[34] Most historians

34. Jacques Derrida, *Writing and Difference,* trans. Alan Bass (1967; Chicago: University of Chicago Press, 1978), 278.

would probably disagree with this assertion or even see it as sounding the death knell of history. In historiography the essay has largely been confined to the so-called think piece such as the extended review or the exploration of a theme. But insofar as one advocates a self-reflexive, critical historiography where one comments on procedures and subjects assumptions to critical scrutiny, the discrete think piece gives way to a more hybridized, internally dialogized or self-questioning historiography that may well include or even take the essay form. As I have intimated, essayistic overtures may be combined with narrative or with other modes of discourse in a critical historiography in ways that should be studied closely and debated.

A crucial conduit for the understanding and evaluation of the linguistic turn in the United States was the seminal essay by John Toews, "Intellectual History after the Linguistic Turn: The Autonomy of Meaning and the Irreducibility of Experience."[35] It is significant that the books he discusses are often collections of essays or extended book-length essays. I discuss Toews's important essay in my own essay, "History, Language, and Reading: Waiting for Crillon."[36] Rather than repeat what I have already written, I would note that in retrospect Toews's essay seems particularly significant not so much for its discussion of a linguistic turn as for its own counterturn to experience, a concept that is given cardinal importance yet not critically analyzed or defined. It becomes in Toews what it is in many others: a black box or a residual category that nonetheless assumes central importance in both criticizing other approaches and authorizing claims. The epistemological privilege of experience has a good Hegelian ancestry, being prominent in *The Phenomenology of Spirit,* and it has been furthered by its role in identity studies and identity politics. How to formulate critically the possibilities and limits of experience in legitimating claims and in expanding the field of historical inquiry, from microhistory to the use of testimonies, is a problem that should be on the agenda of historical studies, including intellectual history, for the foreseeable future, including the important issue of the relation

35. John Toews, "Intellectual History after the Linguistic Turn: The Autonomy of Meaning and the Irreducibility of Experience," *American Historical Review* 92 (1987): 879–907.

36. See my "History, Language, and Reading: Waiting for Crillon," *American Historical Review* 100 (1995): 799–828 (reprinted with some modification in *History and Reading,* chap. 1). See also John H. Zammito, "Are We Being Theoretical Yet?: The New Historicism, the New Philosophy, and 'Practicing Historians'" *Journal of Modern History* 65 (1993): 784–814, and "Reading 'Experience': The Debate in Intellectual History among Scott, Toews, and LaCapra," in *Reclaiming Identity: Realist Theory and the Predicament of Postmodernism,* ed. Paula M. Moya and Michael R. Hames-Garcia (Berkeley: University of California Press, 2000), 279–311. See also my response to Zammito in *History in Transit,* chap. 1, as well as my comments on Toews in chapter 2 of this book.

between experience, trauma, and signifying practices. This is a problem to which I devote sustained attention in *History in Transit: Experience, Identity, Critical Theory.*

Problems addressed in *History in Transit* are further explored and supplemented in the chapters of this book. The bearing of my critical attention is less on a reductionistic or imperialistic social history than on the overextensions of poststructural and postmodern thought as they appear, for example, in Agamben and Žižek. Still, the call for a return to social history or a turn to "practice theory" (even a "unified field theory") requires careful scrutiny, especially with respect to its implications for the kind of intellectual history that interacts with critical theory, is best understood as part of what Bakhtin terms "an uncompleted whole," and cannot be fully absorbed into sociocultural history or a field overly unified in a certain direction. One important horizon of intellectual history and related areas, such as critical theory, is clearly the human-animal problem, which is not a key concern in calls for moving beyond the cultural or linguistic turns. However, interest in the human-animal issue, in one form or another, is prevalent in certain fields, with orientations and arguments, with their necessary leaven of hyperbole, in the process of being worked out.[37] Chapter 6 is an attempt on my part to

37. I would note that my interest in the human-animal problem is long standing and not a response to recent trends. As director of the Society for the Humanities at Cornell, I proposed in the 1990s for a few years running the theme of "Humans and Animals," which the Humanities Council discussed but decided not to accept. Going through the files of a no-longer-in-use computer after the manuscript of this book had gone through its penultimate revisions (which might be seen as the contemporary analog of finding an old manuscript in a drawer), I found the following description of the theme I had proposed (dated September 30, 1996) that, in an uncanny manner, outlines certain of the arguments and guiding questions of chapter 6. I include it here for its historical interest: "Humans have in various ways sought to establish their distinctiveness and dignity through a binary opposition that contrasts humanity with animals and animality. The soul, reason, and language have been three important criteria employed to ground this opposition. And the idea of a 'regression' to bestiality has been standard in characterizing extreme, violent, destructive (perhaps even distinctively) human behavior. Moreover, groups within society have seen other groups as subhumans or as animals in order to degrade, victimize, and exploit them. Conversely, oppressed groups, in defending their rights, have insisted on their own humanity and opposed being treated like cattle or dogs. Does the distinction between human and animal always involve an invidious opposition? How have different religions figured the relation between human and animal? Are religious notions displaced or disguised in secular attempts to distinguish sharply between the two? How is humanism itself defined and constituted? Does it require the representation of the animal as a radical 'other,' a scapegoat or inferior being? More generally, how have animals been treated over time, understood in various theories and ideologies, and represented in different traditions, texts, and images? How do cultures and periods vary in their treatment and understanding of animal life and its relation to humans? Are demands for 'animal rights' to be seen as instances of a 'category mistake' (the idea that the concept of rights applies to animals), symptoms of 'politically correct' thought gone to extremes, or signs of an overdue insistence on the desirability of different relations between humans and animals?"

contribute to this crucial movement of both intellectual and existential importance, notably in its bearing on the relations between humans and other species. Perhaps the broadest and most significant problem I have broached is how to think and act relationally in a nonanthropocentric way that is not entirely within what I termed the grid of victimization with its historically predetermined, to some extent inevitable yet gridlocked, roles. With respect to this problem, working-through is a nonexclusionary, contestatory process that is sociopolitical and attempts to be both critical and constructive.

# INDEX